SOCIETIES AT PEACE

SOCIETIES AT PEACE

Anthropological perspectives

Edited by

SIGNE HOWELL

and

ROY WILLIS

ROUTLEDGE
London and New York

First published in 1989
by Routledge
11 New Fetter Lane, London EC4P 4EE
29 West 35th Street, New York NY 10001

© 1989 Routledge

Typeset in Baskerville
by Pat and Anne Murphy, Highcliffe-on-Sea, Dorset
Printed and bound in Great Britain by
Mackays of Chatham PLC, Chatham, Kent

British Library Cataloguing in Publication Data

Societies at peace: anthropoligical perspectives.
1. Society
I. Howell, Signe   II. Willis, Roy, *1927 –*
301

Library of Congress Cataloging in Publication Data

Societies at peace: anthropological perspectives/
edited by Signe Howell and Roy Willis
p.   cm.
Papers originally presented at a conference in June 1986
at the university of Edinburgh.
Bibliography: p.   Includes index.
1. Ethnopsychology — Congresses.
2. Self-perception — Cross-cultural studies — Congresses.
3. Ethnophilosophy — Congresses.
4. Peace (Philosophy) — Cross-cultural studies — Congresses.
5. Aggressiveness (Psychology) — Cross-cultural studies — Congresses.
I. Howell, Signe.   II. Willis, Roy G.
GN512.S63 1989   306.6 – dc19 88-30271 CIP

ISBN 0-415-01824-2   ISBN 0-415-01825-0 pbk

CONTENTS

CONTENTS

PREFACE

If aggression and violence are part and parcel of what it means to be human, then why is it that there exist societies where aggressive or violent behaviour is conspicuous by its absence? It was with such questions in mind that, in 1985, we invited a group of social anthropologists who had fieldwork experience in societies which, for whatever reason, they described as 'peaceful' to attend an informal seminar to discuss the issues involved in interpreting such societies and how our 'evidence' could be used to question established theories on human nature. We also wished to explore the viability of holding a more formal conference devoted to the topic of peace as a mode of social behaviour. It became evident that there was no shortage of topics, and we decided that a conference was indeed called for in which we could pursue our shared interest in peaceful societies and attempt to challenge what we all regarded as a biased approach which presented human behaviour in terms of how aggressive drives are handled.

Those giving papers were asked to emphasize humans as meaning-makers, rather than humans as biological primates, and to elucidate from their own ethnographic experience the indigenous meanings of concepts relevant for an understanding of human interpersonal and, wherever applicable, intersocietal relations. The title of the Conference was 'Peace, Action, and the Concept of Self', the overall focus being explications on indigenous ideas of what it means to be a human being, how the associated attributes are conceptualized, and patterns of behaviour. The following themes were suggested for consideration by the speakers:

— indigenous concepts of human nature, noting possible differences in values and ideas with regard to different categories within the society, e.g. men and women, 'commoners' and 'aristocrats';
— the whole range of concepts concerning inner states of all kinds and their elaborations and meanings;
— techniques and mechanisms of childrearing;
— techniques and mechanisms of social interaction and control;
— attitudes to, and handling of, deviant social behaviour.

The Conference took place in June 1986 at the University of Edinburgh. In addition to anthropologists, we were fortunate in hearing from two psychologists a report on their research into the development of communication and knowledge in human infants, and the theory of innate human co-operative awareness and the 'need for culture' (Trevarthen and Logotheti). Some of the anthropologists chose not to refer to their ethnographic experience but to address more general issues of methodology and definition (Carrithers, Campbell, Heelas), but the majority of the papers are embedded in the particularity of an ethnographic setting. It is within ethnography that we feel anthropologists have a significant contribution to make to the vexed questions of human aggression and violence. Anthropology is bound up with the understanding of lived circumstances rather than abstract thought, the basis of anthropological knowledge being first and always ethnography. However, description is not a privileged area of objective study, and the presentation of socio-cultural conditions of other societies cannot be viewed as a final explanation of other institutions and values, but must be thought of as part of the observer's reconstruction of their own understanding of the institutions and values. This is particularly so in the case of the topic of the papers in this volume — namely peace as a social value. Western thinkers and the public are concerned — morally and intellectually — with understanding the part played by aggression and conflict in the construction and maintenance of social life. While conflict is taken as given, it is also regarded as problematic. It is, however, largely *our* problem, rather than that of many societies which we study. Papers dealing with the issues of peace and violence are therefore especially influenced by Western preoccupations. For this reason, it is important to examine those societies that appear to contradict much of scientific and commonsensical explanation. We feel that anthropologists are uniquely positioned to introduce a few question marks into the fundamental assumption of the discourse, and it is our hope that this book will provide some such.

We feel that the main contribution of this volume to existing debate lies in the actual ethnographic presentations of peaceful societies, with the overall interpretation being explications on indigenous conceptions of human nature and categories of emotions. We have therefore decided to place that section first. The general theoretical discussion on concepts and definitions is therefore — perhaps surprisingly — put at the end. These parts are separated by two papers which present the key concepts of innate sociality and intersubjectivity.

The Conference received generous financial support from the Seminars Committee of the University of Edinburgh Faculty of Social Sciences and from the Munro Lectureship Fund, University of Edinburgh. We wish to thank both these bodies for the support without which the Conference could not have taken place.

Oslo, June 1988
Signe Howell

INTRODUCTION

SIGNE HOWELL AND ROY WILLIS

WHAT ANTHROPOLOGISTS CAN CONTRIBUTE

Debates about human aggression have been dominated by psychologists and ethologists. Too many of them treat aggression as an innate drive in the individual of the species, so that society enters the picture merely as a modifying influence — if indeed it enters at all.

Although there are important differences between the various theories, the great majority of researchers assert that 'aggression' (however defined; see below for a discussion on definitions) is an integral part of human nature; and that aggressive impulses and behaviour have somehow to be directed and controlled for human relations to be sustained over time in a social setting. Scientists present their ideas to the general public, contributing directly or indirectly to debates in social, legal, and religious domains. Their views on questions of human aggression and violence therefore assume major importance in the moral community of which they form a part. The question of what explanatory status one is to accord 'aggressive drives' in violent (and undesirable) behaviour underlies many socio-legal debates. If part of human nature, to what extent are they legitimate as explanation? To what extent should one draw upon socio-economic factors to explain such behaviour? To what extent must the individual be held responsible for him/herself? These are vexed questions that involve the whole community in Western societies: scientists, professionals, and the general public. The rather surprising introduction of a moral dimension to this apparently scientific debate does, however, render it ambiguous — an ambiguity which becomes even more manifest when scientists present their ideas to a wider audience. It is therefore extremely

1

important that their findings should be presented as theories, not facts (see Kuhn 1962, and Feyerabend 1978 for discussion on the issues involved).

Despite the massive increase in the volume of research in psychology and ethology, little progress seems to have been made. We wish to propose an alternative approach, challenging the assumption that aggression is an innate human drive. It is undeniably the case that in Western society aggression is regarded as part of human nature. But perhaps this tells us more about Western society than about human nature. We wish to suggest that we cannot assume an *a priori* aggressive drive in humans. The presence of innate sociality, on the other hand, has much evidence in its favour. Humans are *a priori* sociable beings; it is their co-operativeness that has enabled them to survive, not their aggressive impulses. Such an assumption underlies the ethnographic papers in this volume, and the argument will be further elaborated below.

Within social anthropology there has, in recent years, emerged a new interest in such questions, adopting a cross-cultural, comparative approach to the study of war, aggression, and violence. Several edited volumes have been published that deal specifically with these issues. However, their sole interest has, in almost every case, been to explain the violent aspects of societies (see e.g. Bramson and Goethals 1964; Bohannan 1967; Fried *et al.* 1967; Vayda 1976; Ferguson 1984; Le Crone Foster *et al.* 1986; Riches 1986). The opposite of violent behaviour, namely peaceful cohabitation on a societal scale, has — with the notable exception of Montagu (1978) — been ignored. As Klama has recently observed in a penetrating critique of the literature on 'aggression', there is a close correspondence between certain popular conceptions of human nature in our society and a number of influential scientific theories to do with the 'biological basis of human behaviour' (Klama 1988: 52).

We believe that social anthropologists can contribute more to the debates, in both empirical and theoretical terms. First, we can present descriptions and interpretations of societies that do not conform to the Western model of humans as essentially aggressive. We can do this by presenting societies whose ideological construction of human nature and behaviour is such as to favour peaceful co-existence. Second, we can offer an alternative way of understanding society, by setting human ideas and behaviour firmly within a socio-cultural context, focusing explicitly on indigenous ideas and values concerning human nature. Most of the anthropologists represented in this volume have worked in societies in which the empirical evidence is such as to cast doubt on conventional wisdom. The typical Western attitude is aptly expressed by David Hume, writing more than two centuries ago in his famous essay *An Inquiry Concerning Human Understanding* of 1748.

> Should a traveller, returning from a far country, bring us an account of men wholly different from any with whom we were ever acquainted; men who were entirely divested of vice, ambition, or revenge; who knew no pleasure but friendship, generosity, and public spirit; we should immediately, from these circumstances, detect the falsehood, and prove him a liar, with the same certainty as if he ha[d] stuffed his narration with stories of centaurs and dragons, miracles and prodigies (quoted in Freeman 1984: 95).

Such, however, seem to be the tales that the anthropologists in this volume have brought home with them. Are we all to be ridiculed? Have we simply not done our job as fieldworkers properly? Or is there some way in which we can accept and make sense of what we found to be the case? Grappling with this problem has led us to reject a sharp either/or dichotomy in terms of innate versus cultural, and instead to posit the existence in human beings of innate potentialities and capacities — as well as innate constraints — that may be turned to peaceful as much as to warlike ends, potentialities and capacities that are necessarily set within the particularity of a moral and semantic universe. As Carrithers and Trevarthen and Logotheti argue in this volume, it is primarily with the construction of such moral and semantic universes (or 'cultures') that the innate potentialities, capacities, and constraints are concerned.

PROBLEMS OF DEFINITIONS

Biological, psychoanalytic, ethological, ecological, social learning, and cognitive theorists have all attempted to further our understanding of aggression. Most would agree that we are far from any theoretical consensus. Marsh and Campbell (1982) attribute the lack of progress to a number of factors, including the difficulty of studying aggression both in laboratory and naturalistic settings, and to the compartmentalization of the academic world which leads to lack of communication across disciplines. While we agree with this, we

3

would add another major obstacle, namely problems of definition of the object of study.

Aggression or violence: emotion or behaviour?

The debate is bedevilled by the problem of definition; a problem which is exacerbated by a common failure to clarify whether aggression is an experiential state or a way of behaving. The conflation of the two confuses the issue, and reinforces the tendency for the behaviour to be reduced to an inner state — and hence rendered less open to investigation.

Thus aggression is often taken as synonymous with violence; violent behaviour being taken as proof of the existence of an inner state called aggression. A brief scanning of the literature reveals numerous unquestioned assumptions and a high degree of confusion and contradiction in what is being talked about. Warfare, for example, is often taken as proof of human aggressive impulses; but as Montagu (1976) tellingly points out, we can assume no aggressive feeling in the pilot dropping powerful bombs from a great height. War is a social, not a psychological, fact.

The problem amounts to isolating criteria according to which we can identify an aggressive act. Is it correct to claim, as Marsh does, that aggression is 'the inflicting of physical hurt' with its associated aim of 'subduing or achieving dominance over a rival' (1978: 33) or should one follow Eibl-Eibesfeldt's broader definition and classify behaviour as aggressive 'if it leads to another party's being hurt; this includes not just physical hurt (injury or destruction) but any kind of hurt, including annoyance, taunts or insults' (1978: 29)?

Siann, in a recent study *Accounting for Aggression* which gives an excellent overview of existing theories and positions, does make a distinction between aggression and violence. According to her, aggression 'involves the intention to hurt or emerge superior to others, does not necessarily involve physical injury (violence) and may or may not be regarded as being underpinned by different kinds of motives'. Violence 'involves the use of great physical force or intensity and, while it is often impelled by aggressive motivation, may occasionally be used by individuals in a mutual violent interaction which is regarded by both parties as intrinsically rewarding' (Siann 1985: 12). While she does have the merit, in contrast to the majority of researchers, of making the distinction between an inner state and an

4

outward act, her definitions do not emerge as analytic categories to be employed for comparative purposes — mainly because they do not avoid the problem of reification, raised below.

Heelas has also given a survey of the different attempts at defining aggression, and the main theories which account for it (Heelas 1982, 1983). In this volume, he argues against 'essentialism', by which he means the application of a cross-culturally applicable definition based on some 'essence' of aggression which then can be 'employed to "read off" the nature of acts'. In a similar vein Gibson (this volume) argues, 'The most basic issue is whether we are to define aggression without reference to native concepts. Those who argue that a universal definition of aggression is possible and even desirable are often interested . . . in whether the members of one society can be said to be "more aggressive" than another according to some quantitative scale'. Both Heelas and Gibson, as well as the rest of the contributors to this volume, are extremely sceptical of the viability of such an enterprise.

In a discussion concerning the use and meaning of the Anglo-Saxon term 'violence', Riches makes the pertinent point,

the analysis could be damagingly influenced by the 'folk' theories about violence which obtain in the analyst's lay culture. Stressing the apparent universality, intractability and unacceptability of the problem of violence, the theories prominent in Anglo-Saxon lay ideas focus strongly on the irrationality and bestiality of violence . . . the approach to violence advocated in the discipline of ethology — in which violence is seen at least partly as having genetic determinants — is rather close to Anglo-Saxon folk ideas. (1986: 2)

Thus, research on humans, or research that has implications for explaining humans, is rarely, if ever, neutral. This of course applies equally to those who make substantive universalistic claims for a fundamentally peaceful drive in humans.

Historically, in the West, the ideas that there is in human nature some intrinsic element or principle which drives human beings to commit damaging and destructive actions is of considerable antiquity and is deeply embedded in the Judaeo-Christian tradition of innate sinfulness. The concept of aggression, however, is of relatively recent origin. Although the Oxford English Dictionary cites several seventeenth-century literary uses of the word, its vogue in academic and popular discourse derives from twentieth-century psychoanalysis and animal ethology. Etymologically, as Fromm reminds us (1973: 189), the English word is based on two Latin words, *ad* and *gradior*, with the combined sense of 'movement towards'. It would appear to have been adopted in psychoanalysis because of its air of scientific detachment and objectivity, its freedom from the objectionable religious overtones of such terms as 'sin' and 'evil'. It is ironic, therefore, that Freud, the anti-religious father of psychoanalysis, should have chosen to use the term aggression as implicitly synonymous with evil and wickedness in his well-known and passionate indictment of his own species:

> Men are not gentle, friendly creatures wishing for love, who simply defend themselves if they are attacked, but . . . a powerful measure of desire for aggression has to be reckoned as part of their instinctual endowment . . . *Homo homini lupus*: who has the courage to dispute it in the face of all evidence in his own life and in history? This aggressive cruelty usually lies in wait for some provocation. (Freud 1939: 50, 51)

In the scientific and popular cultures of our civilization Freud's ideas have acquired the status of virtually self-evident truth. In the widely read book *Human Aggression*, the psychoanalyst Anthony Storr draws our attention to the 'sombre fact that we are the cruellest and most ruthless species that has ever walked the earth' (1968: i).

The above quotes demonstrate, above all, that there is a strong tradition in the West to regard human beings as innately aggressive in our psychic make-up and, resulting from this, violent in our behaviour.

Reification

Many writers, from different disciplines, treat aggression (or aggressive behaviour, if the distinction is made) as a discernible phenomenon, a discrete category which can be studied in isolation from a social and semantic context. Regardless of their theoretical predilections, working definitions, and methods of obtaining data, all such approaches have the effect of hypostasizing something called 'aggression'. In our view all such definitions are generic, subject to the 'fallacy of misplaced concreteness' (Whitehead 1925). Aggression becomes a category or phenomenon whose presence or absence is a matter for empirical investigation. Such has been the assumption underlying much of previous anthropological literature also. But it is precisely the sort of presupposition which anthropologists should challenge, allowing, as it does, so little place for a social construction of knowledge and values and so much for (unexplained) 'human nature'. There is therefore a need to question this assumption that aggression is a given element which somehow has to be accounted for. Campbell (this volume) argues that the search for absolute categories for comparative purposes in various societies is a fruitless enterprise. Instead he proposes an approach that asks the question 'How do these people deal with certain basic human predicaments?' and makes the pertinent point that 'the problem is not the quality we have isolated, e.g., aggression, but how far we can get with an adequate description of what we have found'. If one persists in treating the phenomenon 'aggression' as just that: as a phenomenon or fixed category finding an expression in violent behaviour, rather than treating violent behaviour as the resultant of values acted out, one is forced into simplistic either/or terms, as in the nature versus nurture debates (see below).

In interpreting ideas and behaviour in societies which others might characterize as 'peaceful', we suggest abandoning the focus on the lack of something called 'aggression' (or violence) and the construction of theories that attempt to account for this 'anomalous' absence. Instead, we advocate an alternative approach that dispenses with universalistic definitions and the testing of these. This came out strongly during the Conference, and there was general agreement between the participants that a more fruitful approach is to try to locate interpersonal, or intersocietal, behaviour within the wider discourse of ideology and practice of the society in question. In particular, what is the indigenous theory concerning human nature? What metaphysical constructs embellish the theory? What social and interpersonal practices do they give rise to? What are the mechanisms by which behaviour is directed and controlled? Violent behaviour, in the most general sense, can only be understood in association with other behaviour within the same society. Behaviour is never culturally neutral, but always embedded within a shared set of meanings.

Markedness in language

An accepted notion that aggression is a given characteristic in humans everywhere leads to a search for it in various social settings. This, however, begs the question and determines the formulation of research, phrasing the questions in terms of how aggressive drives are handled. The vocabulary of the debates reflects this, for the contrast is drawn between aggression and non-aggression, violence and non-violence; it is the absence of conflict, not the presence of something else that is noted. The whole emphasis is placed on the terms being negated, thereby reflecting a profound bias towards aggression as the norm. Such a usage of a negation is in conformity with all linguistic markedness and unmarkedness. The marked term is usually short, learned early in life, resistant to acculturative replacement, morphologically simple, generic (as opposed to specific), commonly used, phonologically and orthographically simple; and the unmarked term displays all the reverse characteristics. Hence our preference for the terms 'peace' and 'peaceful' which embody all the advantages of markedness while at the same time better express our general position in this particular instance. 'Peace' and 'peaceful' are not, however, intended as universalistic analytic terms, but their usage is intended to mark a fundamental shift in theoretical focus. Of course these too can be criticized on the grounds that they lack precision, and carry with them built-in biases, impeding both our understanding of our own field experience as well as obstructing cross-cultural understanding. It is our hope that the papers in this collection go some way towards rebutting such charges.

WHAT IS THE APPEAL OF THE INNATE AGGRESSIONIST APPROACH?

Introductory remarks

The view of human nature as fundamentally aggressive can be expected to prevail in those domains where it corresponds with social and cultural ideology. Carrithers (this volume) makes a useful distinction between science and pop science. By the latter he means theories that confirm, unreflectedly, our prejudices. Man thought of as the aggressive animal confirms such Western prejudices.

The view that aggression is an integral part of human nature has been strongly argued for a long time by exceptionally articulate and persuasive individuals. Many of them have directed their writings to a popular audience, and as Ferguson says, 'in doing so, have often sacrificed standards of logic and evidence in favor of the pithy illustration or memorable quote'; and he continues 'Wilson [1978: 99] raises the favorite question of college seminars and cocktail party conversations which is, "are human beings innately aggressive?" His answer is a flat yes. It is this unqualified yes that will be remembered at the seminars and cocktail parties, when his pages of qualification or the tepid conclusions . . . are long forgotten' (1984: 11). The better known propounders of innate human aggression are Lorenz (1966), Morris (1967), Ardrey (1966), Storr (1968), Konner (1984; see Carrithers, this volume), Tiger and Fox (1971), Tiger (1969), and Eibl-Eibesfeldt (1979): all of whom, to varying degrees, base their conclusions on animal behaviour and link these with a theory of the role of violence in hominid evolution. A salutary cautionary note is sounded by Zillmann who concludes after a painstaking review of experimental evidence that 'the amount of relevant data on animal aggression from both laboratory and field investigations is nearly overwhelming. In sharp contrast, research findings concerning the specific differences between animals and man in the mechanics of aggression are almost nonexistent' (1979: 7). While ethologists, like Zillmann, do not necessarily agree with the views of the innate aggressionists, their voices are not heard outside their own circle. The arguments of those who confirm the pop notions have been readily incorporated into popular Western consciousness, finding rich and varied expression in the arts and media.

No doubt there are numerous and complex reasons for the strength of Western adherence to such views. They are to be looked for in our Western indigenous psychological explanations as much as in the domains of scientific pursuit which, as Riches notes above, are not themselves free from such ontological conceptions. To our mind, they can be usefully examined under the following four headings.

Man as animal

Members of most non-Western societies regard themselves as the most superior form of being, in possession of the most desirable qualities. Westerners, on the other hand, attribute to themselves many characteristics they most dislike and, moreover, grant these a powerful explanatory role. The fact that, biologically speaking, we belong to the animal kingdom is frequently used as an explanation for violent behaviour, and the animal metaphor is frequently invoked. William Golding's novel *Lord of the Flies*, read by many British school-children, is seen as an example of the innately brutal characteristics of humans. Schoolboys reveal themselves as having only a thin veneer of 'civilization' which, once the constraints of authority are removed, disappears, laying bare their 'true nature' which is violent, domineering, and competitive, resulting in the survival of the fittest in a most literal sense. Similarly, the violence in many sections of our own society today is, in the media, taken as proof of 'the animal nature of man' which — an insult to many animals — is always understood to be destructively aggressive. Similarly, 'the law of the jungle', meaning, in fact, the absence of any laws, metaphorically links humans and animals. Such theories take the individual as the starting point; and the inherent sociality that we are arguing for — and which precludes any form of methodological individualism — is given little or no credence. As becomes clear from most of the papers in this collection, this particular view of human nature is not one shared by many other societies. They may attribute unattractive and negatively valued characteristics to their enemies or neighbours, but most certainly not to themselves.

Authoritarianism

Second, and related to the first point, the model of man as a violent animal — and hence self-seeking and violent in the pursuit of attaining his goals — is useful as a justification for authority and insti-tutions of authority. It is also found at the base of the neo-classical economic theory of capitalism, with its basic tenet of man as a maximizing individual with limitless needs and desires — a notion Sahlins deconstructed many years ago (1974), but one that still persists in Western economic and political thought, and which under-lies much of the anthropology of conflict. Such thinking is part of a long tradition, finding its most clear formulation in the political philosophy of Hobbes where human society is presented as being in a state of 'warre' in which every man fights every other man for control of resources and for the (presumed) pleasure of dominance. Hobbes' extreme views are often juxtaposed with those of Rousseau, who viewed human nature as innately 'good' and attributes the manifest defects in human behaviour to the corrupting effects of 'society' or of 'culture'. Subsequent debates have tended to favour the Hobbesian view, arguing for institutions of authority, and dismissing Rousseau as a romantic utopianist who simply did not accept people for what they 'really are'. Robarchek (this volume) sets his discussion of the Semai within the frame of what he argues has become a 'sterile dichotomy in Western thought' as a direct result of the ideas of these two philosophers.

Sexism

Third, the views of the innate aggressionists and their followers reflect — and implicitly reinforce — sexism, since it is usually man who is presented in the Hobbesian mould, with a sleight-of-hand extension of man into Man. Here the subject of enquiry purports to be an understanding of human nature, whereas the object of study is in fact the male half of society. Woman is either ignored or presented as innately less aggressive than man. The arguments for a biological difference in the sexes in this regard are far from conclusive, but in cases where such a difference is put forward, the general conclusions of *humanity*'s aggressive nature are not revised. Examples are too numerous to list, but a particularly telling one from members of our own profession, where one might expect some awareness, can serve. In their book *The Imperial Animal*, Tiger and Fox state,

> While possessing females is important to the young males, and is in some sense the whole point of the evolutionary process, it is not necessarily the basic motivating factor [in intra-male fighting]. The possession of a female or females can be viewed as one more valida-tion of male status, which is an end in itself, because, once achieved, the women follow anyway. Whatever the advocates of student power do want — and it is not always clear — one thing they plainly do *not* want is access to their professors' wives (1971: 111).

The 'imperial animal' of the title is exclusively male, whether he be the shaper of human evolution or the intellectual of today. Similar underlying assumptions can be found in Chagnon's famous study of the Yanomamo. He explains male Yanomamo violence as individual competition motivated less by considerations of material well-being than by 'reproductive striving' (1983: 86), i.e., men compete over access to women and the subsequent offspring. These assertions, that men need to compete and that women are an important object of competition, are contradicted by evidence from at least four of the societies described in this volume (Overing, Robarchek, Howell, Willis). Siann concludes that evidence from hormonal studies and ethology is extremely ambiguous and that no conclusions can be drawn with regard to male and female behaviour or emotions, and that psychoanalytic approaches cannot produce any firm answers on questions of sex and gender (Siann 1985: 33–9, 82–4, 123–8). Again, the ethnographic examples of Semai, Chewong, and Piaroa demonstrate that indigenous views regarding emotional and behavioural differences in men and women need not necessarily be conceptualized.

Militarism

Fourth, the Western post-war build-up of defence is partially justified in the above terms. The nuclear arms race, and East–West conflict, is seen as inevitable given that human nature is what it is (namely competitive, aggressive, and combative) and the consequent pessimism shared by a large proportion of Western Europe's population concerning the possibility of nuclear war is again expressed in such terms. War is popularly perceived as part and parcel of what it means to be human, and, with ever increasing deadly weapons, the devastating impact of war is consequently accepted as inevitable.

Some critical comments

Culture, the pre-eminently human factor, has, in much ethology, socio-biology, psychology, and psychoanalysis, been either ignored totally, or at best relegated to a secondary position, a modifying role. Yet Robin Fox, who works from within a socio-biological framework, concedes, rather surprisingly, that 'symbol-making is as much a human attribute as sex and food' (1982: 13). This important point is often ignored, and can in our view be taken further; to suggest that in human society there are *no* natural and neutral phenomena. Acts like eating, sexual intercourse, and fighting are embedded in a socially shared set of associated symbols, and they cannot be isolated from this semantic setting. This is true of human behaviour of all kinds, and of human emotions. None is an objective phenomenon to be studied in isolation; they are all constructed from within the society in

12

question and can only be interpreted in conjunction with other social ideas, in particular indigenous ideas concerning human nature.

AGGRESSION AND VIOLENCE IN ANTHROPOLOGICAL THEORY

Social anthropologists have not, on the whole, been very interested in the general empirical study of aggression, violence, and peacefulness. In British social anthropology, the implicit assumption has been that humans are violent, and that society in various ways controls and constrains. Theories were developed that might be regarded as dealing with such issues only in the field of conflict. Here two main theoretical strands can be isolated. First, how conflict permeates and shapes human interaction and social organization, and second, how the idea of conflict helps elucidate the genesis, escalation, de-escalation, and consequences of combat, violent confrontation, wars, etc. In British and American anthropology, such issues were rarely dealt with directly, but were linked to four main theoretical approaches: cultural relativism, legal and political anthropology, the study of ritual, and bio-ecological determinism. We will allude briefly to the main points, as we see them, of these approaches. (For a detailed presentation of anthropological theories concerning the study of war and conflict, see Ferguson's 'Introduction' to *Warfare, Culture, and Environment* (1984) which, while adhering to a 'materialist' approach, nevertheless provides a useful overview of other anthropological views.)

Cultural relativism

Most social anthropologists probably adhere to some form of 'soft' cultural relativism, whereby the thrust of explanation of human ideas and behaviour is placed within the framework of the particular socio-cultural institutions of a society. They thus decline to proffer a general, universal theory; while at the same time postulating an unexamined 'psychic unity of mankind'. A 'harder' version was expressed in the old 'nurture versus nature' debate of the pre-war era, in which American anthropologists in particular, following the lead of Boas, engaged themselves. The so-called Culture and Personality school of the 1920s, 1930s, and 1940s held that human behaviour was the provenance of culture, not of race, and attempts were made to relate traits of individual personality and symbolic aspects of culture to socialization variables (Lipsey 1985: 180). The debate was recently brought to life again with Freeman's forceful attack on the work by Margaret Mead from Samoa (Freeman 1984). Mead was one of the best-known anthropologists arguing for a nurture perspective on human behaviour. As such, she was an adherent of the particular alliance between psychological behaviourism and cultural relativism which Boas favoured and which won widespread acceptance in American anthropology. Freeman was particularly out to demolish Mead's suggestion (1928) that Samoan society is characterized by values emphasizing uninhibited playfulness and peaceful co-existence, accusing her of having misunderstood Samoan society. This is not the place to discuss the intricacies of the argument and those it gave rise to in the anthropological press (for a cross section of the arguments see, e.g., Strathern 1983; Brady 1983); the purpose in raising it is to note the continued appeal of the debate and to point out Freeman's confident rejection of the possibility of a peaceful society.

Much of the debate surrounding cultural relativism has been polarized into extreme — and ultimately simplistic — either/or terms, as in the nature versus nurture debates. However, the excesses of 'pop socio-biology' should not, as Carrithers points out (in this volume), lead us to a wholesale rejection of the evidence for certain genetically transmitted predispositions in the human animal. To assert that all normal human behaviour is culturally moulded does not necessarily prove that it is also culturally determined. Such has been the assumption behind much work in socio-cultural anthropology. Like pop socio-biology it bears the unmistakable imprint of a particular cultural view of the world, resulting in a projection of ethnographic 'material' onto inert 'other cultures'. Carrithers states, 'My intention is not at all to replace the notion of culture, but to argue that sociality is a necessary precondition for the existence of culture.' Even more importantly, there is every reason to believe, with Mary Midgley, that the basic assumption behind cultural relativism/behaviourism that human beings are totally plastic and devoid of innate structuration is false: 'Sensible psychologists have tended more and more to admit that people do have some genetically fixed tendencies' and she continues that 'What makes this admission hard, is the very strong impression still prevalent that we have to *choose* between considering these tendencies and considering outside conditions' (1979: 20).

As anthropologists we stress context as a methodological necessity. The danger in exclusively privileging the socio-cultural context in the interpretation of human institutions and behaviour is that every social phenomenon becomes so context-dependent that it cannot be translated across cultures. While avoiding strict definitions of social categories, we can nevertheless examine manifestations of how humans in different social settings seek answers to the general existential questions. By accepting an innate predilection to sociality and a fluid range of capacities and constraints, we can focus on indigenous conceptions concerning human nature and human inner states, while avoiding the particularistic errors of cultural relativism.

Political and legal anthropology

Many of the anthropologists dealing with political organization have chosen to approach this from a conflict perspective. Bohannan in his introduction to the *American Museum Sourcebooks in Anthropology* entitled *Law and Warfare* states 'We shall never banish conflict. . . . Rather conflict must be controlled and must be utilized profitably in order to create more and better cultural means of living and working together' (1967: xi). And he continues, 'We need a new "code of aggressions". . . . Conflict is useful. In fact, society is impossible without conflict. But society is worse than impossible without control of conflict. . . . Total repression of conflict leads to anarchy just as surely as does total conflict' (ibid. xii). Such a view echoes that of Freud.

> The existence of this tendency to aggression . . . makes it necessary for culture to institute its high demands. Culture . . . has to erect barriers against the aggressive instincts of men and hold their manifestations in check by reaction-formations in men's minds (1939: 51).

The job of the anthropologist from such a perspective becomes to demonstrate ethnographically how different societies handle conflict through the various political and legal institutions. The 1940s and 1950s saw a great number of ethnographic studies in the British functionalist and structural–functionalist modes, whereby social institutions were analysed in terms of how they maintain the *status quo* of the particular society. One of the most explicit political theories of that period is that of Gluckman. In his famous essay 'The Peace in the Feud' (1955) conflict is again the analytic starting-point for the understanding of society, and the problem is most severe in the analysis of so-called acephalous societies. 'Where do social order and cohesion lie in such societies?' he asks. Gluckman's thesis is that in these societies, the fundamental propensity in men to quarrel is held in check by cross-cutting allegiances. Thus,

> This is the central theme of my thesis — how men quarrel in terms of their customary allegiances, but are restrained from violence through other conflicting alliances which are also enjoined on them by custom. The result is that conflicts in one set of relationships, over a wide range of society, or over a long period of time, lead to the re-establishment of social cohesion (1955: 2).

In other words, paradoxically, feuding has a place in society to maintain the *status quo*.

Similar studies were all analysed with an overall framework of interrelating forms of social organization with the frequency and manifestation of social conflict.

Ritual as catharsis

A different, though often related, approach can be found in one of the several 'displacement of aggression' theories. Here, aggression is taken as a given which must find some outlet. Dollard *et al.* (1969) are generally credited with the formulation of the 'frustration – aggression hypothesis' whereby it is held that the obstruction of goal-oriented behaviour leads necessarily to aggression. This, like most of the purely psychological theories — including psychoanalytic ones — are strictly methodological – individualistic. Thus they are based on the individual psyche and make a theoretical leap from this to the universal psyche. There are, however, some anthropologists who have tried to translate Dollard's ideas into social terms. Frustrations on a group scale may be explained in terms of the group finding release by going to war with its neighbours, or through a collective cathartic experience such as a ritual performance. Internal tensions can be resolved through a creative channelling and thereby reinforce the group's own boundary. But it is probably more at an implicit, unexamined, level that much anthropological writing adheres to the frustration – aggression hypothesis.

Ritual has been regarded by several anthropologists as a social event in which pent-up emotions can find some form of release. Malinowski (1964) argues that ritual served an important function in that it alleviated the anxiety of the participants in areas of uncertainty. Radcliffe-Brown (1952) and Evans-Pritchard (1965) denied this, stating that there was no *a priori* reason for not assuming the opposite, namely that ritual creates anxiety, and that the task of the anthropologist was not to infer psychological states in others, but to focus on the sociological significance of social institutions: ritual being one such. Nevertheless, the 'pressure cooker' metaphor, through which violent and potentially destructive emotions must find an outlet, has frequently been applied in the study of ritual and ecstatic religious behaviour. Turner in his studies of Ndembu symbols and ritual (1957 and 1967) tried explicitly to bring together a sociological and a psychological explanatory framework for the understanding of ritual. He suggested that one of the functions of ritual is the shedding of 'bad' feelings, being the final resort in conflict-solving in what he calls 'social drama'. Turner, however, also allowed for the possibility that rituals do in themselves provoke strong emotions; emotions which then have to be directed.

Such anthropological theories are linked to the catharsis theory, whereby it is held that through some dramatic experience the individual (or group) sheds itself of pent-up, potentially destructive, emotions to emerge cleansed and ready to deal with daily life in a harmonious manner. Like the 'pop' version of innate aggression, there is in the West today a similar 'pop' version of the necessity for catharsis. Howell (this volume) takes up some of these issues in her paper where she argues against the interpretation of ritual as catharsis among the Chewong. Much of Western psychotherapy draws, in various forms, on the catharsis model, whereby it is held as necessary for emotional health to come to terms with the repressed anger that is assumed to be inside the individual, and techniques are developed to make the individual confront these in a dramatic form. The sociologist Scheff is probably the social scientist who has attempted the most thoroughgoing analysis of catharsis in social life. In his book *Catharsis in Healing, Ritual, and Drama* much of previous psychological and anthropological thinking around the issue is incorporated. His is an attempt to put emotions firmly back into studies of social behaviour and he concludes that catharsis is a potentially useful mechanism for psychic health, and that repression of emotions produces instability. Although he allows for many areas of uncertainty in the study of catharsis, Scheff nevertheless accepts the universality of the need to handle destructive emotions, and proposes that ritual, as a cathartic experience, be reinstated in the West as 'a dramatic form for coping with universal distress' (1979: 114). While we agree that emotions should become a legitimate study for anthropologists, we nevertheless feel that the degree of consensus is minimal in such matters and that, for the time being at least, we should abandon universalistic explanatory models, and instead locate such studies within the indigenous understanding.

Socio-biology and ecological materialism

Much of the systematic anthropological work on war and conflict in recent years has been made within an ecological or socio-biological analytical framework. While there are major differences between the two, we have chosen to refer to them together. Socio-biology drew much of its inspiration from the zoologist E. O. Wilson who proclaimed in 1975 the birth of a new synthetic superdiscipline that would merge social science with biology, and which he named sociobiology. This particular theoretical stance has found most of its adherents amongst American anthropologists. Ferguson gives a historical outline of the various approaches which he terms 'materialist'. With regard to their treatment of the present topic, he says, 'A materialist approach to war focuses on war's relations to the practical problems of maintaining life and living standards. Since 1960, this usually has meant studying war in relation to local ecology' (1984: 23). He distinguishes two main types of ecological studies: the origins and evolution of wars and the function of wars.

Much has been written by social anthropologists against the materialist approaches in ethnographic analysis. In our view, we can do no better than quote from Sahlin's direct attack on sociobiology:

> Consider the relation between warfare and human aggression — what Wilson at one point calls 'the true, biological joy of warfare'. It is evident that the people engaged in fighting wars — or for that matter, any kind of fighting — are by no means necessarily aggressive, either in the course of action or beforehand. Many are plainly terrified. People engaged in wars may have any number of motivations to do so . . . ethnographically the energies that move

men to fight are practically coterminous with the range of human motivations (1977: 7).

And later,

For between the basic drives that may be attributed to human nature and the social structures of human culture there enters a critical indeterminacy. The same human motives appear in different cultural forms, and different motives appear in the same forms (ibid.: 11).

AN ALTERNATIVE APPROACH

The idea of human nature and sociality as innate capacity

We have on several occasions referred to the interpretative importance of indigenous constructions of human nature and human emotionality. We know of no empirical examples of a society that does not, however implicitly, hold collective views on what it means to be a human being. Indeed, 'Every religion includes an image of personhood' (Harris 1978: 76). Ideas concerning human nature can thus be said to constitute a human universal. If this is so, then we feel that there is a way out of the various *impasses* discussed above. By placing our theoretical focus in the interpretation of other societies on the social constructions of personhood, we lay the foundation for a legitimate comparative enterprise.

Moreover, by accepting the overwhelming evidence that there *are* innate human capacities, predilections, and constraints, we can take a step further in such an enterprise. Thus human beings come prepackaged with a set of potential capacities and constraints, but these in themselves are not fixed or determined. Rather, they are a set of directives for an imaginative negotiation which seek specific definition in the cultural setting. Among these may be listed the capacity for co-operative behaviour and the capacity for uncooperative, competitive action (both conceptual and physical). The important point to stress is that humans appear to possess an innate capacity for finding common cause in a great number of cultural activities, a capacity Carrithers in this volume calls 'sociality'. Such a capacity would not explain the specific instances of human socio-cultural arrangements in their immense variety — that could only be done by reference to local histories, local circumstances, and local causes —

19

but it could explain how such a range and history of variation was possible at all. Such suggestions are borne out by Trevarthen and Logotheti (this volume). They argue, from the evidence of infant behaviour, that *Homo sapiens* is born with the capacity to participate in the collective understanding; to learn the meanings of his/her particular culture. On the basis of many years' detailed observation of infants, they argue for the existence of what they call 'innate inter-subjectivity' as a universal motivation, present in the newborn and peculiar to our species, that leads the child to acquire symbolic understanding. This means that we have an innate predisposition to experience and act inter-subjectively, beginning with an awareness of ourselves as social beings with emotions in relationship to other social beings who have the same emotions, interests, and intentions which we can perceive. We regard such a theory as providing us, as anthropologists, with a concept of useful explanatory power. Moreover, it allows us to talk more confidently of a psychic and cognitive unity of humanity without limiting us to absolute categories.

However, it is important to note that a theory of innate human sociality is not a reductionist theory. Unlike pop socio-biology, which appeals to the gene as the ultimate and fundamental causal factor in human evolution and behaviour, innate sociality supposes a predisposition in human beings towards the continual absorption of existing meanings and the creation of new meanings in local universes of thought that are constantly being discovered, destroyed, and negotiated anew in the process of social interaction. The relation between these inherent motives for culture and society is a matter that requires analysis of the epigenetic regulations of brain growth, about which little is yet known.

Thus sociality, together with indigenous theories of human nature, provide a framework for comparison between different societies and cultures, including the various 'peaceful societies' described in this volume. As we (Carrithers, and Trevarthen and Logotheti) have already noted, sociality, as an innate, presumably genetically inscribed predisposition in all human beings, explains both the existence of the characteristic human ability to construct systems of cultural meaning and the enormous empirical variations observed to occur in such systems. More, the fact that this being, *Homo sapiens*, is from the moment of birth aware of itself in relation to others, and experiences and defines itself in such a relational mode, suggests the universal, pre-cultural basis of a relational concept that appears to occur in one form or another in all human cultural systems: the complementarity of Self and Other; Us and Them. Innate 'I – Thou' appears, then, to be the origin of cultural 'Us – Them'. Always shifting, always situationally determined like the ever-changing systems of cultural meaning in which it is embedded, the Self – Other/Us – Them boundaries are also the emic ground of kinship and enmity, affiliative and 'aggressive' behaviour, peace and war (see also below).

It may perhaps have been valid in the past to dichotomize theoretical stances into endogenous (formulated in terms of what is natural to humans) and exogenous (formulated in terms of socio-cultural factors) (Heelas 1983); but many biologists today think that there is a built-in capacity for change through learning capable of giving directive impulses for change. Thus, while we may be born with a certain 'equipment' this does not necessarily determine behaviour; and, furthermore, behaviour can alter the equipment.

The view that co-operation, not competition, is more conducive for survival is also gaining ground among biologists and ethologists. The ethologist P. Bateson abhors the way competition is used as an explanatory factor in evolutionary theory, and says,

> The pattern generated by co-operative behaviour could distinguish one social group from another and could mean the difference between group survival and communal death . . . It is a travesty of Darwinism to suggest that all that matters in social life is conflict. One individual may be more likely to survive because it is better suited to making its way about its environment and not because it is fiercer than others. Individuals may survive better when they join forces with others (1985: 3).

Similar ideas are expressed by Leakey and Lewin:

> Throughout our recent evolutionary history, particularly since the rise of a hunting way of life, there must have been extreme selective pressures in favour of our ability to co-operate as a group: organized food gathering and hunts are successful only if each member of the band knows his task and joins in with the activity of his fellows; a good deal of restraint on natural impulses during the stalk and capture of the prey is likewise essential. The degree of selective pressure towards co-operation group awareness, and

identification was so strong, and the period over which it operated was so extended (at least three million years, and probably even longer), *that it can hardly fail to have become embedded to some measure in our genetic makeup* (1977: 209, emphasis ours).

While we find this second passage of great interest, we feel that the concept of 'natural impulses' is problematic in two ways. First, there would appear to be an assumption that these are in their essence unco-operative, something which we would question, and second, the restraint itself would have to be a natural impulse!

However, if the general points of our argument are right, it seems to us that the innate versus learnt debate loses most of its force; indeed, the papers in this volume corroborate such findings.

We are suggesting, then, that the term 'human aggression' as conventionally and commonly used is doubly skewed by ideological influences that are deep-rooted in our Western culture. On the one hand aggression, though 'natural' (particularly in males) is also condemned as 'bad'. On the other hand, its perceived opposite, peacefulness, carries with it the negatively valued connotations of being passive and inert (qualities which furthermore are associated with females).

THE ETHNOGRAPHIC PAPERS

The ethnographic papers do not provide the 'answer' to why human beings are aggressive (or peaceful). We have argued throughout that such a formulation of the problem is inappropriate, for it leads to a reification of human qualities for the purposes of comparison. Violent and peaceful social interaction is not to be understood through the search for a thing called 'aggression', but through the sensitive and detailed explication of the values and meanings that embody and shape behaviour in different social settings.

The aim of the ethnographic papers is to understand violent and peaceful behaviour in different societies. We believe that the novelty of our approach lies in the focus adopted for interpretation. We accept the fundamental premiss argued by Carrithers, and Trevarthen and Logotheti that sociality is an innate and necessary capacity in humans. From this we put a major explanatory weight on the indigenous construction of human nature and emotions. This approach is novel insofar as the interpretation of behaviour is embedded in moral values directly associated with what is held to constitute a human person.

While we wish to avoid the pitfalls of many earlier studies on 'peaceful' or 'violent' societies by pulling out one behavioural feature as overridingly important in the analysis, we feel nevertheless that several issues of general interest have emerged, all of which are suggestive for the further understanding of societal peaceful co-existence, and we turn now to a brief consideration of some major points that are raised in the ethnographic papers.

Us/Them

It is not uncommon among non-Western societies that humanity is denied to members of other societies. We are the true human beings, they lack something or other, or they are witches, or cannibals (see Arens (1979) for a discussion of this theme). A stark opposition is drawn between the desirable (and 'good') human qualities that we have, and the undesirable (and 'bad') qualities that they, the others, the outsiders have. This is a juxtaposition found in many of the societies discussed in this volume. Although they attribute violent characteristics to outsiders, they all see themselves as inherently peaceful.

For the Buid, the Chewong, the Semai, the Balinese, and the Piaroa it is always 'Them', the dangerous, non-human outsiders who are violent and warlike. In contrast, the social domain of 'Us' is characterized by the absence of combative and destructive behaviour. Buckley's peaceful Northern Ireland community also conforms to this pattern, seeing itself as an island of human values under perpetual 'siege' from dangerous, barely human outsiders.

On the other hand, the Fipa, and the Zapotec do not make such a distinction meaningful. Indeed the Us/Them opposition itself, which Fipa perceive as one between Settlers and Strangers, is culturally 'played down' in favour of the continuing process, by which as a deliberate matter of social and State policy, outsiders are incorporated into the society.

A related point of significance in several instances is the deliberate preference for avoidance rather than confrontation in situations perceived as threatening. This is often accompanied by a self-presentation as 'fearful'. These characteristics are most manifest among the Chewong, Semai, Zapotec, Piaroa, and Buid.

Egalitarian social organization

In several of the societies discussed, institutionalized authority is minimal, and personal autonomy appears to be highly valued. It is possible that this form of political organization is more conducive to non-competitive peaceful behaviour but, as many instances from New Guinea and Amazonia show, it is certainly no guarantee of it.

But in a highly stratified, caste-like society like Bali with a complex division of labour it is understandably difficult to maintain the Chewong-like idea of peaceful interaction between individuals. The ideal and the actual conceptualization of Balinese personhood, as Howe describes it, certainly is one that centres round peace and calm. However, there is a lack of fit between social order and cosmological system, and what are seen by less fortunate Balinese as gross inequalities of wealth and power serve as grounds for occasional breaches of the 'peaceful' ethic.

In contrast with Bali, the Fipa as described by Willis provide an example of a hierarchical and centralized society that has successfully generalized a norm of peaceful interaction originating at the local community level. Here a combination of favourable ecological and economic conditions, at a particular historical moment, appears to have made this achievement possible. And here also gender differences are minimized.

Gender relations

When non-hierarchical, uncentralized societies — like the four hunter-gatherer examples here described — are divided internally on Us/Them lines, it is often the case that gender differences define and establish social distinctions. Such appears to be the case among the unstratified, yam-cultivating peoples of Papua New Guinea (see Strathern, Godelier, etc.). This is also the case among the Shavante, near-neighbours of the 'peaceful' Piaroa. In contrast, Piaroa minimize gender differences and maintain the same normative code of non-violent behaviour for both males and females.

Indeed, an interesting correlation has emerged in the field studies presented between 'peacefulness' as a moral value and gender equality. The Piaroa perception that male and female natures are essentially identical is shared by the Chewong, Semai, Buid, and Fipa. This is an important point in the comparative study of ideology,

24

and brings out the usefulness of focusing on ideas concerning human nature. Most of the literature that deals with indigenous psychologies fails to take into account the possible variations in this respect between not only the sexes, but between other social categories such as chiefs and commoners. Different characteristics and qualities may be attributed to different social categories of humans, accompanied perhaps by different moral demands, and proper account must be taken of these in the study of behaviour. It is a perspective that Freeman in his criticism of Mead totally failed to appreciate, and one that might have reduced the savagery of his attack.

The gender perspective is one that could fruitfully be pursued further in anthropological studies on values in connection with social behaviour. So far the information available is too small to draw any conclusions, but the correlations from the papers in this volume are suggestive and deserve further investigation on a comparative basis.

Cosmological charter

Many of the papers in this volume set the human agent within a cosmology, a total moral universe of meaning. More particularly, there is a focus on indigenous ideas concerning human nature, and the psychological attributes associated with it, and behaviour is interpreted in terms of these ideas. In many of the societies described it is found that the collective is emphasized rather than the individual. This applies very clearly to the Zapotec, who, as O'Nell puts it, ask 'not so much, "Who am I?", but "How am I a part of something?" '. But this is not invariably the case; Robarchek, for example, sees a push for individual autonomy among the Semai and Overing similarly stresses the value of autonomy among the Piaroa. What is common to all, however, is that an emphasis is placed on peaceful interaction among the members of the society, and this emphasis is cosmologically constructed and morally embedded in a cosmological universe of meaning.

CONCLUDING REMARKS

Within the overall acceptance of innate sociality in humans we have tried to shift the debate on human aggression or peacefulness away from definitions and absolute categories, to an investigation of alternative moral orders in which the human person is perceived of as

25

radically different from that constructed through the Judaeo-Christian tradition. Agreeing with Sahlins that 'Culture is not ordered by the primitive emotions of the hypothalamus; it is the emotions which are organized by culture' (1977: 13), we have presented some different social orders where fighting, competition, and other violent behaviour are not part of the order, or part of the people's ideas of what a human being is. We hope we have contributed to the debate surrounding human aggression in a constructive and novel way; and that we have raised some questions surrounding a number of basic notions that have remained unexamined by both the scientific and lay communities.

© 1989 Signe Howell and Roy Willis

REFERENCES

Ardrey, R. (1966) *The Territorial Imperative*, New York: Atheneum.

Arens, W. (1979) *The Man-eating Myth: anthropology & anthropophagy*, Oxford: Oxford University Press.

Bateson, P. (1985) 'Co-operation', *Cambridge Review*: 150–2.

Bateson, P. (1986) 'Sociobiology and human politics', in S. Rose and L. Appignanesi (eds) *Science and Beyond*, Oxford: Blackwell.

Bohannan, P. (ed.) (1967) *Law and Warfare: studies in the anthropology of conflict. N. American Sourcebooks in Anthropology*, New York: The Natural History Press.

Brady, I. (ed.) (1983) 'Speaking in the name of the real: Freeman and Mead on Samoa', *American Anthropologist* 85 (4): 908–47.

Bramson, L. and Goethals, G. W. (eds) (1964) *War: studies from psychology, sociology and anthropology*, New York: Basic Books.

Chagnon, N. (1983) *Yanomamo the Fierce People*, New York: Holt, Rinehart & Winston.

Dollard, J. *et al.* (1969) *Frustration and Aggression* London: Academic Press.

Eibl-Eibesfeldt, I. (1979) *The Biology of Peace and War*, New York: Viking Press.

Evans-Pritchard, E. E. (1965) *Theories of Primitive Religion*, Oxford: Clarendon Press.

Ferguson, R. B. (ed.) (1984) *Warfare, Culture, and Environment*, Orlando: Academic Press.

Feyerabend, P. (1978) *Against Method*, London: Verso.

Foster, Le Crone, M. and Rubinstein, R. A. (eds) (1986) *Peace and War: cross-cultural perspectives*, Oxford: Transaction Books.

Fox, R. (1982) 'The violent imagination', in P. Marsh and A. Campbell (eds) *Aggression and Violence*, Oxford: Blackwell.

Freeman, D. (1984) *Margaret Mead and Samoa*, Harmondsworth: Penguin Books.

Freud, S. (1939) 'Civilization and its discontents', in J. Richardson (ed.) *Civilization, War and Death*, London: Hogarth Press.

Fried, M., Harris, M. and Murphy, R. (eds) (1967) *War: the anthropology of armed conflict and aggression*, New York: The Natural History Press.

Fromm, E. (1973) *The Anatomy of Human Destructiveness*, New York: Holt, Rinehart & Winston.

Gluckman, M. (1955) 'The peace in the feud', in *Custom and Conflict in Africa*, Oxford: Blackwell.

Harris, G. (1978) *Casting out Anger: religion among the Taita of Kenya*. Cambridge: Cambridge University Press.

Heelas, P. (1982) 'Anthropology, violence, and catharsis', in P. Marsh and A. Campbell (eds) *Aggression and Violence*, Oxford: Blackwell.

Heelas, P. (1983) 'Anthropological perspectives on violence: universals and particulars', in *Zygon* 18 (4): 375–403.

Heelas, P. (1984) 'Emotions across cultures: objectivity and cultural divergencies', in S. B. Brown (ed.) *Objectivity and Cultural Divergence*, Cambridge: Cambridge University Press.

Klama, J. (1988) *Aggression: conflict in animals and humans reconsidered*, London: Longman.

Konner, M. (1984) *The Tangled Wing: biological constraints on the human spirit*, Harmondsworth: Penguin Books.

Kuhn, T. (1962) *The Structure of Scientific Revolutions*, Chicago: Chicago University Press.

Leakey, R. and Lewin, R. (1977) *Origins: what new discoveries reveal about the emergence of our species*, London: Macdonald & Jane's.

Lipsey, M. (1985) 'Culture and personality', in A. and J. Kuper (eds) *The Social Science Encyclopedia*, London: Routledge & Kegan Paul.

Lorenz, K. (1966) *On Aggression*, London: Methuen.

Malinowski, B. (1964) 'An anthropological analysis of war' in L. Bramson and G. Goethals (eds) *War: studies from psychology, sociology and anthropology*, New York: Basic Books.

Marsh, P. and Campbell, A. (eds) (1982) *Aggression and Violence*, Oxford: Blackwell.

Marsh, P. *et al.* (eds) (1978) *The Rules of Disorder*, London: Routledge & Kegan Paul.

Mead, M. (1928/1943) *Coming of Age in Samoa*, Harmondsworth: Penguin Books.

Midgley, M. (1979) *Beast and Man: the roots of human nature*, Hassocks: Harvester Press.

Montagu, A. (1976) *The Nature of Human Aggression*, Oxford: Oxford University Press.

Montagu, A. (ed.) (1978) *Learning Non-Aggression: the experience of non-literate societies*, Oxford: Oxford University Press.

Morris, D. (1968) *The Naked Ape*, New York: McGraw-Hill.

Radcliffe-Brown, A. R. (1952) *Structure and Function in Primitive Society*, London: Routledge & Kegan Paul.

Riches, D. (1986) *The Anthropology of Violence*, Oxford: Blackwell.

Sahlins, M. (1974) *Stone Age Economics*, London: Tavistock Publications.

Sahlins, M. (1977) *The Use and Abuse of Biology: an anthropological critique of sociobiology*, London: Tavistock Publications.

Scheff, T. J. (1979) *Catharsis in Healing, Ritual, and Drama*, Berkeley: University of California Press.

Siann, G. (1985) *Accounting for Aggression: perspectives on aggression and violence*, Boston: Allen & Unwin.

Storr, A. (1968) *Human Aggression*, Harmondsworth: Penguin Books.

Strathern, M. (1983) 'The punishment of Margaret Mead', in *London Review of Books* 5–18 May 1983: 5–6.

Tiger, L. (1969) *Men in Groups*, New York: Random House.

Tiger, L. and Fox, R. (eds) (1971) *The Imperial Animal*, London: Secker & Warburg.

Turner, V. (1957) *Schism and Continuity in an African Society*, Manchester: Manchester University Press.

Turner, V. (1967) *The Forest of Symbols: aspects of Ndembu ritual*, Ithaca: Cornell University Press.

Vayda, A. P. (1976) *War in Ecological Perspective*, New York: Plenum Press.

Whitehead, A. N. (1925) *Science and the Modern World*, London: Macmillan.

Zillmann, D. (1979) *Hostility and Aggression*, Hillsdale, New Jersey: Lawrence Erlbaum Associates.

Part One

ETHNOGRAPHIC STUDIES OF SELF, EMOTIONS, AND BEHAVIOUR IN PEACEFUL SOCIETIES

Chapter One

HOBBESIAN AND ROUSSEAUAN IMAGES OF MAN:

autonomy and individualism in a peaceful society

CLAYTON A. ROBARCHEK

Western social science theory seems to be perennially torn between two contradictory images of human sociability and of human nature: the Hobbesian war of each against all, and the idyllic existence of the Rousseauan noble savage. The former image is particularly conspicuous in discussions of human aggression and violence, especially by ethologists, socio-biologists, and many psychoanalysts (Paul 1978; Wilson 1978; Eibl-Eibesfeldt 1979; Freeman 1983), while the latter image predominates in many accounts of peacefulness (Benedict 1934; Nance 1975; Turnbull 1961; Thomas 1958). In keeping with the ethnographic focus of this book, my primary objective is to explore the psycho-cultural dynamics of non-violence in a specific society, the Semai Senoi of Malaysia. Doing so, however, will challenge the modern counterparts of both the Hobbesian and Rousseauan views of human beings and human behaviour. (The facts that Rousseau never used the phrase 'noble savage', and that Hobbes has been widely misinterpreted are irrelevant here, since my concern is not with the conceptions that two seminal thinkers actually articulated, but is rather with the stereotyped dichotomous conceptions of human nature and human society that have come to be associated with their names.)

These two images, however irreconcilable they may be on the surface, are, nonetheless, merely variants of a single conception of human beings and human behaviour, exemplars of a paradigm within which the character of human relations is seen not as growing out of human purposes and choices, but as determined by some natural state of human beings. Both images ultimately deny the humanity of their subjects by maintaining the deterministic role of these predispositions, thereby reducing human beings to mechanically reactive

31

automata. The most commonly seen current formulations of this model alternatively emphasize either a maximizing human nature determined by biology, or a *tabula rasa* wholly tractable to the collective will of society, either the 'selfish gene', or the selfless primitive communist at one with the collective consciousness of his group.

The Semai Senoi, the ethnographic subjects of this paper and victims of purveyors of both images, seem to have suffered particularly in this regard. Senoi peoples have been portrayed on the one hand as the quintessential noble savages by perpetrators of 'Senoi Dream Theory' (Stewart 1951, 1954; Garfield 1974) and on the other as raging bloodthirsty killers by proponents of instinctive human aggression (Paul 1978; Eibl-Eibesfeldt 1979; Wilson 1978). (See Robarchek 1983; Dentan 1983; Domhoff 1985 for discussions of Senoi dream theory; see Robarchek 1986b; Robarchek and Dentan 1987 for a refutation of allegations of Semai bloodthirstiness.) One objective of this paper will be to transcend these human nature-based caricatures by examining the psycho-social dynamics of individualism and autonomy in Semai society, a society which is, in fact, virtually free of violence. The approach taken here exemplifies what emerged in our discussions during the conference as a major theoretical orientation: a view of human action — peacefulness or violence — as the outcome of choices made by people actively in pursuit of particular purposes and goals, choices made and enacted within particular psychologically and culturally constituted realities which they themselves are actively constructing (see Buckley, Howell, O'Nell, Overing, Gibson, Howe, Campbell, this volume).

Both in popular accounts and in much social science literature, the image of a peaceful society seems to carry with it a number of associated conceptions: co-operation, communalism, absence of self-interest, and so on. In short, when we hear of a peaceful society, we are likely to envision a society that is somehow the antithesis of the self-absorbed individualism of the modern urban-industrial world. This image seems to be as appealing to romantic capitalists as it is to millenarian marxists, both of whom see it as a sort of primitive grace from which the modern world has fallen (e.g. Diamond 1972; Wolf 1981; Durdin 1972; MacLeish 1972; Montagu 1976). The implicit underlying assumption seems to be that non-violence and individualism are incompatible or, more likely, the converse: that individualism necessarily entails competitiveness, conflict, and, ultimately,

32

violence. While such logical consistency may be entailed in human nature-based conceptions of human relations, it is not, as we shall see, implied in a perspective that takes purposeful human actions in service of a variety of culturally defined (and often contradictory) goals as the primary fact of human relations.

The relative scarcity of ethnographic descriptions of peaceful societies has resulted in focusing a good deal of interest on those that do exist: Colin Turnbull's description of the Ituri Forest Pygmies (1961), Elizabeth Marshall Thomas' characterization of the 'harmless people', the Kalahari Bushmen (1958), Robert Dentan's description of the Semai as 'non-violent people of Malaya' (1968), Robert Levy's ethnography of the Tahitians (1973), Jean Briggs' descriptions of the Inuit (1970, 1975), and Melford Spiro's accounts of life on Ifaluk (1950, 1952), being among the most notable. While the primary ethnographic accounts of life and character in such peaceful societies usually present multi-dimensional pictures of complex human beings, these pictures tend to become more and more one-dimensional as the material is employed in secondary and tertiary works, where the original complexity is often reduced to little more than caricature. That has certainly been the case with the Semai ethnographies.

The effects of observers' values and predispositions on their perceptions, descriptions, and analyses of ethnographic reality is, of course, an issue that has long been a matter of explicit concern to anthropologists. The problem, in many cases, seems to lie less with the original ethnographic descriptions than with secondary and tertiary applications where these data are put into service in the construction of grand theoretical schemes. In the tendency to portray non-violent peoples as lacking the egoism, selfishness, pettiness, and acquisitiveness so typical of the modern world, the issue is less one of distortion of the data, than of greater or lesser degrees of selectivity and emphasis in reporting and analysis. I can see something of the sort as I look over my own published attempts to describe and account for the peaceful way of life followed by the Semai, and I think I can also see some of the reasons for it. In these analyses, I have clearly stressed the affiliative, dependent, nurturant, accommodative, non-competitive aspects of Semai society, culture, and character over other aspects, because these seemed particularly relevant as factors in the complex psycho-cultural dynamic that contributes to the Semai abhorrence of overt conflict and violence. I still feel that to be true.

Nonetheless, there is another side to Semai character, one involving a large measure of social and emotional isolation and jealously guarded personal autonomy. While I have noted these before (1977a), I have not previously stressed their importance in Semai daily life and their place in the dynamic of non-violence. (It was my wife and ethnographic collaborator, Carole Robarchek, who, recognizing the importance of autonomy as a factor in her data on economic decision-making, suggested that it was perhaps time to address this imbalance.)

THE AFFILIATIVE/DEPENDENT SIDE OF SEMAI CHARACTER

This section briefly sketches some elements of a culturally constituted image of Semai reality, and the motivational context which it helps to define. The discussion centres on two centrally important psychocultural themes — dependency and danger — as they interact in constituting the individual, social, and cultural contexts of action. These themes infuse cultural beliefs and values, individual cognitive and affective orientations, and the institutional orders within which these are manifested. As such, they comprise central components of the motivational context of Semai social relations — the behavioural environment within which choices are made and actions undertaken. This is a context where, as we shall see, affiliation and dependence are major social and psychological goals and where violence is not perceived as a legitimate behavioural option. Since I have described this context in detail elsewhere (Robarchek 1977a, b; 1986a), I will only sketch it here.

The themes of dependence and danger are ubiquitous in Semai life and are intricately intertwined. Dependence, together with its reciprocal nurturance, is an important structural and emotional dimension in nearly all social relationships, both between human beings and between humans and the 'spirit' helpers who have come to them in dreams to seek affiliation with the human world. In the day-to-day world of human interactions, this is expressed most clearly in the symbolic equivalence of food and nurturance as manifested in the ethic and practice of food sharing. The injunctions to share food and to avoid violence are the most important moral imperatives in Semai society and, as such, are constantly reiterated. Nearly any public gathering, and certainly any meeting to resolve a dispute, will begin and end with statements by elders stressing the interdependence of the group, recalling past aid given and received by individuals, emphasizing that each is dependent on the others for survival, asserting that the band is really a group of siblings, and so on (see Robarchek 1986a for discussion of additional cultural expressions of this complex).

Danger is likewise omnipresent; virtually every entity and activity entails the possibility of illness, injury, and death. In the human world, potential dangers range from the non-kinsmen and non-band members whose intentions can never be known with certainty, to the homicidal *mai kahnoh kuui* — 'the cutting-off-head-strangers'· — who are believed to lurk along forest paths to decapitate the unwary, selling the heads to lowland Malays for ritual purposes. In the natural world, even the most objectively benign creatures, dragonflies and butterflies for example, can precipitate disaster, bringing thunderstorms with high winds, torrential rain, lightning, falling trees, and landslides. The natural world is also populated with a vast array of *mara'* — 'they that kill us' — the vast majority of which harbour malevolent intentions toward human beings. These include tigers and other dangerous creatures that may or may not have material form at any given time, ghosts, as well as 'spirits' — the waterfall *mara'* that causes tuberculosis; the tree *mara'* that kills a person's 'soul' by breaking its neck, bringing sickness and death in a single day; the hilltop *mara'* that twists and shrivels limbs, and so on. Avoiding making these latent potentialities manifest is a constant concern, evidenced by the multitude of taboos that bracket even the most mundane activities in a (usually vain) attempt to forestall the dangers that lurk on all sides.

These two themes — danger and dependence — are inextricably interwoven in individual cognitive and affective orientations. I have described the enculturation of these orientations elsewhere (Robarchek 1977a, 1979a). Suffice it to say here that, during enculturation, individuals acquire, first, an image of themselves as helpless and dependent in a hostile and malevolent world that it is largely beyond their ability to control and, second, a set of habits and expectations that lead them to seek and expect aid and comfort from others in times of distress. These orientations are subsequently given cultural expression and concrete content in beliefs, such as those described above, in a vast number of malevolent situations, forces and beings, nearly all of which are actively bent upon the destruction of human beings. *In toto*, these constitute an image of a world filled with dangers, human and non-human, known and unknown, which constantly menace from all sides, and against which the lone individual is helpless.

The only source of security, the sole refuge from this malevolent world, is in the kindred and the band, that tight little group of 100 or so other people with whom one's life is bound up from the cradle to the grave. The subjective significance of this group is reflected in the paramount importance, noted above, of the values of nurturance and group affiliation. This can also be seen in the responses to a series of sentence-completion test items directed toward eliciting cultural values. Of 102 value-related statements elicited from nineteen individuals, only two were not clearly related to two core values of nurturance and affiliation. 'Goodness' was shown to be defined primarily in terms of nurturance (generosity, helping, etc), and 'badness' in terms of behaviours inimical to affiliation, especially fighting and anger (see Robarchek 1986a).

Of major significance in the relationship of self-concept to non-violence is the fact that this value system and the ideals of self which it informs are shared by both men and women (I owe the recognition of this significance to Joanna Overing's paper in this volume). The male/female distinction is not an important structural principle in Semai society: the sexual division of labour is clear, but not rigid; there are no counterparts to the Mehinaku bachelor described by Gregor (1985) who goes hungry and cold rather than undertake the women's tasks of preparing manioc and hauling firewood; to a Semai, such behaviour would simply be absurd. Here, there are no strictly male or female tasks or roles (there are even a few female 'headmen'); there are no purely male or female personality attributes; there is no gender difference in access to ritual knowledge, no 'men's clubs' or 'men's houses'; and there are no puberty rites or other rites of passage defining differential ideals of manhood and womanhood. In short, and unlike most societies, there is no separate cultural ideal of womanhood against which an aggressive ideal of manhood might be cast in structural opposition.

What all of this shows is an image of a world fraught with dangers that are beyond the control of any human being, a world where the only refuge is in the protection and nurturance of kin and community. Without this, a person is completely at the mercy of the dangers that menace from without. The perceived importance of this refuge can be seen in another of the sentence-completion test responses. To the item 'More than anything else he/she is afraid of', the model response, more frequent than 'tigers', 'spirits', or 'death' combined (all of which were cited), was 'becoming embroiled in a dispute'. Becoming so embroiled strains the relations with kin and co-villagers, threatening the only bulwark against the malevolence of the world outside. In a world so construed, and a motivational context so defined, it is clear why violence is not perceived as an acceptable behavioural option in interpersonal relations. (Howell, in this volume, describes a similarly non-violent orientation among the closely related Chewong, but one apparently built on a much less fearful world view.)

The ubiquitous expression of dependence and nurturance through the essentially mandatory giving and receiving of food does not, contrary to what might be expected, significantly constrain individual autonomy, at least in part because 'balanced' reciprocity (Sahlins 1972), involving the accounting of gifts and the expectation of equivalent return, is neither expected nor, in fact, permitted within the community. The Semai ethic of sharing mandates that aid be given when it is needed (with the expectation, to be sure, that it will be reciprocated by someone at some later date when the giver is in need), but any accounting or direct reciprocation is unacceptable. This was made very clear to me early in my fieldwork when I offended a neighbour by trying to make explicit return of food that had been given to my wife and me. Accepting help thus does not entail an accumulation of debt nor does it imply subordination, and is not a route to subjugation. Nor is sharing or giving help a route to dominance; it is merely what is expected, part of the minimal definition of what it is to be a member of a Semai community (see Robarchek 1986a; see Dentan 1968: 134 for a discussion of implications of the distinction between reciprocity and sharing).

ENCULTURATION OF AUTONOMY

From an early age, the autonomy of the will of the individual is culturally affirmed. No child can be forced to do anything he or she does not wish to do. The most respected elder in the community may order a child to fetch something, but if the child refuses, that is the end of the matter (see Dentan 1968: 59). This even extends to for-bidding children to do things that are positively dangerous: playing with sharp knives, climbing tall trees, and so on. Parents may order children not to do these things, but such orders have little effect and no punishment is forthcoming if they are disobeyed.

From infancy through early adolescence, Semai children are largely unconstrained and free of external domination. This is somewhat less the case for girls, who are expected to help their mothers with child care and other household chores, than for boys, of whom very little is expected. None the less, both sexes spend much of their time in pairs or small groups, doing largely as they please: playing, fishing, catching butterflies for sale to traders, and so on. Although schools are becoming more accessible to more and more Semai communities, children often attend only sporadically, simply refusing when it suits them. Similarly, medicine, and especially inoculations and hospitalization, cannot be forced on anyone. If a small child rejects medicine dispensed by one of the medical posts scattered throughout the region, parents will not persist in the face of the child's refusal (see Robarchek 1980). Children are taught to share, are encouraged to contribute to the household, and are praised when they do so, but little real social pressure is brought to bear until adolescence. Even then, this is likely to be little more than an insistence that they begin to make some regular contribution to the household in the form of dried fish, tobacco, and so on. Finally, sexual experimentation, which begins at an early age, is entirely free from adult concern or interference. Only with marriage are young people expected to put aside the freedom of childhood and assume adult responsibilities, and it is often several years after marriage before young people (especially young men) finally settle into domesticity. Long before this, however, the groundwork has been well laid for a sense of personal autonomy that is not in conflict with attitudes of dependency (since assistance is simply to be expected and does not, as we have seen, entail subordination) and that persists throughout life.

CULTURAL EXPRESSIONS OF AUTONOMY

Several concepts reinforce and give explicit cultural expression to this sense of individual autonomy; especially significant in this regard are the concepts of *pehunan* and *segat*.

Pehunan refers to a state of extreme vulnerability to dangers of all sorts that results from the frustration of an individual's wishes (see Dentan 1968; Robarchek 1977b, 1986b). While such a state most frequently results from the frustration of a person's expressed desire for some material object, especially food or tobacco, Dentan (1968) notes that it can also be the result of forcing someone to do something against his or her will. Thus attempting to coerce a person into doing something he or she does not want to do — i.e. infringing on the person's autonomy — places that individual in increased peril of illness, injury, attack by wild animals or malevolent 'spirits', or any of the other innumerable dangers that menace constantly. Moreover, the person responsible for inducing this state is likely to be held at least partially liable if misfortune does occur. Thus, while this concept and associated beliefs are central to Semai attitudes of dependency (by entailing the responsibility of the group to nurture the individual by satisfying his needs, see Robarchek 1986b), it also buttresses the sense of individuality by giving a privileged position to individuals' wishes and motives.

This privileged position of an individual's wishes over the wishes of others also finds its expression in the concept of *segat*. The term is obviously cognate with the Malay '*segan*': 'reluctant' or 'shy' (Dentan 1968); however, the Semai meaning is rather more complex. It labels an attitude that can be roughly glossed as 'don't feel like it' (see Dentan 1968). The word is most often heard in response to an order to do something: fetch firewood, haul water, etc. The response, '*nye', egng ng segat*' ('no, I don't feel like it') is its own justification, requires no further elaboration, and is generally final.

Segat is also frequently used to 'explain' why one has chosen not to do something, collect rattan for sale, for example, or attend a curing seance: '*Egng ng segat ci'niib*' ('I don't feel like walking [that far]'). Once again, no further explanation is deemed necessary. Too frequent reliance on *segat* to avoid one's responsibilities would, of course, eventually bring social pressure to bear: gossip, scolding, shaming, and so on. On any given occasion, however, the contravention of one's own desires is sufficient justification for refusal to comply with the wishes of others.

The resistance to being coerced has a variety of more or less typical expressions, shaped by other values and ideals. Dentan, for example, describes the Semai concept of *persusah* — to make difficulty or unhappiness for someone by meddling in his affairs — and notes that the prescribed response to such interference is withdrawal or passivity (1968: 63). A typical instance can be seen when one person attempts to persuade another to do something that the latter doesn't want to do, or to tell him something that he doesn't want to hear. The paramount value which Semai place on avoidance of conflict or confrontation precludes a direct response, so a strategy of passive resistance is adopted: the person who is being importuned begins, without responding directly, to turn slowly, almost imperceptibly, around, until the one who is importuning him is speaking to his back. (Briggs (1970: 59–60) describes a similar value on autonomy and resistance to its infringement among the Inuit.)

One of the consequences of this reluctance to surrender autonomy is an extreme difficulty in organizing any collective action unless everyone can be convinced that it is in his or her best interest. In more than two years of living with one band of Semai, my wife and I witnessed only two instances of large-scale co-operative action, one of which I had to organize myself to mobilize a labour force to repair a dangerously deteriorated suspension bridge which nearly everyone in the band used every day, and which was literally on the verge of collapse. The other involved the building of a fence to keep goats owned by members of one hamlet from ravaging the swiddens of another hamlet of the same band. Both projects, but especially the latter, required numerous meetings and much cajoling. In the case of the fence, those whose swiddens were being devoured argued that it was the responsibility of the goat owners to contain their animals; the goat owners held that the swidden owners should contribute to the protection of their own gardens. Some semblance of co-operation was finally attained only on the grounds that it was everyone's responsibility to protect the band from the internal dissension and strife which the affair was creating. On numerous other occasions I saw attempts to mobilize band-wide agreement or co-operation fail utterly when faced with the passive but intractable opposition of individuals to yielding their freedom of action to group consensus.

The other side of this culturally defined autonomy is a sense of separateness, of isolation, that has both psychological and sociocultural components and consequences. I have described elsewhere the truncation of strong affective ties that occurs in childhood and the emotional estrangement this engenders (Robarchek 1977a). Dentan cites an informant who asked rhetorically 'what good does it do an unhappy person to have another person upset?' (1968: 64). This attitude can, for example, be seen in a limited expression of empathy (teenage boys and girls laughing and joking together as they help relatives of a dead baby dig a grave, for example). None of this, however, should be interpreted as implying that Semai are callous or indifferent to the welfare of their neighbours and kin, which is certainly not the case; it merely demonstrates that another person's problems and affairs are pre-eminently his own; '*hal mai, hal mai; hal hii*', *hal hii*'' is the apposite aphorism: 'their affairs are theirs; our affairs are ours.'

This non-identification with the feelings of others is linked to a per-ceived impossibility of knowing the thoughts of others as well. I recall, while discussing with a neighbour the psychiatric disorder of a co-villager, asking 'Is his thinking confused?' Although, on reflec-tion, that was an exceedingly dumb question, my neighbour's response was, none the less, informative. He looked at me with a sense of utter incredulity and answered: 'I don't know how he thinks.' (Most Westerners would, I think, have little difficulty in assuming that they could infer confused thinking from the observa-tion of confused speech and behaviour.) This same attitude can also be seen in the exasperating, but typical, response that we received whenever we questioned a third party's motives for doing something: '*Oh, sara' li kaa*'' — roughly: 'Oh, it's his business.'

Emotional isolation is also manifested in a rather high level of insecurity in the relationships between husbands and wives. This insecurity, along with a felt need for some stable focus of emotional security, can be seen in responses to the sentence-completion test item 'more than anything else he/she worries about. . . .' The modal response was 'rejection by his/her spouse'. The genuine vulnerability of the marriage relationship can be seen in the high frequency of adultery and divorce that is typical of Semai communities. This should not, however, be taken to imply that extra-marital affairs are taken lightly. Quite the contrary; the emotions engendered by such rejection can overwhelm a person's coping resources, sometimes leading to suicide. (See Levy (1973) who saw, in Tahiti, an associa-tion between a desire for a measure of interdependence and autonomy, a certain degree of emotional remoteness from others, and a resistance to dependence.)

The subjective threat perceived in rejection by a spouse or lawyer is given cultural expression and concrete content in the concept of *sasoo*, which refers to a malevolent *mara'* called a '*sasoo* woman' or '*sasoo* man', that may attack the rejected party. Assuming the form of the lost love, the spirit comes in a dream to sexually possess the abandoned one. Persons so possessed lose their senses, periodically or permanently, withdraw from contact with others, and may wander

41

off into the forest, perhaps never to return. The longer one is so possessed, the more difficult it is to exorcise the *sasoo* spirit, since, 'like a real spouse', it merges with the very flesh and bone of the victim. Such possession is, in fact, the primary explanation for actual instances of psychiatric disorder in the community where my wife and I worked (see Robarchek 1977b).

In sum, alongside group orientation and dependence, individualism and autonomy are significant components in the psycho-cultural dynamics of life in a Semai community and are given explicit cultural expression in notions such as *pehunan* and *segat*. Social implications include a resistance to co-operative activities growing out of a reluctance to surrender one's freedom of action or to subordinate one's wishes to the will of others. Psychologically, the dark side of this individualism entails an emotional remoteness from others which can be seen in the limited expression of empathy and in the fragility and insecurity of many marriage relationships. The intense threat of further isolation is given cultural formulation in the concept of *sasoo* possession, and individual expression in withdrawal and even suicide.

CONCLUSION

I have attempted, in this paper, to sketch the background of human interaction in a particular milieu, to describe some aspects of a behavioural environment within which people organize their lives in pursuit of particular goals. More specifically, I have attempted to trace some of the interrelationships among several 'orientations' or 'themes' in Semai life — dependence and nurturance, danger, individualism, and autonomy — that interact in constituting, socially, psychologically, and culturally, a reality where individuals are, on the one hand, at risk of being alone in an unremittingly hostile world and, on the other, tightly enclosed in a network of kin and co-villagers upon whom each is dependent for his very survival. In such a situation, individualism and affiliation, autonomy and dependency, are not social or psychological opposite poles on a Hobbesian-Rousseauan dichotomy but, rather, mutually reinforce one another in defining a particular phenomenal reality. Expressed in behaviour, the result is neither the self-obsessed maximizing of Adam Smith and E. O. Wilson, nor the self-abnegating communalism of Marx and Engels. Rather, a context of action is defined where autonomy continues to be valued and guarded, but where the paramount cultural values stress generosity and affiliation, and where kindred and community, protected by these values, remain the sole sources of nurturance and security. In a world so defined, peacefulness does not require suppression of individuality and renunciation of autonomy; it is simply the only sensible way for people to behave, and it has, for Semai, become a crucial part of a definition of self and a positive goal in its own right.

© 1989 Clayton A. Robarchek

REFERENCES

Benedict, R. F. (1934) *Patterns of Culture*, New York: Houghton Mifflin.

Briggs, J. (1970) *Never in Anger: portrait of an Eskimo family*, Cambridge, Mass.: Harvard University Press.

Briggs, J. (1975) 'The origins of nonviolence: aggression in two Canadian Eskimo groups', in W. Muensterberger (ed.) *Psychoanalytic Study of Society*, 6: 134–203, New York: International Universities Press.

Dentan, R. K. (1968) *The Semai: a nonviolent people of Malaya*, New York: Holt, Rinehart & Winston.

Diamond, S. (1972) 'Anthropology in question', in Dell Hymes (ed.) *Reinventing Anthropology*, New York: Random House.

Domhoff, G. W. (1985) *The Mystique of Dreams*, Berkeley: University of California Press.

Durdin, P. (1972) 'From the space age to the Tasaday Age', *New York Times Magazine*, 8 October 1972.

Eibl-Eibesfeldt, I. (1979) *The Biology of Peace and War*, New York: The Viking Press.

Freeman, D. (1983) *Margaret Mead and Samoa: the making and unmaking of an anthropological myth*, Cambridge, Mass.: Harvard University Press.

Garfield, P. (1974) *Creative Dreaming*, New York: Ballantine Books.

Gregor, T. (1985) *Anxious Pleasures: the sexual lives of an Amazonian people*, Chicago: University of Chicago Press.

Levy, R. (1973) *Tahitians: mind and experience in the Society Islands*, Chicago: University of Chicago Press.

MacLeish, K. (1972) 'Stone Age cavemen of Mindanao', *National Geographic* 140: 8, 216–49.

Montagu, A. (1976) *The Nature of Human Aggression*, Oxford: Oxford University Press.

Montagu, A. (1978) *Learning Non-Aggression: the experience of non-literate societies*, Oxford: Oxford University Press.

Nance, J. (1975) *The Gentle Tasaday*, New York: Harcourt Brace Jovanovich.

Paul, R. (1978) 'Instinctive aggression in man: the Semai case', *Journal of Psychological Anthropology* 1 (1): 65–79.

Robarchek, C. A. (1977a) 'Semai nonviolence: a systems approach to understanding', unpublished Ph.D. dissertation. University of California, Riverside.

Robarchek, C. A. (1977b) 'Frustration, aggression and the nonviolent Semai', *American Ethnologist* 4 (4): 762–70.

Robarchek, C. A. (1979a) 'Learning to fear: a case study of emotional conditioning', *American Ethnologist* 6 (3): 555–67.

Robarchek, C. A. (1979b) 'Conflict, emotion and abreaction: resolution of conflict among the Semai Senoi', *Ethos* 7 (2): 104–23.

Robarchek, C. A. (1980) 'Mothers, ghosts and shamans: Semai world view and ethnomedicine', in *Health, Food and Nutrition in Malaysia*, Penang, Malaysia: Penang Consumers Association.

Robarchek, C. A. (1983) 'Senoi anthropologist speaks up', *Dream Network Bulletin* 2 (8): 8.

Robarchek, C. A. (1986a) 'Helplessness, fearfulness, and peacefulness: the emotional and motivational contexts of Semai social relations', *Anthropological Quarterly* 59 (4): 177–83.

Robarchek, C. A. (1986b) 'Primitive warfare and the ratomorphic image of mankind', paper presented at a conference entitled 'The anthropology of war', sponsored by the Harry Frank Guggenheim Foundation and the School of American Research, Santa Fe, New Mexico, 24–28 March 1986.

Robarchek, C. A. and Dentan, R. K. (1987) 'Blood drunkenness and the bloodthirsty Semai: unmasking another anthropological myth', *American Anthropologist* 89 (2): 356–65.

Sahlins, M. (1972) *Stone Age Economics*, New York: Aldine.

Spiro, M. (1950) 'The problem of aggression in a South Sea culture', unpublished Ph.D. dissertation. Northwestern University.

Spiro, M. (1952) 'Ghosts, Ifaluk, and teleological functionalism', *American Anthropologist* 54: 497–503.

Stewart, K. R. (1951) 'Dream theory in Malaya', *Complex* 6: 21–33.

Stewart, K. R. (1954) 'Mental hygiene and world peace', *Mental Hygiene* 38: 387–407.

Thomas, E. (1958) *The Harmless People*, New York: Random House.

Turnbull, C. (1961) *The Forest People*, Garden City, NY: Doubleday & Company.

Wilson, E. O. (1978) *On Human Nature*, Cambridge, Mass.: Harvard University Press.

Wolf, E. (1981) Foreword to *In Search of the Primitive*, by Stanley Diamond, pp. xi–xiii. New Brunswick: Transaction Books.

Chapter Two

'TO BE ANGRY IS NOT TO BE HUMAN, BUT TO BE FEARFUL IS':

Chewong concepts of human nature

SIGNE HOWELL

INTRODUCTION

In this paper I shall consider an alternative theory of human nature, that of the Chewong of Peninsular Malaysia which, I shall argue, is closely linked with the 'peaceful way of life'. My argument is that ideology is also a moral system, and that moral values must be directly related to ideas of human nature: what it is to be a person. An integral part of any theory of personhood concerns inner states of all kinds, and I shall be centring my discussion on indigenous ideas relating to some inner states important to the Chewong, an understanding of which, I shall argue, is necessary in order to understand their interpersonal behaviour and associated values.

Such an approach is in keeping with the guidelines for the original conference, which stressed the interpretative importance of indigenous concepts of self. To avoid becoming embroiled in psychological or philosophical debates concerning selfhood, most of which are individually oriented as well as universalistic in their conclusions, I prefer to use alternative expressions; either concept of personhood, or concept of human nature.

The Chewong are a hunter-gatherer, shifting cultivating group of people who live in the tropical rain forest of the Malay Peninsula. Linguistically and culturally they are related to the Semai about whom Robarchek is writing in this volume. The Malaysian aboriginals are usually classified as non-violent, non-aggressive, peaceful etc., as well as non-hierarchical (see Dentan 1976, 1978; Robarchek 1977, 1979; Robarchek and Dentan 1987; Howell 1981, 1984, 1988). The problem lies in how to account for this, to the Western observer, astonishing phenomenon.

HUMAN NATURE ACCORDING TO CHEWONG
PHILOSOPHY

By human nature, I here mean Chewong nature: what it means to be a Chewong human being. As is commonly found in small-scale societies, the definition of humanity excludes all but the we-group. The we-group of the Chewong, however, extends into the domains of non-human beings, that is, it includes all those things in the environment such as trees, stones, rivers, mountains, which are supposed to have consciousness — and thus in Chewong parlance are 'people' (*beri*), as well as the large number of beings who are said to exist, but who are invisible to the ordinary eye. They are all 'people' with identical person attributes to the Chewong. In order to understand the guiding ideas of the Chewong moral universe, it is necessary to examine the ordinary human beings in relationship with this large world of non-human or superhuman beings. I have argued elsewhere (1984) that Chewong society is co-existent with their universe, and for this reason ideas concerning all categories of conscious beings must be taken into account when establishing indigenous person attributes.

A healthy, rational, and fully functioning person is one whose being is in balance. This means that the body; the 'soul' (*ruwai*) — the main indicator of consciousness and rationality; the liver — seat of inner states of all kinds and reference point for personality; the smell — an integral and unique part of the individual; and the eyes — the medium which allows one to perceive reality in conformity with those of one's own species, are all present and in the correct state. In addition, certain specific characteristics associated with the liver (shy and fearful) are also required, while others (angry, quarrelsome, brave) are definitely not part of the Chewong person. These will be discussed in detail below. It is important to stress that the Chewong do not conceptualise specifically male characteristics as opposed to female ones. Unlike many other societies, including our own, Chewong ideas about human nature are truly applicable to both sexes. This is particularly clear in childrearing practices where boys and girls are treated identically, and are expected to develop similar person characteristics. While the Chewong are fully aware of the physiological differences between the sexes, these are not valued relative to each other, nor do they constitute any base for symbolic ordering (see Howell 1983, 1988 for further discussion on Chewong gender).

Another aspect of humanness is an egalitarian social order. Thus neither the Chewong nor any of the superhuman beings are organized in a hierarchical ranking system. They are explicit on this point. Social stratification with a chief at the top is part of the outside world, not theirs.

Ideas of health and disease are integrally linked to personhood ideas, and it is therefore important to consider these. To the Chewong, disease is always explained in terms of one of the above-mentioned attributes being upset in some way, usually through the interference of a non-human being. When an illness occurs, those who are knowledgeable in such matters proffer a diagnosis. This means trying to identify which kind of being might be responsible, based on evidence from the patient's recent behaviour (this includes improper experiencing and/or expressing of emotionality; see Howell 1981, 1984 for a more detailed discussion). Once this is done, healing is attempted. This may be done by spells directed at the harmful being, hoping to negate its influence, or by the performance of a large-scale shamanistic seance in which those who have spirit guides send their 'souls' (ruwai) out into the worlds of the various non-human beings looking for the one responsible. The most serious forms of illness are those where the patient's ruwai or smell has been taken by one of these beings. In such cases, it is of utmost importance to retrieve it lest the patient dies.

To assist the healing process, humans need the co-operation of others. Anything or anyone non-human may become the spirit guide of an individual human. The relationship is initiated by an encounter when the object or being reveals itself as 'people' (beri) — a person with consciousness — in a dream, trance, or during a waking state in the jungle. During a seance, humans request their spirit guides to come and to help them. Various preparations must be made to entice them. Spirit guides, regardless of what kind, are always described as extremely timid. The slightest disturbance makes them retreat in fear (I shall return to this point below). The most common species of spirit guide, and those most loved by the Chewong, are the so-called 'leaf-people'. They are beings who live in plants, trees, and flowers. There is a perceived identity in looks and dress between Chewong and the leaf-people — and, as I shall show, in their personalities.

The other main kind of beings with whom the Chewong claim close affinity is the 'original people' who live on Earth Six, above the human Earth Seven. These beings used to live on Earth Seven a long

47

time ago, but they retreated to Earth Six because it was too hot and too dirty here. They are immortal because of the cool temperature on Earth Six and because they eat nothing but fruit, a cooling food. The Chewong are mortal because the reverse conditions prevail on their earth. The jungle is hot, and they eat meat, a food which is hot and dirty because of the blood content. The leaf-people are also cool, their food being the morning dew and the cool incense smoke offered them by the Chewong.

What about the rest of the superhuman beings in the Chewong universe? There is a vast number of these, and they fall into several distinct kinds. However, the broadest distinction being made, and one which is of most relevance in the present context, is that between the 'good' (*baig*) and the 'bad' (*yabud*) — or, as I prefer, the helpful and the harmful, designations which have less of Western moral connotations and which in the particular context correspond more closely to Chewong associations. Related attributes are beautiful and generous, and ugly and stingy respectively. These are directly congruent with the beings' activities: whether they cause harm, in the form of disease and mishap, or whether they help to set things right following such a damaging occurrence.

There are many different beings in the Chewong universe who may inflict harm upon them. With the possible exception of only two — Tanko, who causes the thunder and lightning, and a group of beings known collectively as *keoi* (or *nlab*), beings who are transformed humans but who have lost their humanness completely — none of them is portrayed as evil, malicious, or in any way seeking to harm humans. Rather, their intentions and activities are perceived as identical to those of humans: to feed themselves and to prevent or overcome mishaps.

One major distinguishing feature between all conscious beings is the eyes. The actual constitution of the eyes is different in all species. This means that they all perceive the world in slightly different ways. All beings who live on Earth Seven — with the exception of the leaf-people — are carnivorous. What constitutes their meat, however, differs and this is linked to their perceptions of the environment. Thus the Chewong see a wild pig, or any other animal normally hunted, primarily as potential meat and they set about trying to catch it. Similarly, the harmful beings see meat when they look upon the human body, the human 'soul' (*ruwai*), or human smell, and they will also set about trying to catch these. Just like humans, they go hunting with their blowpipes and they erect snares and traps in the jungle. The Chewong do not perceive these activities as expressing any anger or aggressive feelings, however, even when they themselves are the victims. Rather, they explain it in terms of each species behaving according to its 'nature'. In this regard they make no distinction between animals and superhumans. Dangerous animals do not attack unless an individual has made this possible through his or her incorrect behaviour. I shall return to this below.

INNER STATES AND THEIR RELATIVE VALUE

I now wish to look at some Chewong words that pertain to inner states and relate these to ideas of what it means to be human. I have examined this vocabulary elsewhere (1981) and will here confine myself to noting that the range and elaboration of emotional and mental terms is relatively limited. People are not concerned with discussing their emotional states; emotionality in most instances is negatively valued. However, a few such are heavily elaborated culturally, and I propose that an examination of these is one means by which we might achieve an understanding of Chewong 'peacefulness'. I shall look at five indigenous concepts which I think throw some light on the particularity of Chewong social and individual behaviour. Two are highly valued, namely *lidya* (shy, timid, ashamed) and *höntugen* (frightened, fearful), and can be said to be integral aspects of the Chewong person (Howell 1988). The other three are subject to severe cultural condemnation and can be said to represent the non-Chewong person, by which I mean people outside the wider social universe of humans and superhumans, in effect Malays and Chinese. These are *chan* (angry), *oklahi* (quarrelsome), and, of a somewhat different but related order, *berani* (brave, daring).

Shy and fearful

The Chewong learn to fear as very young children. Adults take great delight in frightening them by invoking unexperienced horrors, such as being confronted by a Malay or a tiger. Parents speak approvingly of their timid children, and adults are constantly at great pains to convince others of their own fearfulness. Similarly, shyness is constantly invoked as a legitimate reason for failure to do something. There is no ambiguity about the value of these characteristics. They are integral parts of the Chewong concept of human nature — and valued ones at that. However, it is important to stress that the Chewong mainly fear the unknown, or the uncontrollable. The jungle presents no terror to them. They know how to behave properly in it, thereby avoiding danger (for a contrasted view of Malaysian aboriginals' attitude to their jungle environment, see Robarchek, this volume).

It is interesting to examine various superhuman beings and determine which of them are presented as inherently shy and fearful. Whenever confronted with perceived danger the leaf-people and the original people flee. This is of course the way the Chewong themselves react under similar circumstances. To flee from danger is the explicit mechanism of Chewong defence. There are numerous incidents to exemplify this. They fled from the marauding Malays of earlier times; they flee from the approach of any stranger today; they flee from any imagined threatening event or confrontation. Such immediate and terror-filled reaction is a constant topic of conversation, just as is the fearfulness of the leaf-people and the original people. While sharing many similarities, the relationship between humans and the original people, and humans and the leaf-people, is not identical. The original people are ancestors of the Chewong in so far as they represent the mythical past, but not in the sense that they are transformed dead of today. The leaf-people are not linked to humans in such a direct way, but structurally the relationships are analogous. These two categories of superhuman beings occupy a very special place in Chewong philosophy; they are both — in their different ways — the *alter ego* of humans. It is interesting therefore to note that the chief emotional and behavioural characteristic of them both is timidity, fearfulness, and retreat in the face of perceived danger. None of the other superhuman beings is described as inherently shy or fearful, a further indication of their being conceptually set apart from human beings.

However, we cannot posit an opposition in terms of fearful, helpful, and good beings versus brave, aggressive, harmful beings. There is a set of rules which inform and direct human behaviour, and the transgression of any of these usually leads to some form of superhuman intervention in the form of illness and mishap. None of the superhuman beings — with the exception of the two already mentioned — can thus interfere with a human being unless a rule has been broken. So with regard to these beings, the Chewong know that they are vulnerable to attack, but that if they take proper care in their day-to-day behaviour and avoid places where potentially harmful beings are known to live and set their traps, they have a fairly good chance of being healthy and fit. The important point is that none of these beings is referred to as evil, nor their harmful acts as aggressive or violent. They are just carrying out their life in accordance with the rules given them, as all 'people' including Chewong do. The potentially harmful beings may be described by the adjective *yabud* (bad, harmful, ugly), but whenever thus designated, the speaker will invariably qualify this by saying that they are not 'truly bad' because they only cause harm if a person breaks a rule, or inadvertently falls into a trap.

Contrary to influential theories in primatology and ethology, hunting among the Chewong cannot be described as an aggressive or violent activity (see the Introduction, this volume, for discussion of problems in connection with the definition of these terms). Hunters do not portray the hunt in ways that could be construed as aggressive, either in the hunter's emotional state or in his attitude to the prey. The various non-human beings who hunt humans are not portrayed as violent or aggressive either. Everyone, visible and invisible, has to eat according to Chewong notions of the world order. Part of the diet is meat, and to many the human body, soul, and smell constitute meat. If someone catches a human soul or throws their spear into a human body thereby causing illness to the victim, then this is either plain bad luck or the direct result of some transgression which permits the animal/being to attack. Humans must diagnose who has done the deed and try to rectify it. The point is that hunting, whether performed by humans, animals, or superhuman beings, is not an activity associated by the Chewong with any aroused inner state. It is not a violent act; it is not conceptualized as an attack. The words used make this clear. There are numerous words for the hunting activity, mainly dependent upon the object of the hunt or the tools employed, but none corresponds to words denoting violent acts. Of course there are several such words, for the Chewong are not ignorant of other modes of behaviour than those practised by themselves. They have in their language, and frequently use, Malay imported words for attack, fight, war, to quarrel, and to be angry. However, there appear to be no words for compete or coerce. It is an interesting feature of Chewong social relations that no competitive games are played, either between adults or chilren. Hunting is not an occasion for male striving after status. On the contrary, the Chewong in hunting as in other matters tend to ignore or negate any demonstration of individual superior skill.

While to some extent the harmful and the helpful beings in the Chewong universe can be thought of as opposed, they do not fall into neatly discernible complementary categories. A previously harmful being may change and become a helpful spirit guide to an individual, at which point it will also become circumspect, if not fearful, in its relationship with humans. However, the leaf people and the original people alone are described automatically as shy and fearful. Only these two kinds of helpful people are unequivocally desirable spirit guides. The Chewong wish for their attendance and assistance. Ideally, they do not wish for any interaction at all with the other kinds of superhuman beings. The myths which describe encounters with superhuman beings of all kinds never describe the various harmful ones as shy or fearful, whereas they always do with respect to the helpful.

The two beings who unanimously are characterized as not fearful are Tanko and *keoi*. Tanko is a very complex character (see Howell 1984), but in several of his aspects, Tanko is described as deceitful. He is portrayed as having a voracious sexual appetite. He tricks young girls into having sexual intercourse with him, and he steals children whom he gives as food to his dogs. He is untrustworthy, pretending to be something pleasant when he has harmful designs. This is also the case with the group of beings called *keoi*. *Keoi* look like ordinary human individuals — men and women — and in fact they were this at some time, but they performed a forbidden act which transformed them into *keoi*. As *keoi* their eyes are completely different, and they see other humans as potential meat and set about catching them. But their hunting is qualitatively different to that of other species — animal or superhuman. While living amongst their intended victims they brazenly plot to catch them, all the while lying and playing tricks. In the myths both Tanko and *keoi* take the wildest risks to achieve their ends. They are explicitly said not to be fearful. As such, humans fear them, and as such, they are firmly set apart from the Chewong. Interestingly, *keoi* are the only beings the Chewong may kill. This can be explained, I think, in terms of the former Chewong status of these beings. Through their wholly unacceptable behaviour, *keoi* mark themselves apart from humans, while reminding them of the possibility of such behaviour. In conformity with their special status, *keoi* cannot be killed with ordinary weapons, but only with fire.

Brave, angry, and quarrelsome

If we examine an inner state/behavioural model possibly opposed to that of shy and fearful, namely brave, we find that this is not a characteristic the Chewong associate with themselves. The word they use for this (*berani*) is Malay but, more commonly, they simply negate the word fearful. An example of what it means to be brave (or not fearful) was provided by myself. I had left my mother and father and husband to go alone to a place which was completely unknown to me in order to live with people who were equally unknown. Every Chewong, man and woman, insisted that they would never be able to do such a thing, they would be much too frightened. 'What if we had been bad people?' they kept asking. Their image of non-Chewong is that they are 'bad' (*yabud*) — they cannot be trusted not to harm one. This attitude explains the general terror that my arrival provoked. Outsiders, in their experience mainly Malays and Chinese, are portrayed as thieves and cheaters who will not stop at physical violence. The meaning of *yabud* in this instance is therefore qualitatively different from that used in the context of harmful superhumans. Malays and Chinese *are* bad. They are also fearless. Of course they are not part of the Chewong wider social universe of humans and superhumans, and hence they fall outside their moral universe. There are no shared 'rules' governing their relationship which enable individuals to avoid dangers through correct behaviour. Ideologically speaking, the Malays and Chinese are not human. There were numerous adults, mainly women but also some men, who had never left the jungle to visit the nearby Malay villages or Chinese trading station. They declared they were much too frightened. Even those who went regularly, and who spoke Malay fairly fluently, were always tense and on the look-out for danger. Stories of alleged atrocities performed by Malays or Chinese were frequently brought back. When hearing such tales those in the jungle would become quite terrified, and I once met a group of Chewong on the move with all their worldly belongings, having abandoned their settlement in order to resettle much deeper in the jungle because they had heard rumours that the Malays wanted Chewong heads.

Fleeing has always been the Chewong response to violence. To remain and confront the aggressors is not a viable alternative. 'No, no, we are not brave, we are very frightened', was the inevitable response when I asked why they always fled. This was not a matter of excuse, but a statement of fact. To be brave is not desirable. I suggest that if this were not so, the conceptual link between humans and the leaf and original peoples would be severed.

Another emotion which is somewhat elaborated upon by the Chewong is that expressed by the word *chan* which I translate as anger or angry. What are the circumstances in which they use this word and what are their attitudes to a person thus described? While it is recognized that anyone might experience anger at some time, and engage in a quarrel, most would not admit to having done so. I never witnessed a serious quarrel or observed anyone I would describe as angry. This, of course, does not mean that the Chewong think the same; their standards are very different from mine in this regard. Very occasionally a small child would throw a tantrum when denied something, and it would be described as *chan*. Adults ignored such outbursts as much as possible, occasionally shouting at the child to stop. They offered no theory as to why the child behaved in such a way, no external event was allowed an explanatory status; rather the outburst was reflected back to the personality of the child, who was said to have a very angry liver (the liver being the seat of inner states).

When adults get upset about someone's behavior, they tend not to confront the protagonist, but withdraw into themselves. A frequent cause is marital infidelity. The injured parties say that their livers are 'not good' (we would say we were feeling depressed), they 'miss their spouse'. It was my experience that they took an extremely passive line, waiting to see if the situation would change and the spouse return. Alternatively, an illness may befall the injured party. The adulterer is the cause of this in so far as his/her act has allowed a superhuman being to attack the spouse. Illness is thus one way of coping with jealousy. The sick person would not be described as *chan* in such instances, although the cause would be identified as directly related to the behaviour of the spouse. Alternatively, it is possible to take a retaliatory line and attack the errant spouse, either verbally — the most common form — or by attacking his/her things; never their person. For instance, one woman who was described by all as extremely jealous of her husband (he was said to be innocent) had an angry liver, and she was always quarrelling. Thus she not only shouted at him, she once took his best blowpipe, broke it in two and

54

stamped on it. This was a most amazing act; the Chewong continued to talk about it for weeks. Everyone was extremely upset and disturbed by her. Institutionally, there are no mechanisms for punishing someone for deviant behaviour of any kind. This woman did behave antisocially. Several families who lived in the same settlement decided to leave as a result of her behaviour, and others insisted that they would never go to live in the same place as her. But such an occurrence of anger was extremely rare. When I cited instances when I thought anger might have been appropriate, I was always told 'this is not our way'.

So again, we find that Chewong reaction to perceived violence — which is how I would describe the abuse of the jealous woman — is to retreat from it. Anger is ignored as much as possible, as with angry children, but when it becomes too manifest, people physically remove themselves, just as they flee from outsiders. Those Chewong who behave in unacceptable ways cannot be confronted directly. This is the case with all deviant social behaviour, such as incorrect marriages or theft. In such instances the culprit would normally leave, but never at an explicit request. More violent crimes than that performed by the jealous woman did not occur among the Chewong while I was with them, nor could anyone tell me of others in the past. Their mythology has no instances of human physical violence. I asked about murder. They insisted it never happened. When I pressed them to imagine the result of such an event, they replied the murderer would be so ashamed (*lidya*) that she/he would leave the region altogether never to return; again withdrawal.

The host of different beings attributed with consciousness that exist within the Chewong universe have structurally similar qualities to humans. With the possible exception of Tanko and *keoi*, none is perceived as hierarchical, aggressive, competitive, quarrelsome, angry, or domineering. Neither are they brave. Humans and the rest of the conscious non-humans are shy and fearful. Of these, semantically and ideologically the leaf-people and the original people stand closest to the Chewong, while Tanko and *keoi* stand closest to the outsiders. On the whole, the terms bad, brave, quarrelsome, and angry are associated with outsiders, not with the Chewong or the various superhuman beings who participate in the wider Chewong social universe. The Malays and Chinese represent the prototypes of these characteristics. They are therefore to be feared and avoided. There is very little the Chewong can do to prevent the Chinese and Malays from harming them, except to stay out of their way as much as possible. Not being part of the Chewong social universe, they operate according to different rules but, interestingly, this does not mean that they can be treated in qualitatively different ways — such as be attacked. There are thus no circumstances in which the Chewong may behave in contradiction to their ideologically constructed concept of human nature. To them, the meaning of human is to be fearful, and this permeates their cosmology. Conversely, to be angry, quarrelsome, or brave marks one off as not human. Such characteristics, in effect, either prevent social relations from being established or, whenever manifested through behaviour, they cut them off.

CONCLUSION

In the Introduction to this volume we ask: can anthropologists contribute anything to questions concerning human aggression? Have I done so in this paper? I have tried to present a society where aggressive behaviour as we understand it — however loosely defined — is not much in evidence. Robarchek (1979) has suggested that the Semai, from the earliest childhood, learn to fear arousal of all kinds, resulting in a general ethos of low-key emotionality. I agree with much of his interpretation and find that my understanding of the Chewong coincides in many instances with his of the Semai. But I would place a somewhat different emphasis, and suggest that in the Chewong case fear is a positive emotion and encouraged in children because to be fearful is to be human, while the arousal of other inner states is negatively valued and discouraged — as manifest in the various rules that forbid them (see Howell 1981). They are not part of being human. In an earlier paper (1977) Robarchek argues that Schachter's frustration – aggression theory can be found to hold among the Semai when we examine one of their rules, *punan*, whereby any kind of 'frustration' (I call it 'unfulfilled desire' as found in the rule *punen* among the Chewong) must never be allowed to persist. It is only by alleviating frustration immediately, or even before it becomes experienced, Robarchek argues, that the Semai are able to be so non-violent. Thus he seems to be arguing from within a position which holds that aggression is an innate attribute of sufficient strength that it needs to be redirected in some way for it not to manifest itself in interhuman relations. However, he argues strongly for the claim that successful handling of aggressive impulses is culturally possible (see also his paper in this volume).

I have argued throughout this paper against the various theories that hold that human aggression is so formidable as to require special mechanisms for handling or redirection. Thus, in the anthropological literature, ritual is often explained in terms of 'letting off steam'. Various pent-up emotions can be released and an emotional equilibrium restored (Scheff 1979; Gluckman 1963; Heelas 1983; Briggs 1970). Heelas (1982) has also discussed the usefulness of catharsis as a general explanation for shedding undesirable violent emotions, and argues that the catharsis view of aggression may be too simplistic. Not only does the contradictory nature of the evidence preclude any generalization, but it is difficult to conduct any cross-cultural comparisons because there is no agreement as to what should be compared. While admitting that the actor's definition of violence may differ from culture to culture, thereby making a universal definition impossible, Heelas nevertheless accepts *a priori* the presence of the 'thing' violence in all of us. '. . . [I]t cannot be argued that violence exists solely as a cultural phenomenon . . . violence is almost certainly embedded in the natural world' (1982: 54). Explicitly or implicitly, the various theories treat aggression as an absolute discrete 'thing', which, when it appears to be absent in a particular society, has somehow to be accounted for. It is this assumption which I have been questioning in this paper.

If one is still searching for ways to explain this absence, believing with most ethologists, socio-biologists, and even some social anthropologists that aggression is part of human nature, then the obvious place to look is for some form of ritual as catharsis, or try to identify some other culturally constructed behaviour pattern which allows the individual Chewong to shed negatively valued arousal states, like anger, which according to such theories would build up and erupt in uncontrolled violent behaviour. Not only have I been unable to identify any such ritual — it would, for instance, be incorrect to interpret the shamanistic seance as practised by the Chewong in such terms — but other practices, analogous to eskimo dog beating as presented by Briggs (1970) are equally absent. However, I would argue that it begs the question to phrase it in such a way. I do not disregard the possibility that some rituals in some societies do indeed perform such a function, but this interpretation would be meaningful only if the members of those societies could be shown in their various ideas and practices — in particular those concerning personhood — to endorse such an interpretation. In other words, let us avoid *a priori* assertions about human nature and try instead to perform a systematic explication of indigenous ideas concerning human nature and social and cosmological relationships.

The question I think we should ask is not, 'Is violence learnt or innate?', but rather, 'What are the ideological constructs that encourage violent or peaceful behaviour and make it meaningful and proper?', and the closely related one, 'What do the behaviour patterns *mean* to the participants?' Do *they* perceive themselves as 'aggressive' or 'peaceful', and if so, 'What are the semantic connotations of the words used?' In order to ascertain the indigenous meanings, I suggest that indigenous concepts be explored, and the vocabulary denoting inner states examined. Which experiential and behavioural characteristics are valued by the members of a particular social group? There are only a few societies where all members hold the same characteristics to be applicable to everyone. Men and women, for instance, may in many cases be characterized as different in this regard — their human nature may not be identical — and proper interpretative emphasis must be given in such cases. While such an approach may seem inconclusive, it is one that allows each cultural situation to be interpreted in internally appropriate ways, while at the same time giving full credence to the psychic and cognitive unity of humanity.

Empirical examples of peaceful societies, which do not need some release mechanism for assumed aggressive drives, should at least alert us to the possibly false linking of human aggression and human nature. As Montagu (1976) has stated again and again, the social activity of war need have no relationship with the inner state of aggression. To confuse the two confuses the issue in general. As fearful, angry, brave, quarrelsome, competitive, kind, generous, co-operative etc. do not exist in the world as measurable qualities, but humans as social beings may develop all, or none, to varying extents, so social behaviour like war can only be explained with reference to complex social factors, not to some assumed universal inner state.

© 1989 Signe Howell

REFERENCES

Briggs, J. (1970) *Never in Anger*, London: Harvard University Press.

Dentan, R. K. (1976) *The Semai: a non-violent people of Malaya*, New York: Holt, Rinehart & Winston.

Dentan, R. K. (1978) 'Notes on childhood in a nonviolent context', in A. Montagu (ed.) *Learning Non-aggression*, Oxford: Oxford University Press.

Gluckman, M. (1963) 'Rituals of rebellion in south-east Africa', in *Order and Rebellion in Tribal Africa*, London: Cohen & West.

Heelas, P. (1982) 'Anthropology, violence, and catharsis', in P. Marsh and A. Campbell (eds) *Aggression and Violence*, Oxford: Blackwell.

Heelas, P. (1983) 'Anthropological perspectives on violence: universals and particulars', *Zygon* 18 (4): 375–403.

Howell, S. (1981) 'Rules not words', in P. Heelas and A. Lock (eds) *Indigenous Psychologies*, London: Academic Press.

Howell, S. (1983) 'Chewong women in transition; the effect of monetisation on a hunter-gatherer society in Malaysia', in *Women and Development in South East Asia*, Occ. Paper 1, Centre for Southeast Asian Studies, University of Kent.

Howell, S. (1984) *Society and Cosmos: Chewong of Peninsular Malaysia*, Oxford: Oxford University Press.

Howell, S. (1988) 'From child to human: Chewong concepts of self', in I. M. Lewis and G. Jahoda (eds) *Acquiring Culture: comparative studies in childhood*, London: Croom Helm.

Montagu, A. (1976) *The Nature of Human Aggression*, Oxford: Oxford University Press.

Robarchek, C. A. (1977) 'Frustration, aggression and the non-violent Semai', *American Ethnologist* 4 (4): 762–70.

Robarchek, C. A. (1979) 'Learning to fear: a case study of emotional conditioning', *American Ethnologist* 6 (4): 555–67.

Robarchek, C. A. and Dentan, R. K. (1987) 'Blood drunkenness and the bloodthirsty Semai: unmasking another anthropological myth', *American Anthropologist* 89 (2): 356–65.

Scheff, T. J. (1979) *Catharsis in Healing, Ritual, and Drama*, Berkeley: University of California Press.

Chapter Three

SYMBOLIC REPRESENTATIONS OF TRANQUILLITY AND AGGRESSION AMONG THE BUID

THOMAS GIBSON

This chapter will describe the symbolic representations of *uway* ('tranquillity'), *isug* ('aggression'), and related moral concepts among the Buid, a group of shifting cultivators inhabiting the highlands of Mindoro, Philippines.[1] In my view, the Buid may be fairly described as a society 'at peace' because of the extremely low *value* they attach to 'aggression' and the extremely high *value* they attach to 'tranquillity'.

DEFINITIONS

At the conference in which this paper was first presented, there was a great deal of discussion about how one is to define concepts like 'peace' and 'aggression' for comparative purposes, and, as always in such discussions, a fair amount of pessimism about the possibility of success. Since some of the issues raised in these definitional discussions and addressed elsewhere in this volume have a bearing on the approach adopted in this paper, it is necessary to say something about them first. The most basic issue is whether we are to define aggression without reference to native concepts. Those who argue that a universal definition of aggression is possible and even desirable are often interested in determining whether a universal human proclivity toward aggression exists, or whether the members of one society can be said to be 'more aggressive' than another according to some quantitative scale.

For my part, I doubt the feasibility of such attempts to disengage the meaning of the word 'aggression' from local systems of meaning. In this paper, I shall treat 'aggression' as a moral concept like that of 'good' or 'evil'. My usage therefore represents a 'translation' of a native Buid concept, and is defined in opposition to other Buid concepts. The comparative implications of adopting this approach are that the meaning of what we are labelling 'aggression' will necessarily vary from case to case, depending on how the native concepts to which it is opposed vary from case to case. It then becomes impossible to rank societies as more or less aggressive than one another, just as it is impossible to say that one society is more or less evil than another. Evil and aggression, in this sense, exist in every society, as a means of defining the good and the peaceful (or cowardly) (see Campbell, this volume).

Of course, our decision to translate a particular concept as 'aggression' presupposes a very general similarity between the place of that concept in the native system of moral categories and its place in our own system. My point is simply that once an 'emic' definition is attempted, we must go beyond looking for an 'essential' definition of an isolated concept, and discuss the whole structure of moral categories. It is these structures which must then be compared, not their elements. In any one society, the meaning of 'aggression' will be determined by the presence or absence of related concepts such as 'bravery', 'cowardice', 'honour', 'peacemaker', 'bully', and so on.

Once we turn to actual ethnographic cases, it is usually not very difficult to identify concepts which seem to overlap with our concept of 'aggression', at least in some of its usages. For the purposes of this paper, only a portion of the total semantic field covered by the English term is relevant. This is because the term is rather ambivalent in English, having both 'good senses' and 'bad senses'. The bad senses cluster around the notion of deliberately causing harm to another being or entity. In the extreme case this is done without provocation and through pure malice. These notions are also central to the Buid concept of *isug*. In the English case, the positive usages, particularly of the adjective form 'aggressive', cluster around the notions of being 'self-assertive', 'driven to succeed', and so on. These may be more common in American than in British English. They are absent in the Buid case.

But here a central ambiguity creeps in. While the notion of 'deliberately causing harm' may be central to a culture's concept of aggression, actual instances of 'aggressive conduct' are always open to interpretation and reinterpretation. This is true of all conduct interpreted as having a moral relevance, as being a sign of virtue or vice. Immoral or antisocial conduct demands an explanation in terms of inherently unobservable causes, be they 'motives', 'intentions', 'desires', 'proclivities', 'spirit attack', 'witchcraft', 'disorders of the humoural system', and so on. What is more, the same conduct may be subjected to a series of different interpretations as subsequent events show it to be part of a pattern of conduct or as an isolated instance, as implicating a wider or narrower range of social relationships, and so on. This notion is familiar from accounts of the diagnosis of disease in traditional societies. What may in the first instance be attributed to physical causes and treated by an herbalist may, if it persists or grows more severe, be redefined as caused by mystical forces requiring treatment by a diviner (see Horton 1970: 142). Indeed, in many societies disease may itself be viewed as a sign of moral failure, either of the victim or of some 'witch'.

Among the Buid, momentary expressions of anger may be viewed in the first instance as indicative of a momentary desire to harm another, but if such conduct becomes persistent or habitual it is almost always reinterpreted as being caused by hostile mystical forces and thus as not being under the deliberate control of the individual. Now, even if all instances of 'aggressive conduct' were ultimately reinterpreted as being caused by an external agency, the ideal model of aggression as 'deliberately causing harm' would still exist as a model. Indeed, the very necessity of reinterpreting an act as not deliberate presupposes the idea that it might have been.

What I would like to suggest here is that the Buid view aggressive conduct as a sort of moral infirmity requiring explanation in much the same manner as does a physical infirmity. As the conduct in question enters the public arena of moral argumentation, what lies behind it, and so what kind of thing it 'really is', changes. Given the inherent uncertainty of moral interpretation in social life, it would be foolish to believe that we could come up with a definition of aggression that would allow us to unambiguously classify, much less measure, instances of aggressive conduct in unfamiliar societies.[2] The fact that acts of violence, aggression, or even boastfulness (*buagun*) are consistently condemned, and the lack of any positive evaluation of acts of 'bravery' or 'courage', may result in a lower rate of deliberate maiming and homicide among the Buid than among populations which attach positive evaluations to such acts (everything else being equal).[3] Homicide rates are interesting in themselves, but they can never be explained simply in terms of cultural definitions or psychological dispositions. They represent the product of a number of other factors as well, including political, economic, and demographic ones as they intersect at particular moments in history (see Howe, this volume). They are not my primary concern in this paper.

While I question the possibility of ranking Buid society as more or less 'peaceful' according to some culture-free, quantitative standard, I think it can be placed in a category of relatively 'peaceful' societies because of the complete absence of any social situation in which aggressive conduct is assigned a positive value. This is not to say that acts which we, or the Buid, would interpret as aggressive never occur, but that such acts are viewed as deviations from the ideals of Buid political culture.

In the following sections, I begin by discussing Buid attitudes toward aggression and its opposite, tranquillity, in the daily life of the community. In the next part, I describe Buid attitudes towards what they perceive as the intrinsic aggressiveness of their lowland Christian neighbours, before turning to the activity in which the symbolism of tranquillity and aggression receives its greatest elaboration: animal sacrifice. The discussion thus begins with relations internal to the human community, proceeds to those between the community and its human neighbours, and ends with the relations between the human and non-human worlds.

RELATIONS WITHIN THE BUID PERSON

When treating the meanings of moral concepts such as aggression and tranquillity, it is necessary to say something about the local theory of the moral agent, or person. Among the Buid, an individual is made up of three components: a physical body (*abilugan*), a soul or vital principle (*falad*), and a mind (*fangayufan*). The soul is said to reside in the upper torso, and is the seat of the emotions. It is vulnerable to attack by predatory spirits of various types, who are said to 'bite' the souls of their victims. Death results when the soul becomes detached from the body. At death, the soul is transformed into a 'ghost' (*labang taw*). Ghosts represent the soul in a pure state, as it were, dissociated from both a body and a controlling mind. Now, ghosts are regarded as being greedy for meat and as possessive of their former spouses, both forms of behaviour condemned as anti-social among the living. They are also regarded as being capable of causing illness or even death to get their way. In this sense, one of the components of the personality is regarded as being inherently 'aggressive', except that in life it is normally held in check by the mind.

63

The mind is less closely associated with the body than is the soul. It is associated with perception, especially sight and hearing, but above all with speech and understanding. Although it does not survive death, it is closely associated in life with a category of immortal spirits, the *lai*, which act as spirit familiars to mediums. It is the mind of the medium, not the soul, which travels during a seance and which acts to defend the community in an altruistic manner. Spirit mediums may not be paid for their services, and their power comes primarily from their collective efforts in large group seances. Virtually every adult man, and a few older women, possess familiars. Working in teams, groups of mediums and their familiars mount an almost continual watch on the predatory spirit world, protecting the souls of the living from attack. The mind and spirit familiars are thus inherently social and associated with language and perception, while the soul and ghosts are inherently egocentric and associated with eating and desire. I shall return to the opposition between speech and eating toward the end of this paper.

Persistent aggression is a deviation not only from social convention, but from the way people 'naturally' are, since the mind is thought to be properly in control of the soul (cf. Strathern 1980; 198). Persistent aggression requires an explanation in terms of exogenous, supernatural forces. An aggressive person is open to accusations of being in league with or under the control of malign mystical powers. Small children who engage in anti-social acts like tantrums and quarrelling are equally apt to be diagnosed as having been 'bitten' on their *falad* by one of a number of invisible beings: *fangugyab*, 'that which causes crying', *fangarisugan*, 'that which causes quarrelling', *fansungun*, 'that which causes depression', and so on.

The very old and the young have a weaker mind than those in their prime and are for this reason more vulnerable to spirit attack. They are also more vulnerable to uncontrolled emotional states, such as anger or jealousy. Buid describe these feelings in terms of the soul rising up from the chest into the neck and issuing forth in bitter words or even violence if not held in check by the mind. The mental community formed by adult mediums in collective seances must then add its protection and control to the souls of the vulnerable old and young to maintain the peace and order within the community as a whole. Peace and order on the empirical plane is established and maintained through a series of *tultutlan*, 'collective discussions', in which the unruly emotions of those who have been involved in quarrelling (*garisugan*, 'mutually aggressive acts') are brought back until order and peace, *uway*, is restored.

RELATIONS WITHIN THE BUID COMMUNITY

Elsewhere I have described Buid childrearing practices and I will merely summarize that account here (Gibson 1985). Within Buid society, the only social relationships in which hierarchy and dependency are legitimate are those between children and adults, and these relationships are governed by an idiom of shared physical and spiritual substance I call 'kinship'.[4] The aim of socialization is to bring children to a point at which they are no longer dependent on their senior relatives. Instead, they should be able to participate in the community of autonomous adults as equal members engaged in the sharing of labour, food, and speech without ever becoming indebted to other specific individuals. I employ the term 'sharing' in a technical sense to distinguish it from 'reciprocity' as a specific type of transaction. Reciprocity implies dualism or symmetry: a give and take between two equivalent groups or individuals, in which the potentiality for debt is always present (Polanyi 1957). Sharing implies an asymmetry: it is a transaction between an individual and a group. The individual gives to the group as an undifferentiated whole, and receives only as a member of a larger group. The potential for dyadic relations of indebtedness is thereby eliminated.[5]

As an individual matures, the idiom of kinship is increasingly replaced by an idiom of companionship, in which social relationships are governed by an idiom of shared activity. The point of the idiom of companionship is that it allows individuals to form and to dissolve ties with one another with greater ease and frequency than would the idiom of shared substance. The gradual detachment of the child from dependency on specific adults is accomplished through three principal mechanisms: a high rate of divorce, peer-group learning, and a minimization of the authoritarian aspect of the parental role. Children are likely to be brought into contact with, and dependence on, a large number of 'step' relatives because of the first mechanism. Their subordination to adults in general is minimized by what might almost be called an avoidance of them: from the age of five or six, they return home only to eat and sleep, and spend the rest of their time in unsupervised gangs. Finally, children are never punished for disobedience. Indeed, it is more likely that a small child will attempt to command an adult than the other way around. I never witnessed an adult raise his or her hand, or even voice, to a child.

Among adults, the ideal is that everyone treats each other as an autonomous equal, and that everyone performs their material and ritual obligations to the community. Conflict is dealt with through simple avoidance — Buid traditionally lived in isolated family homesteads — or through the submission of a dispute to a formal *tultulan*, 'collective discussion', in which a sum of compensation is mutually agreed and paid. The most common type of dispute is divorce, since spouses cannot, by Buid cultural definition, avoid one another for long. One or other spouse is generally recognized as the one being 'abandoned', and is entitled to damages for emotional upset. No one has the authority to enforce a settlement, but through extended discussion and diffuse moral pressure, divorces are normally settled without undue disruption. The emphasis throughout is on preserving communal harmony (*uway*) through the separation or reconciliation of the disputants.

Individuals who are reluctant to go along with the sentiments expressed in a collective discussion may be castigated as unduly *kaingli*, 'jealous', or *kongit*, 'possessive', of their spouses, an infringement of the legitimate autonomy of the latter. While individuals have certain rights in their spouses, rights recognized by the compensation they receive when they are 'abandoned', these rights are always subordinate to the rights of individuals to freely choose their consociates. Worse than jealousy or possessiveness, however, is the attempt to establish superiority over others. In a mild form this is simply boastfulness, *buagun*, a term whose root can also mean simply 'lying'. A boastful individual is apt to be deflated through ridicule, or simply ignored, an art at which the Buid are true masters. If an individual attempts to assert superiority through force, the line is crossed into aggressive, *maisug*, behaviour.

As I noted above, simple withdrawal is the preferred solution to conflict. The socially approved response to aggression is avoidance or even flight. The Buid language is rich in words for fear, fleeing, and escape from danger, none of which carries negative moral overtones. It is not uncommon for people when telling stories about themselves to stress how frightened they were by some experience. Far from rendering them subject to ridicule, such a stress is one of the best ways to hold an audience and gain sympathy. By contrast, the only Buid words which might be used to translate our concepts of 'courage' and 'bravery' carry strongly negative moral overtones: words like *isug* denote not so much an indifference to personal danger as a tendency to fierceness or violence. The emphasis is less on an individual's inner resources than on the danger he or she poses to others.

Withdrawal from conflict can be emotional as well as spatial. Sulking is a common occurrence, but it may sometimes be carried to an anti-social extreme. Extreme emotional withdrawal, or suicidal depression (*sungun*), is viewed as a common affliction of those whose desires have been thwarted, especially in affairs of the heart. Like aggression, it may be blamed on attack by a predatory spirit. Suicide is carried out according to a culturally standardized formula: after two weeks of sulking, one finally withdraws into the deep forest away from all human habitation, and hangs oneself from a tree. The body of a suicide is not buried, but left to hang until the rope breaks. The ghost associated with it remains a permanent threat to the living, as it wanders the earth with a stretched neck looking for companions. It is only after the death and complete dehumanization of the suicide that they threaten physical harm to those who offended them in life. As I explain further below, aggressive behaviour is regarded as typical only of lowlanders and spirits. But before turning to Buid relations with neighbouring lowlanders, I will bring out the specificity of Buid attitudes toward violence and aggression by comparing them with other Philippine groups who have a less negative attitude toward these phenomena.

COMPARISON WITH OTHER PHILIPPINE GROUPS

A sharp contrast to the Buid is provided by the Tausug, a Muslim group inhabiting the Sulu archipelago in the southern Philippines. During the heyday of the Sulu sultanate from 1780–1880 the Tausug conducted frequent slave raiding and plundering expeditions against the Spanish-dominated Philippines, especially Mindoro. Among the Tausug today, one's social position must be continually revalidated, and this depends on one's ability to respond to assaults on one's honour with immediate violence. Interestingly, they use the same term for aggression as the Buid, but give it precisely the opposite moral evaluation: 'A *maisug* person is combative and not deterred by physical danger and risk, one who has strong feelings and is not afraid to express them. . . . Public cowardice or a refusal to respond to an insult or affront is shameful in the extreme' (Kiefer 1972: 53).

Having said this, however, Kiefer goes on to point out that the masculine ideal of violent pride is in tension with the religious ideal of revenge as being God's prerogative. There is a similar tension inherent in the ambiguity of the Tagalog concept of *tapang*. The Tagalog people traditionally inhabited central Luzon, and their language now serves as the basis for the Philippine national language. While being called *matapang* is taken as a compliment among Tagalog-speaking lowlanders, it describes fierce or dangerous men, ready to fight without regard to personal danger, rather than those willing to risk themselves for others. It is taken as a compliment because a man with a reputation as dangerous will be respected.

The contrast I am trying to draw between courage on the one hand, and *isug* or *tapang* on the other, is similar to that between guilt and shame. The former stresses the individual's internal state, the latter his or her relations with others. The Buid rejection of *isug* does not imply a readiness to submit to the will of others. Their belief in individual autonomy is such that even children are not required to obey their elders. What is rejected is the necessity or even possibility of maintaining or augmenting one's social position through violence. One's social position as an autonomous, equal adult is ascribed: Buid youths do not have to achieve equality with or autonomy from adult men through acts of violence, as among so many headhunting societies in Southeast Asia. Nor do adult men have to defend their position by recourse to force: there is no shame attached to fleeing from aggression. And the devaluation of violence puts Buid women at an advantage relative to women in warlike societies. Given women's lesser upper-body strength as compared with men's, a positive evaluation of violence helps to legitimate male domination.

The connotation of internal strength attached to the English concept of bravery is expressed in Buid with the phrase *marigun fag fangayufan*, literally 'strong minded'. The equivalent in Tagalog is *lakas ng loob*, or 'internal strength'. In these instances, the stress is on an individual's ability to bear misfortune stoically, to overcome hardship by drawing on one's internal resources. The association between fortitude and capacity for violence is absent in the Buid concept of *isug*, present to a certain extent in the Tagalog concept of *tapang*, and quite clear in the English concept of bravery. I would suggest that in each case the strength of the association is a measure of each culture's commitment to the overcoming of adversity through aggressive or violent acts. For the Buid, this is always illegitimate. For Tagalogs, it is a rather amoral possibility: violent individuals are respected, but there is a less than human quality about them and violent acts are often carried out under the cover of a real or assumed drunkenness.

RELATIONS WITH OUTSIDERS

Tagalog concepts are directly relevant to the present discussion because the Buid with whom I lived are in daily contact with Tagalog-speaking immigrants from neighbouring islands. As is the case with the Semai and the Chewong, the Buid define their values in opposition to those of their aggressive lowland neighbours (Dentan 1975; Howell, this volume). Many other writers working in Southeast Asia have drawn attention to the fact that particular ethno-linguistic groups cannot be treated in isolation, but must be regarded as forming part of a larger social system. The classic example is, of course, Leach's work on highland Burma. Nearer to the Buid, Morris has described the Melanau of Borneo as living in a 'highly diversified social environment in which many cultural and linguistic groups are interspersed with and closely related to one another' (1967: 216). Morris goes on to argue that the Melanau image of the spirit world reproduces this social environment by representing the cosmos as 'a kind of loose composite or ''international'' society knit together by a commonly held ''rule of law'' ' (1967: 214). Now, while such a description can be applied to Buid relations with neighbouring highland groups and with certain types of spirit, it is not applicable to their relations with lowlanders. The Buid do not regard themselves, and are not regarded by the Christians, as belonging to the same social system, and as sharing an underlying set of political values. Between the Buid and the Christians there is a difference in outlook so profound that one might almost say that a state of permanent antagonism and hostility prevails between them. In this conflict the society of the Christians is incalculably more powerful.

Lowland Philippine political culture is relevant to the Buid because lowlanders are continually trying to draw the Buid into it, and the Buid are continually trying to resist it. It is a political culture in which the strong man dominates a series of lesser men through intimidation and debt. Patrons attach clients to themselves by extending loans to the latter in times of crisis. The fundamentally asymmetrical relationship between a landlord and his tenant is expressed as one of reciprocity, however: a landlord and his tenant are both called *kasama*, 'companions' or 'partners', the former supplying the land and sometimes the capital and equipment for farming, and the latter the labour. After the harvest, each is said to receive his 'share' (*bahagi*) of the product. This dependency of the weak on the strong has a moral component. Because the client or tenant is in a state of long-term indebtedness, he owes his patron a 'debt of gratitude' and should be ready to help the latter on a diffuse, non-contractual basis. Patron– client ties often receive ritual sanction through the institution of godparenthood. The parents of a sponsored child become the *comadre* or *compadre* of the patron. Now, the term *compadre*, or its abbreviated form *pare*, is normally used in address to indicate intimacy and equality. By converting a patron into a *compadre*, a client is again trying to represent a fundamentally hierarchical relationship as one of mutuality and reciprocity.

Compadrinazgo ties cannot be created between Buid and lowlanders because the Buid reject the Christian rituals on which they are based. Instead, Christian traders attempt to implicate the Buid in the ancient Filipino institution of blood brotherhood. Christians now use *sandugo*, 'one blood', as a universal term of address and reference for the Buid. Like *compadre* it carries the same moral connotations of diffuse, enduring obligation and the same quality of masking a hierarchical relationship in the mutuality of kinship relations. The Buid resent the use of the term and the attempt to place them in the moral as well as material debt of the lowlanders. The lowlanders are sub-moral beings in Buid eyes, given their aggressive and domineering customs. The poor Christian settlers in the mountains view the Buid as standing in the same relationship to them as they stand to their own patrons. The Buid are sub-moral in Christian eyes because of their refusal to 'properly' acknowledge their debts.

Contemporary tensions between the Buid and Christian settlers from the lowlands must be placed in historical perspective. When the Spanish arrived in Mindoro in 1570, they discovered coastal settlements paying tribute to the Sultan of Brunei. The Spanish expelled the Muslims from the island, but were not able to bring it under their full control, or defend its inhabitants from Muslim raiders, until nearly the end of the nineteenth century. The last recorded raids occurred in 1870 and 1874. During this 300-year period, coastal settlements were repeatedly raided for captives to supply the slave markets of Sulu in the southern Philippines, and the once prosperous ports were reduced to impoverished and depopulated backwaters.

Mindoro served, in effect, as a battleground between the Spanish based in Manila and the Muslim traders based in Sulu.

While little direct evidence is available on the fate of the mountain populations during this period, there is little doubt they were too weak numerically and organizationally to put up any effective resistance to either power. While the Muslims were after captives, the Spanish were after tribute-paying subjects and converts. The Hispanized inhabitants of the lowlands viewed the unconverted pagans as little better than animals, whose lack of sophistication in dealing with a market economy allowed them to be exploited through debt bondage and coerced trade. More recently, the primary threat has been to the highlanders' land, although coerced labour and unequal trade continue. But however the goals of their lowland neighbours have shifted over time, they have remained essentially predatory.

The fluidity of Buid social groupings, and the ease with which the institution of sharing allows individuals to integrate into new groups, provide the best protections a weak society can have against predatory neighbours. There are no internal bonds or hierarchies which the outside powers can use to control the behaviour of more than one individual at a time. An enemy who will not stand and fight, and who has sufficient room to move and hide cannot be 'defeated' or absorbed. This fact accounts for the continued autonomy not only of the Buid but of many other shifting cultivators and hunter-gatherers in Africa and Asia (Gibson, in press). These peoples cannot allow themselves much investment in fixed assets they would need to defend, but just as importantly they cannot allow themselves much investment in social ties to specific others. Hence the positive value attached to mobility and sharing in their societies. Of more direct relevance to the thesis of this paper is the association of acts of violence and aggression, both material and mystical, with forces external to the society. Unable to profit through such acts under any conditions, the Buid never associate aggression against humans with the generation of wealth or vitality. But there is one form of aggression which is not only legitimate, but positively enjoined: the sacrifice of animals.

RELATIONS WITH THE ANIMAL AND SPIRIT WORLDS

I already introduced certain mystical categories above in my discussion of Buid personhood, particularly those relating to spirit mediumship. Here I wish to focus on the employment of carefully controlled acts of aggression against the animal world as a means of modifying their relations with the spirit world. The Buid perform at least five different kinds of animal sacrifice, each intended for a different type of spirit. But the Buid also view themselves as constituting a sort of animal ultimately destined to provide a feast for a class of spirits after death. They say that '*Taw an labang babuy*': 'People are the pigs of the predatory spirits.' They also say that '*Labang taw agkagat taw maskin kasamuk taguban*': 'Ghosts bite people because they are hungry for meat.' An examination of these five kinds of sacrifice, and of the system of belief underlying these two statements, reveals a symbolic world in which aggression and tranquillity are viewed as opposing principles held in uncertain balance by ritual action (see Gibson 1986 for a full account).

Animals are killed only to avert mystical dangers which cause illness and death. The more animals a household is obliged to sacrifice, the greater has been its misfortune. Because of this, a household obliged to sponsor many feasts gains no prestige, but becomes rather an object of pity. Whenever a pig or chicken is killed, it must be shared out in exactly equal portions among all the members of the community, without regard to their age, sex, status as kinsman, or previous relationship with the sponsor of the sacrifice. The size of the 'community' involved in these distributions varies depending on the nature of the occasion and the number of animals killed. This variation is due to the amount of interest generated by a particular ritual among members of distant settlements. It is not due to the exclusion of certain categories of people from attendance. Most meat distributions involve a local group numbering between fifty and one hundred individuals. On certain occasions, representatives from all the local communities in a region containing 700 individuals or more will attend. One such occasion is the final ritual performed to terminate the funeral cycle three months after a death. On the whole, an individual may expect to attend a sacrifice every one or two weeks, so that there is a constant circulation of meat throughout the community. In fact, the sharing of meat is the most frequent form of material transaction between households, and a key means of integrating new members into the local community.

Thus while all domesticated animals belong to, and are closely identified with, particular households, they are all destined to be consumed by the community as a whole. One might say that when a particular household is confronted by a mystical threat, it dissolves its individual identity into that of a larger social unit whose size is determined by the severity of the threat. It does this by sharing something closely identified with its members, the animals they have domesticated by hand, with the encompassing community in a commensal ritual.

Although carefully controlled, aggression is an inescapable aspect of Buid animal sacrifice. In all of the rituals described above, animal vitality is deliberately concentrated and transferred to those members of the human community most in need of vital reinforcement, such as small children and nursing mothers. The animals are always chopped into small pieces and further reduced by boiling. The life-giving qualities of pork broth are brought out in a *lisbay*, or myth, concerning the culture hero Litaw:

> During an extended period of wandering in the sky world, Litaw met Inabay, who gave him some dust from her eyes. This dust gave Litaw magical powers. When he returned to earth, he discovered that his father had died. Litaw said: 'Never mind. Get me a big pig and we shall cook it.' The pig made five pots of broth. Litaw fetched his father's corpse, which was still rolled up in its burial mat and starting to decay. Litaw poured the pots of broth over the body, one by one. As he began pouring the fifth, the body stirred, and Litaw's father said: 'That's enough, I'm being scalded.' And so he came back to life.

Another method for concentrating animal vitality is the stew prepared for ghosts, in which elements of every part of the animal are cooked together with rice. When a wild pig is caught, the meat of the head is set aside for small children, for the vital principle is associated with it.

The point is that violence is a necessary part of human interaction with the non-human world, but absolutely illegitimate within it. Violence and aggression tend to be associated symbolically with eating, which is a one-way relationship of domination, and so is incompatible with mutuality which is symbolically associated with speech, a two-way relationship between equals. The opposition between aggression and mutuality, eating and speaking, is underlined in Buid symbolism by the presence of a taboo against speaking to animals. This taboo belongs to the same category, *fayawan*, as incest and other rules against mixing things which should be kept separate. The existence of an explicit prohibition on treating animals as social beings indicates that the Buid might in fact have ambivalent feelings on the subject. Other evidence of this ambivalence concerns the way they treat young animals, raising them by hand inside the house to encourage their attachment to their owners. When a particularly close rapport develops between a human and an animal, such that the animal will follow its owner through the forest, the animal is called a *batiti*, 'pet'. One must still not talk to the pet in human language, however.

In Mindoro, domesticated pigs and chickens often go wild, and wild pigs and chickens can be domesticated if captured young. Every generation of pig and chicken must be deliberately domesticated or incorporated into human society lest it go wild. One may employ uncontrolled violence only against wild animals which are totally independent of human society. The Buid make an effort to reduce the suffering, or, at least, the struggling, of domesticated animals when they are slaughtered. They are usually partially asphyxiated before being stabbed. That is, they do this in every case except that of an exorcism ritual where the point is to make a deliberate display of violence and aggression, in the sense of 'intentionally causing suffering to another being', to frighten the predatory spirits. Even then, the slaughter is carried out without malice toward the animal. The predatory spirits, on the other hand, are described as if they bore actual malice toward humans.

Commensality provides the most powerful means by which both the Buid and the predatory spirits assert the internal solidarity of their respective collectivities. From the perspective of humans, solidarity is expressed in opposition to a category of predatory beings which regard humans as their prey, on the one hand, and to a category of prey which regard humans as their predators, on the other. The human community is, in fact, regarded as but one level in a cosmic system of stratification defined in terms of the inherently unequal relationship between the eater and the eaten. The higher the stratum, the more aggressive and evil are the beings. Pigs, for example, eat only plants. The latter are essentially passive and do not suffer before they are consumed. Humans eat pigs, but only after killing them, and cooking them, in a controlled and 'humane' manner. They have, moreover, previously fed and cared for them, or in the case of wild pigs, they have paid their spirit 'owners' proper compensation. In a sense, the pigs already 'owe' their masters their lives. The predatory spirits, finally, obtain human flesh by invading human territory and seizing, through force, what they have not produced. What is more, they begin to consume their victims while they are still alive, or, alternatively, once they have begun to rot.

The most powerful and feared of all the predatory spirits are the *fangablang*, 'those who are encountered'. These are said to resemble giant Christian lowlanders, and are continually invading Buid settlements in search of human flesh. Cannibalism is a subject of fascination and exquisite horror for the Buid, as it is for Europeans (see Arens 1979). It condenses in a vivid image the most extreme form of violence and domination imaginable: the treatment of a social being as an animal, and the incorporation of its substance into one's own body. Through their transitor radios, the Buid are aware of various *gira* (Spanish *guerra*, 'war') being fought in different parts of the world. Significantly, they are convinced that such extreme instances of violent behaviour can have only one purpose: killing and eating the enemy.

Standing in opposition to the predatory spirits are the spirits of the earth, who are closely associated with the spirit familiars discussed above under Buid personhood. The Buid say that the growth and well-being of their crops and children derive from the spirits of the earth. In general, the Buid place far more stress on the process of growth than on the acts of planting seed or of conceiving children. This process is guaranteed by the spirits of the earth, who withdraw their protection from the human community when it is divided by quarrelling. Thus persistent aggression (*garisugan*) within the community places all its crops and children in mystical danger. The need to restore tranquillity, particularly between husband and wife, in order to regain the protection of the spirits of the earth is a major incentive for resolving *tultulan*, 'collective discussions', quickly and smoothly. Now, the spirits of the earth are the only spirits which can be addressed in ordinary human speech in the course of a ritual. Speech and communal peace represent life and unity just as eating and individual desire represent death and division.

CONCLUSION

In conclusion it may be said that the structure of the spirit world constitutes both a model of and a model for the larger social system in which the Buid are embedded. At one extreme are the relations of permanent hostility between the Buid and Christians, paralleled on the mystical plane by the permanent struggle between the spirit familiars and the predatory spirits. At the other extreme are the relations of mutual help and sharing within the Buid community paralleled on the mystical plane by the solidarity between the humans and the spirits of the earth. Continued life and growth depend ultimately on the maintenance of tranquillity within the human community, which is a prerequisite for the continued assistance of the spirits of the earth. But it is equally necessary that humans engage in a ceaseless and violent struggle with beings which attack from outside the bounds of society. The rejection by the Buid of any form of legitimate hierarchy or aggression within their society must be set within the context of a larger cosmological system in which humans are under constant attack by both predatory spirits and lowlanders, and in which they must commit parallel acts of aggression against their animals.

Buid attitudes toward tranquillity and violence are the product of a long historical process, in which they were consistently the victims of outside forces. During this period, acts of aggression and domination came to be identified symbolically with the agents of disease and death, while a state of internal tranquillity, equality and individual autonomy came to be identified with the agents of health and growth. These identifications are part of the reason for their continued autonomy from the lowlands, in that they prevent the Buid from developing internal hierarchies which could be manipulated by more powerful state societies. They are also partly the result of the Buid's occupation of a habitat marginal to the economy of the lowlands: unable to permanently occupy Buid territory, the lowland powers have been content until now with sporadic, predatory incursions. An ideology of peace is thus both cause and effect of the Buid's situation in a larger regional system (Gibson, in press).

It should now be clear that Buid attitudes toward peace and violence cannot be understood in terms of innate psycho-biological dispositions, or in terms of their adaptation of the natural environment. The Buid have as much of a capacity for violent behaviour as the members of any other society. What is interesting is that this capacity is not developed, or its exercise rewarded in Buid society. An instructive example of members of a peaceful society being suddenly propelled into a situation in which violence was rewarded is provided by the Semai of Malaysia.

Many people who knew the Semai insisted that such an unwarlike people could never make good soldiers. Interestingly enough, they were wrong. Communist terrorists had killed the kinsmen of some of the Semai counterinsurgency troops. Taken out of their non-violent society and ordered to kill, they seem to have been swept up in a sort of insanity which they call 'blood drunkenness' . . . Talking about these experiences, the Semai seem bemused, not displeased that they were such good soldiers, but unable to account for their behaviour. (Dentan 1968: 58–9)

In other words, the Semai had always been *capable* of violence, but this capability had never had any *meaning*. Even after the fact, their violent behaviour just did not make sense.

The Buid and Semai examples should also serve as a caution against theories about violence and aggression which treat them as typically involving a contest between two balanced opponents competing for access to a scarce resource. In most of human history, including the modern period, the most significant types of violence involve the institutionalized oppression of a weaker group (gender, class, ethnicity, nation) by a stronger one. Warfare, preparations or war, and negotiations for 'peace' by the elites of opposing stratified social formations often distract attention from, and may be *meant* to distract attention from, the permanently installed violence perpetrated by dominant strata against subordinate strata within each formation (see Chomsky 1987: 105–6).

NOTES

1 The writing of this paper was made possible by a grant from the Harry Frank Guggenheim Foundation. I should also like to thank Anthony Carter and Grace Harris for their careful commentaries on this paper. Any remaining confusions are my own.
2 One of the problems with Heelas' excellent discussion (this volume) is that while he develops the ambiguities concerning intentionality in our own concept of 'aggression' very well, he does not seem to recognize that this may be a very general feature of related concepts in other cultures. Another problem is that he does not deal with the fact that an 'intent to harm' may itself be ambiguous: in certain contexts, it may be seen as a good thing, in others as bad. Indeed, I believe the Buid to be highly unusual in their condemnation of aggression in their dealings with all but the animal and spirit

worlds. (There are signs that they are beginning to view it as legitimate, in theory, in their dealings with Christian lowlanders, although they still find it difficult to apply in practice.)

3 Notice that the determination of such rates presupposes an understanding of what counts in a culture as 'deliberate', and that a high rate need not necessarily be viewed as a bad thing by the culture concerned.

4 The Buid attitude toward 'kinship' is perhaps as unusual as their attitude toward 'aggression', but that is another paper (Gibson 1985).

5 Elsewhere I argue that transactions among the Buid are dominated by a principle not recognized by Polanyi, and that Sahlins' reduction of Polanyi's three categories to a single continuum is even more misleading. Sharing is characteristic of a certain kind of non-competitive egalitarianism because it eliminates the possibility of debt (cf. Sahlins 1972: 193–6; Gibson 1988).

REFERENCES

Arens, W. (1979) *The Man-eating Myth*, New York: Oxford University Press.

Chomsky, N. (1987) *On Power and Ideology*, Boston: South End Press.

Dentan, R. K. (1968) *The Semai*, New York: Holt, Rinehart & Winston.

Dentan, R. K. (1975) 'If there were no Malays, who would the Semai be?', *Contributions to Asian Studies* 7: 50–60.

Gibson, T. P. (1985) 'The sharing of substance versus the sharing of activity among the Buid', *Man* 20 (3): 391–411.

Gibson, T. P. (1986) *Sacrifice and Sharing in the Philippine Highlands*, London: Athlone Press.

Gibson, T. P. (1988) 'Meat sharing as political ritual: forms of transaction vs modes of subsistence', in T. Ingold, D. Riches and J. Woodburn (eds) *Hunters and Gatherers Volume II: property, power and ideology*, London: Berg.

Gibson, T. P. (in press) 'Raiding, trading and tribal autonomy in insular Southeast Asia', in J. Haas (ed.) *The Anthropology of War*, Cambridge: Cambridge University Press.

Horton, R. (1970) 'African thought and western science', in B. Wilson (ed.) *Rationality*, Oxford: Basil Blackwell.

Kiefer, T. (1972) *The Tausug*, New York: Holt, Rinehart & Winston.

Leach, E. (1954) *Political Systems of Highland Burma*, London: Athlone Press.

Morris, H. S. (1967) 'Shamanism among the Oya Melanau', in M. Freedman (ed.) *Social Organization*, London: Frank Cass.

Polanyi, K. C. (1957) 'The economy as instituted process', in *Trade and Markets in the Early Empires*, Glencoe: The Free Press.

Sahlins, M. (1972) *Stone Age Economics*, London: Tavistock.

Strathern, M. (1980) 'No nature, no culture: the Hagen case', in C. MacCormack and M. Strathern (eds) *Nature, Culture and Gender*, Cambridge: Cambridge University Press.

Chapter Four

STYLES OF MANHOOD:
an Amazonian contrast in tranquillity and violence

JOANNA OVERING

INTRODUCTION: MORAL UNIVERSES AND THE BOUNDARIES FOR PEACEFUL AND VIOLENT ACTION

The Piaroa, a jungle people who dwell along tributaries of the Orinoco in Venezuela, equate the value judgement of 'good' with that of 'the tranquil': both carry the label of '*adiwa*'. For them, the person of good character has what is said to be the imagination to live tranquilly, or literally 'the wizardry to live tranquilly' (*mariya adiunaku*). The good social life, the Piaroa insist, is the tranquil one where individuals are never coerced by or subjected to the violence of kinsmen and neighbours. Social action among the Piaroa is congruent with their discourse on harmonious existence; for their evaluative rhetoric is coupled with a social state of extremely peaceful living. Piaroaland is almost free of all forms of physical violence, a place where children, teenagers, and adults alike never express anger through physical means. The Piaroa place immense value upon personal moderation in behaviour and are therefore appalled by most display of excess, especially if violent in intention.

This is not to say that the Piaroa have formed a totally peaceful society, and I have written elsewhere (1986a) on their discourse of predation, cannibalism, and revenge. Through sorcery, the Piaroa shaman leader is highly violent on a daily basis toward the end of protecting his community from the dangers of disease and death, both being considered to be attacks by cannibalistic beings from both this and other worlds. A state of violence or peace is always relative and depends somewhat upon the boundaries of the moral universe, but also upon the nature of the moral system at hand. Violence belongs to the domain of foreign politics for the Piaroa, while for their neighbours, the Yanomami, close kin can easily transform into dangerous 'others'. A Yanomami may assault, perhaps fatally, a wife, brother, or cousin (see Lizot 1985: 45, 68, 69ff.). The Shavante leader of the Brazilian Amazon may kill a fellow villager whom he views as an intolerable competitor (Maybury-Lewis 1971: 186ff.). In contrast, the moral universe within which the Piaroa cannot inflict violence is very wide, encompassing all of Piaroaland. The Piaroa say that all their deaths are caused by outsiders, and their own powerful revenge rituals are aimed at villages outside of Piaroaland (Overing 1986a).

The moral dogma of the Piaroa disallows, then, violence toward anyone who is part of their this-worldly political and social universe, that is, anyone who is not a total stranger. Most important, enemies are not seen. Foreign sorcerers enter Piaroaland in the guise of butterflies; thus, even those who inflict violence upon Piaroa are unseen in human form. In contrast, for the Yanomami and the Shavante the moral universe within which violence is not allowed slips and slides: today you are a friend, but perhaps tomorrow you are not. Such variation in the conception of stable moral boundaries that delimit friend and extreme otherness reflects the considerable difference between the Piaroa and such groups as the Shavante and the Yanomami in their *everyday* display of hostilities. Yanomami and Shavante violence occurs within both community and tribal boundaries.

The particular contrast between peaceful and violent action in which I am interested falls outside any simple dichotomy which might distinguish between a state of war and peace. While it is the hostility of 'outsiders' that often legitimates violence, the definition of who counts as 'outsider' is a highly relative matter, as the cases cited above suggest. Nor is the fashionable 'mode of production' argument a likely key to the matter. Despite recent generalizations about the violence and aggression which supposedly typify societies of tropical forest in South America (see, for instance, Sanday 1981: 193), these peoples vary considerably in the degree and the kind of violence allowed in everyday life. Yet most would fall into the category of 'brideservice society', a social formation that Collier and Rosaldo (1981: 280) have defined as radically different from that of the 'bride-wealth society'. These authors argue that in the 'brideservice societies', a category encompassing the relatively egalitarian hunting and gathering peoples and those that have a mixed economy of hunting, gathering, small-scale horticulture, the association of sexuality and violence, which is but a particular type of sexual oppression, plays a central role in all political and much social action. Collier and Rosaldo are linking a particular mode of production ('brideservice economies')●with a specific type of politics ('sexual politics') and a particular theory of personhood '(Man the Hunter, Warrior, Life Taker and Giver' vs. 'Woman his Sexy Partner') (see Collier and Rosaldo 1981: 275–6, 315).

While Collier and Rosaldo have relatively successfully characterized one type of 'brideservice economy', they are too sweeping in their wider generalization; for brideservice economies are not always associated with the cultural values these authors stipulate. For many groups with such 'economies', community and even inter-community relations are conceived as properly being harmonious ones (for example, see the following literature on South America: Santos 1986 on the Amuesha of Peru, Thomas 1982 on the Pemon of Venezuela, and Overing Kaplan 1975 on the contrast in 'peaceful' and 'bellicose' peoples of the Orinoco Basin at the time of the Conquest). The sample of groups used by Collier and Rosaldo, upon which they constructed their model, skewed the data; for they were all peoples who place immense value upon 'Man the Hunter and Warrior', and who also elaborate ritually upon the violent, destructive, and fertile potential in men. Such values work at the expense of a positive evaluation of females. They also work against a high value being placed upon the creation of peaceful everyday relationships.

The remainder of my paper will deal with the extreme contrast between two South American groups, the Shavante and the Piaroa, in their respective valuation of male maturity. The exploration will revolve around the systematic development in youngsters of the desired, and contrasting, characteristics the two valuations entail. For the Shavante, the essence of manhood is what Maybury-Lewis (1971: 268–9) summarizes as 'sexual bellicosity', while for the Piaroa it is the ability to co-operate tranquilly with others in daily life. The Piaroa view the arrogant and dominating character, which the Shavante would highly esteem in a mature male, as odious. What is even more striking in these contrasting evaluations of maturity is their treatment of gender. The Piaroa definition of ideal maturity for men is identical to that for women; but the Shavante define ideal manhood as the achievement of a state that is both opposed and superior to the feminine.

Gender antagonism is, therefore, to a certain extent built into the definition of manhood for the Shavante. The flamboyant ritual celebration of male bellicosity and the male collectivity among the Shavante appears to carry with it a corresponding devaluation of women, and indeed to be built upon it. A Piaroa man, on the other hand, must, ideally, co-operate equally well with men and women, and, as is true also for women, achieve harmony in these relationships. Such a difference in conceptions of gender and gender roles has strong implications for the event of peace or friction in the play of daily life, and cannot be too much emphasized. It is this issue, the interplay of ideas about gender and gender roles with the creation of discord or harmony in community relationships, about which I shall be concerned below. The focus will be upon systems of morality that vary greatly in their images of manhood and styles of manhood.

Much anthropology has been written on the ways in which culture and social rules constrain women. A modern variant of this view is the Marxian argument of Meillassoux, who sees the formation of the sexual division of labour, itself, as entailing the socio-political subjugation of women, making 'the woman (or slave) a servant of men' (Meillassoux 1981: 21). He argues that kinship institutions, such as marriage, conjugality, and paternal filiation, were then imposed upon women by men as the means through which men constrained women to gain control over both the means of reproduction and labour (ibid.: xxi–xxiii, 20).[1]

My concern is to show that, on the contrary, culture and social rules may well constrain males to fit a given society's ideas about virtuous male behaviour. This is not a merely tongue-in-cheek reaction to such arguments as that of Meillassoux. When the Shavante train boys to become warriors who can both take and give orders, they systematically *constrain* the youngsters in age-set seclusion for a period of five years during which time they are trained to endure suffering (see below). In contrast to the position taken by Meillassoux above, when I speak of 'constraint' my interest is with the overt institutionalization and effects of intentional physical constraint. In a paper on peace and violence this is probably a proper focus, for it is men who are usually in charge of techniques of attack against outsiders. The treatment and definition of enemies are matters forthcoming from the domain of 'the political', which is to a large extent a male domain. Also, it is more than likely the case, however, that how a society designs manners for close personal and social relationships cannot be totally separated from its understanding of the 'proper' treatment of its enemies.

AN IMAGE OF MANHOOD:
THE VIRILE SHAVANTE HUNTER AND WARRIOR

The Shavante are an Amerindian group of some 2,000 people who dwell in the Mato Grosso of Central Brazil. In terms of dietary needs and actual consumption patterns, they have a gathering economy supplemented by both hunting and horticulture. However, if one looks at Shavante rhetoric and desire, they have a hunting economy. According to Maybury-Lewis (1971: 33–6), the Shavante, both men and women, have a passion for meat, and consider it the prime delicacy: in fact, however, they subsist primarily on wild roots, nuts, and fruits from the collecting trips of women.

Hunting, then, serves other needs in Shavante society than just dietary ones. Its technicalities interest the men above all else, and it is the activity upon which they spend most of their energy and about which they talk endlessly (Maybury-Lewis 1971: 33). Hunting also provides the men with a public stage for the stylized display of virility. The unsuccessful hunter is met with marked coldness by the women, while the successful hunter flings down his kill for the women to prepare, and with studied indifference goes to lie down. Such a conclusion to a hunting trip is evidence that the man is endowed with proper male virtue. Endurance, fleetness, wakefulness, watchfulness, and bellicosity, all attributes that for the Shavante lead to good hunting, are also indicative of valour, the most esteemed characteristic of Shavante manhood.

Collier and Rosaldo (1981: 276) have noted that in societies where valour in men is associated with the role of hunter, there is often an ideological linking of hunting, killing, and male sexuality. This is no less the case for the Shavante, as evidenced by their great *Wai'a* ceremony which, as Maybury-Lewis describes it (1971: 243ff.), is a ritual representation of the sexual aspect of male ferocity. Shavante men in this ceremony act out the glorification of the essence of manhood, comprised for them of both the bellicose, destructive aspect of male power and its sexual/generative side (ibid.: 266). Ferocity is demonstrated, and the force of it received, through: (a) the ritual killing of a mythical, fierce and excellent hunter, (b) the ceremonial (and actual) rape of women, where a woman from each clan is chosen as object, and (c) a ceremonial pantomime of attack which opposes the moieties one to the other: one side in fierce, scowling stamping dance moves against a man of the opposite moiety who must not flinch, even if trampled (Maybury-Lewis 1971: 257). As Maybury-Lewis remarks (ibid.: 66), 'the combination of sexuality and aggression could hardly be more aptly expressed than in a ceremonial rape'. The women are also warned by the men that if they, the women, should set eyes on the masks of the ceremony, the men would manhandle, rape, and disfigure them. The ceremony is at its base one that celebrates opposition and division, the division between the genders, between the clans, between the moieties. Through such opposition, men both act out their power and receive it.

The institutions of Shavante society are such that women are usually excluded, except as 'objects', from its public aspects.[2] In adulthood, spouses spend little leisure time together: men in leisure, if not at their parental home, spend most such time in the men's house. Women are prohibited from approaching the mature men's council, which takes place daily in the men's house when most decisions about the affairs of the community are made. Women are also excluded from most features of the highly elaborated age-set system. Women have no say in their marriages: often they are married when still babies, or at least by the age of five in a group ceremonial marriage, for youths, held for them at the close of their bachelor hut initiation period. Older men are usually polygynous; thus a youth rarely has available for marriage an age-mate female, and he must wait for a younger generation of females to mature before cohabitation with them. Much of Shavante life, in Maybury-Lewis's words (1971: 104), 'is a function of politics, and Shavante politics is based on competition between groups of males'. Or, as Lopes da Silva observes (1986a), the Shavante conceive of society through the male model.

The characteristics of Shavante leaders are also telling of the value placed upon ferocity in the Shavante ideal of manhood. As is true in general for lowland Amerindian leaders, the Shavante leader has no power of coercion for the organizing of daily economic activity. He can make suggestions and harangue in the man's council meeting, but he cannot order people into action. His qualities, nevertheless, are those of the successful hunter/warrior: he must demonstrate his ideal manliness through self-assertiveness, forceful oratorical skill, athletic prowess, and ceremonial expertise (Maybury-Lewis 1971: 198; also see Seeger 1981: 183 on the Suya leader whose temperamental characteristic is that of 'uncontrolled belligerence'). As is also the case for other Amerindian leaders, he has the responsibility for peacemaking. However, if he is a particularly strong leader, the Shavante chief has no compunction in killing factional opponents within his own village. Should he go too far, the only repercussion, so long as he remains powerful, is for some of the village members to leave the village.

Belligerence is systematically instilled in males as proper behaviour from a very young age (the information on the training for proper female maturity is unclear), and boys and girls at a very young age are separated from one another as playmates (also see Lizot 1985: 39 on the Yanomami, and Seeger 1981: 155ff. on the Suya). Small children are encouraged to be small tyrants, to react violently if thwarted. Yet the scolding and punishment of children are rare (see Lizot 1985: 73 on the Yanomami). Tantrums by small children are frequent and condoned by parents: Shavante fathers encourage their children to displays of violence against the mother (Maybury-Lewis 1971: 71). Children are taught to retaliate any hurt, a 'blow for blow' principle (see Lizot 1985: 74 on the Yanomami).

Shavante youths are trained not simply to be warriors, but also to learn co-operation with other men as a group in adversity against other groups of men (see Seeger 1981: 155ff. on the Suya). To instil the characteristics of the co-operative warrior, the Shavante seclude boys as age-sets for at least five years, during which period they undergo continual harassment and daily haranguing by older men, suffering endurance tests, such as all night exposures and duels at dawn. The boys during this period of seclusion learn athletic prowess and how to display belligerence. Through the lengthy and arduous training during seclusion, they are: (a) to develop a lifetime corporate spirit within the group, (b) to learn to accept the dominance of older men, and to be prepared in general for (rather violent) dominance relationships among men, and (c) taught to act violently as a group.

This seclusion period is closed by an elaborate ceremony that emphasizes the spatial and emotional removal of young men from the world of women. After this stage, the young men, who are the warriors *par excellence*, are relatively free of obligation until mature. These young warriors are characterized by Maybury-Lewis (1971: 140 – 2; also see Seeger 1981: 162 on the Suya) as exceedingly vain, proud of their bellicosity and beauty. The training for bellicose action nevertheless continues: the mature age grade of men imposes anger and ferocity upon these young men, goading them continually into violent action.

In conclusion to this section, the factors internal to Shavante society that contribute to the formation of a particular type of hunter/warrior complex, one similar to that described by Collier and Rosaldo (1981), and to the playing out of violence within the community on a more or less daily basis, and indeed which build such violence into everyday life, can be summarized as follows:

1. the image of ideal manhood is that of the bellicose and handsome hunter/warrior;
2. political leadership corresponds to this image;
3. public leadership in general is associated with the principle of male dominance, of men over men, of men over women;
4. political ideology is male-biased and associated with the values of male supremacy and ferocity;
5. women are disallowed from participating in most public decision-making and from the political process in general; they are associated with the domain of the domestic;
6. most public co-operation is between men, and not between men and women, or between women;
7. the genders are systematically separated from an early age;
8. children are trained into violent reaction;
9. initiation is focused upon the lengthy constraint of boys, during which period the boys are separated off from female society, taught male solidarity, bellicosity, and endurance, and trained to accept the dominance of older groups of men;
10. ceremonial displays of male virility, ferocity, and sexuality are highly elaborated, as too is ritual violence against women;
11. the ritual celebration of fertility focuses upon male generative abilities, and not female ones;
12. male economic activities and the products of male labour are prized over female economic activities and the products of female labour.

In short, the Shavante image of society can almost be equated with the social organization of men, and their notions of personhood with 'manhood'. Such an image fits well with the Collier and Rosaldo characterization of a 'brideservice society'. *None* of the above summary statements applies to the Piaroa.

AN IMAGE OF ADULTHOOD: PIAROA TRANQUILLITY AND THE MASTERY OF EMOTIONS

For the Piaroa, the ideal of man the hunter and sexy warrior is not culturally elaborated, nor is the value of male political supremacy. They do not associate valour with the handsome and arrogant hunter, and young men are taught to pity such evidence of 'lack of control'. The Piaroa attitudes toward food reflect their devaluation of the status of the practical hunter. They rely on four food sources, that from garden cultivation, from collecting, from hunting, and from fishing. With respect to desire, they insist on the equal value of products of the hunt and products of the garden. A proper meal, they say, should be comprised of both meat (the product of men's labour) and manioc bread (the product of women's labour).

For the Piaroa, the ideal of social maturity is the same for men and women; it is one of controlled tranquillity. The individual, both male and female, is responsible for mastering emotions and the poisonous creative powers within the person which come from the crystal boxes of the *Tianawa* gods (see below). Through such mastery, the individual can achieve the moderation in behaviour to allow him/her to lead a tranquil and therefore moral life within a community of relationships. It is through this mastery that one achieves ideal manhood and womanhood in Piaroaland, and through it one can then creatively participate in the building of community. The arrogant and handsome hunter is an image seen to be as disruptive to community relations as that of the 'promiscuous woman'. The image that a Piaroa wishes to present to the world is that of 'dignified difference'. The Piaroa judgement about the 'handsome hunter' is a complex one which can be understood through their theory of knowledge and personhood, a topic for below.

Today there are approximately 7,000 Piaroa living in the Amazon Territory of Venezuela. Until about 1970, the population was highly dispersed with great distances separating both houses and territories. In contrast, life within the multiple-family house was carried out within densely populated spaces. If antagonisms or competition became overt within the house, it disbanded into separate units (Overing Kaplan 1975). Since 1970, the Venezuelan government has encouraged the Piaroa to form larger communities in downriver positions closer to the administrative centre. Thus, although I use the present tense, the physical organization of communities and the economic organization that I discuss are more relevant to the pre-1970 period.

Each territory, comprising six to seven multiple-family houses, has its own 'master of the territory', who is the *ruwang* that holds the supreme position in a loose hierarchy of *ruwatu* (pl.) within it. The *ruwatu* are politico-religious leaders who are basically 'men of knowledge' who deal with forces of destruction and regeneration from other worlds. The politicking between the *ruwatu* is kept at a relatively low-key level, for they rarely meet as a group. Competition among *ruwatu* between communities is usually expressed through the accusations of sorcery attack, often in the wake of marriages which shift the residential alignments within the territory, and thus respective follower size. While the drama of such shamanic battles can be high, there are many mechanisms that allow for their peaceful resolution (Overing Kaplan 1975; Overing 1985). Competitors are rarely accused of deliberately killing a kinsman, though they might well be accused of inadvertently doing so.

Despite the fact of achieved *ruwang*ship, the Piaroa are relatively speaking highly egalitarian, for they place great value upon personal autonomy. The status labels of '*ruwang*' and '*ruwahu*' are the only ones used in reference by the Piaroa outside of kinship terms to think about and to classify social relationships. Typical of Amerindian groups of the Guianas (see Rivière 1984), Piaroa social life is very unformalized. There are no age sets, no descent groups, no warrior societies, no formal council of mature men, no moiety organizations for the playing out of community life. There exist no mechanisms for corporate group decision-making with regard to disputes or economic matters. Rivière (1984: 4) has argued that such informality is a product of the emphasis by the Guianese Amerindian upon the value of individualism. I wish to add, at least for the Piaroa, that their 'informality' is also a product of their high valuation of peaceful living.

Unlike the Shavante case, leadership pertains not to 'manhood', but to the role of *ruwang*. In other words, an adult man does not automatically assume a political role on the basis of his gender, any more than does a woman. If one wishes to speak of specifically 'political' roles, the divide is between the individual *ruwatu* and their wives (*ruwahutu*), on the one hand, and everyone else, on the other (Overing 1985). However, power in Piaroa social life, as for the universe in general, is highly dispersed and individualized.

The community does not hold land in perpetuity: no Piaroa can 'own' land, nor can the community. No one, no leader, and no group can order the labour of another, or demand the products of it (Overing Kaplan 1983/4). All products from the jungle are shared equally among members of the large house, while garden products and artifacts are privately owned by the individuals whose labour produces them (or literally creates them; see below). Loosely organized work parties (all male, all female, male and female) within the community characterize economic life. Each woman is mistress of her own fertility for which she alone is responsible: the community has no legal right to her progeny; nor does her husband if they should divorce.

The Piaroa are as allergic to a notion of social 'rule' as to the idea of 'the right of command'. While there are proper ways of doing things, it is up to the individual to *choose* or *not to choose* to do them. The Piaroa emphatically told me that there was no residence 'rule'. Although there are kinsmen and in-laws with whom it is proper to live, the final choice is always left to the individual as a private decision. The Piaroa daily express to one another their right to private choice and their right to be free from domination over a wide range of matters, such as residence, work, self development, and even marriage.

For the Piaroa, coercion has no place within the domain of the social, including any power a 'collectivity' might have. The notion of giving up one's rights to a 'whole community' or of submitting to a decision forthcoming from the community or a portion of it would be a strange and abhorrent idea to them (Overing, in press). Sovereignty is in large part in the hands of individuals. Even the gods have no powers of coercion over individuals.

Despite the fact that any notion of 'the will of the collectivity' would be alien to the Piaroa, the ability *to be social* is considered to be the most important *and valued* characteristic of humans living on this earth. According to Piaroa theory, the human condition is unique in that humans are the only beings that are today able to achieve a social life and to live in a community. The Piaroa live on earth beneath 'the sky of the domesticated', and it is the sociality of living in communities beneath this sky that sets humans apart from all others. Only humans can acquire the capacities for creating tranquil and moral (non-competitive) relationships of co-operation which allow for the forming of a moral community. Both sociality and the powers to transform the earth's resources for use, powers upon which sociality depends, are capabilities distinct to earthly humans. *Achieving the social*, then, is the primary goal of the Piaroa community. In great contrast to that type of political thought which equates 'the social' with the constraint of a collectivity and with relations of domination, the Piaroa insist upon the opposite where 'the social' is viewed as the means through which humans could actively prevent the establishment of (immoral) relations of dominance (Overing, in press).

The work and the skills for building community are considered to be skills of wizardry (*maripa*), and each individual acquires such skills, as appropriate to gender, through 'lessons in wizardry' (*maripa teau*). Such skills, which fill one's 'beads of knowledge' within the person, are the poisonous creative powers for transformation that come from the crystal boxes of the *Tianawa* gods. All powers for building community, for reproducing and producing, come, then, from another world, that of the gods. *This earthly world was depleted of all powers* at the end of creation time history; after that time the community could only be achieved and continuously recreated through individuals carefully taking, with the help of the *ruwatu*, *limited* amounts of transformational forces to do so from the gods.

In contrast to peoples who believe that their communities have existence through time through rules of corporation, the Piaroa do not understand 'community' and the relationships of which it is comprised as a political given that allows for continuity through time. Rather it is for them a process of existence that has to be daily achieved by individuals through work, that is through the individual mastery over emotions and the skills of wizardry. The Piaroa, for instance, place emphasis upon marriage ties in the development of community rather than upon the ties of descent. Through marriage and affinity the work of reproduction and production can be achieved.

For the Piaroa the social can only be created through the skills and the personal autonomy of individuals. Humans can act as moral, social agents because unlike all other present day beings they acquire both a 'life of the senses, or desires' (*kaekwae*) and a full 'life of thoughts' (*ta'kwaru*) to be used on earth. Moderation in behaviour, which allows for the ability to interact tranquilly, is achieved by attaining mastery over one's 'life of senses' and one's 'life of thoughts' (Overing 1985).

Ta'kwanya and *ta'kwakomenae* are the two components, or forces, of

90

ta'kwaru, 'the life of thoughts', both of which come from the crystal boxes of the gods. *Ta'kwanya* refers to all those particular cultural capabilities a specific type of people have that enable them to live as they do: it is their means of living and fulfilling their material needs; it is their way of doing things in the material sense. It is a category that includes both reproductory capabilities and the knowledge and abilities to transform the earth's resources for use: for acquiring food, for making tools, for processing food, for being fertile, for doing ritual. It also includes language and social norms. There is a strong sense of violence attached to the notion of *ta'kwanya*; for this category of creative, cultural capability is comprised of poisonous forces and carries with it the idea of *predation* (see Overing 1986a). For the Piaroa, reproduction, production, and language are all placed on the same level as basically predatory capabilities, or the means for predation. Thus, the transformational capabilities for fulfilling material needs are dangerous to the self if one takes too many of them, and they can be dangerous to others in contact with one. For instance, the transformational forces of men are dangerous for women, and vice versa; both are dangerous for children. Each person is responsible for preventing his/her danger to others (Overing 1986b).

It is through the other aspect of one's 'life of thoughts', i.e. *ta'kwakomenae* (will, rationality, consciousness), that a Piaroa acquires the autonomy to 'master' within one's self both the dangerous *ta'kwanya* and one's 'life of the senses'. It is through this mastery that one achieves ideal manhood and womanhood in Piaroaland, and can then creatively participate in the building of community.

The Piaroa leaders, the *ruwatu*, take more skills of wizardry within themselves than normal people. They therefore have greater responsibilities than the layman for the building of community. They, for instance, display in self-deportment great tranquillity, or mastery of emotions; for one of their greatest duties is to create the tranquil relationships which would allow for the work of building community, and therefore for its wealth. Because the *ruwang* takes more creative capabilities within himself, he is also the most productive member of the community, and the most dangerous. It is he who brings into this world all the powers to be used in it; at the same time it is he who could become predator through sorcery of his own people (see Overing 1985). A tranquil demeanour then is also *required* of the powerful *ruwang* by the members of his community as evidence of his mastery over his powers and his emotions. A display of too much arrogance or 'excessive' behaviour leaves a *ruwang* sitting alone, with no followers.

To sum up, *Ta'kwaru*, 'the life of thoughts', is a concept about human agency that conjoins within the person a specific culture and the autonomy to use this culture socially in a moral or immoral way. *Ta'kwakomenae* (will, etc.) is that crucial aspect of *ta'kwaru* that allows for responsible or irresponsible behaviour. It is one's motivation or intentionality in using one's customs (i.e. one's poisonous capabilities); it is one's comprehension of them, and one's responsibility or irresponsibility for their use, power, and force. Virtue for the Piaroa demands the mastery through the will of both emotions and cultural capability toward the end of achieving social responsibility.

LESSONS IN WIZARDRY

The skills of wizardry to build community are acquired gradually through life. A child's first lessons occur when she or he is 6 or 7 years old when the *ruwang* gathers a group of boys and girls together to teach them *ta'kwakomena* (consciousness, will, responsibility), or basically social morality. They are taught what our moral philosophy calls 'the other-regarding virtues', those that enable one to take responsibility for one's actions towards others (see Overing 1985). The Piaroa see the virtue of living peacefully with others as more important than 'the self-regarding virtues' (which in contrast the Shavante favour), such as personal courage, ambition, talent, and industry. The *ruwang* also teaches the children what the Piaroa view as social deficiencies: such traits as ferocity, ill-nature, cruelty, malice, arrogance, jealousy, dishonesty, vanity. The teaching *ruwang*, then, in these first 'lessons in wizardry' teaches the value of mastery over the emotions. However, *ta'kwakomena* not only refers to responsibility, but to personal autonomy in general. It is therefore the children's own decision which virtues they develop, as too it is a personal decision later which other aspects of knowledge, types of capabilities, one develops (Overing 1985, 1988).

Before the child is 'tamed' through its first *ta'kwakomena* lessons, it plays with a mixed-gender pack of free-roaming, small children. Since the Piaroa totally disallow physical violence, and children are never physically punished, the children have no model of such action. Their play, although robust, is accompanied by very little obvious dissension. Temper tantrums are discouraged, met by mocking and teasing, and strong anger is expressed by both adults and children through pointed silence (Overing Kaplan 1975; Overing 1988).

After the initial 'lessons in wizardry', the child is expected to take increasing responsibility for its actions and to co-operate with others in everyday activities. As children begin to participate in daily tasks, they gradually leave the mixed gender pack of children to join the company of young people who are of their own gender.

Boys undergo no period of constraint, in contrast to their lot among the Shavante. The Piaroa have no competitive sports, or ones that require endurance: there is no duelling, wrestling, or log races. Shuttlecock is the only sport I saw teenagers playing. The leisure time of teenage boys is spent wandering in the forest, from house to house, and in hammock gossip. By working unsystematically with adults of their choice, they slowly learn the skills of their choice, those of hunting, fishing, or the making of artifacts. Girls have less leeway than the boys. A young daughter will help her father distribute game or follow her mother into the fields, but by the age of 9 or 10 girls are participating in the total range of tasks normal to female status. Unmarried young people, male and female alike, provide a labour force upon which all adults of the communal house may draw, a preparation for the general co-operation upon which the Piaroa place such value among adults within the community.

It is particularly the case with men that they slowly over time increase their knowledge and mastery over self. Many ceremonies for both males and females are privately conducted, often at the most in the company of a *ruwang*. Marriage as a ritual is a private one between bride and groom, who are usually of approximate age. That such stages in development go relatively unmarked in community ritual is significant as one of the factors contributing to the peacefulness of the Piaroa.

Both boys and girls continue their 'lessons in wizardry' at puberty. For a woman, her most important acquisition of wizardry are her 'beads of menstruation'. The *ruwang* chants to fill her beads of knowledge with the knowledge of fertility. Menstruation, and the fertility with which it is associated, form a woman's 'thoughts' (her *ta'kwanya*), as similarly hunting and fishing capabilities are the 'thoughts' of a man. When a girl receives these 'beads of knowledge' from the gods, she then has the power to master her own fertility. It is understood, in Piaroa thought, that women have control over their own biological processes and must take responsibility for them.

All boys when about 12 undergo a great increase festival, the *Sari*, their second 'lessons in wizardry', which gives them the internal clothing of the hunter and fisherman. Far from being distressed by the initiation of the boys, the women as a group ritually congratulate each boy at its close, and praise him. The *Sari*, however, is not primarily an initiation ceremony; for it will be held by a great *ruwang* and his wife (the *ruwahu*) regardless of whether there are boys of appropriate age for initiation. It is at this ceremony that the sacred instruments, which the women must not see, are played. The *ruwang*, who is with the men outside the house, chants with the *ruwahu*, who is inside it with the women. In such chants the two leaders re-enact the roles of the creator god of the Piaroa and his sister.

Typically for the Piaroa, the women are not warned against seeing the instruments with a threat of rape; rather, it is said that if a woman should see the flutes, the entire village must commit mass suicide by joining hands and jumping off a cliff (and I must admit that their reasoning on this is not clear to me). However, the *Sari*, as a great increase ceremony, is one of the most dangerous rituals the Piaroa perform, and, as such, only a great *ruwang* and his wife may present it. Through his powers, he makes fertile the jungle and rivers: he travels to all the sacred homes of the 'parents of the animals and fish' beneath the earth, and transforms the inhabitants of these subterranean villages into the form of animal and fish. He then transports them to earthly space for human use. The ceremony is, then, a demonstration of the 'fertility' of the *ruwang*, and not of Piaroa men in general. The great 'secret' of the rituals is that the Piaroa are cannibals; for the meat they eat each day is human in its origin.

After their first 'lessons in wizardry' for the hunt, men may undergo, if they wish, more powerful lessons to slowly increase their internal 'beads of knowledge', their source of power as hunter, fisherman, chanter. The most powerful 'lessons in wizardry' are those taken for the learning of shamanic powers, and in the Piaroa theory of knowledge, men who do undergo them are the best hunters in Piaroaland, even if they rarely hunt (Overing 1988).

The excellent, practical hunter who has had no further lessons in hunting-wizardry than his introductory ones as a teenager is said to know little about hunting. Thus, for the Piaroa, 'hunting' includes all capabilities for acquiring animal meat and for making it edible for human consumption. The hunter who strikes down a wild peccary with a blowgun dart is participating in only one aspect of this process, and the critical role is played by the *ruwang*. It is the latter who has the transformational capabilities for the very creation of animal meat. The Piaroa consider the most powerful creative capabilities to be those of the woman, who bears children, and those of the *ruwang*, who transforms humans to animals (Overing 1986b). Thus, the *ruwang*, who transforms human to animal flesh, who transports it to earth, and then, after earthly kill, transforms the animal flesh into edible vegetable form (see Overing Kaplan 1975), is the greatest of all hunters.

It is through the power of his 'thoughts' that the Piaroa *ruwang* is their great warrior and hunter, while the physical prowess of the practical hunter is considered to be a minor capability, not one to place much value upon. Danger, from the Piaroa point of view, is from the predatory activities of beings from other worlds, and the responsibility for protection from them is in the hands of the shamanic *ruwatu*. Dealing with outsiders, with the enemy, is the duty of the *ruwang*, and not of men in general. Therefore, Piaroa boys are not constrained into learning the aggressive stance of young warriors to fight men of this world; they do not learn to accept the dominance relationships of groups of men over other groups of men. Males are not placed in age sets to mark their development and to rank their status as men: beyond certain learning, all maturity is both a relative and an individual matter. Nor do Piaroa young men learn the self-regarding virtues of manhood that would set them as males against females, and, as such, superior to them.

The Shavante have no shamans, and the duty of protection, fighting, and hunting in Shavanteland is carried out through group debate by men and through their physical violence. In Piaroaland, the *ruwatu*, individually, have the power that men as a group have in Shavanteland. All protection is carried out through the power of the 'thoughts' of individuals, and not through the physical bellicosity of men in groups. It might be added as an aside that it probably takes much more cultural energy to teach bellicosity and to produce warriors (with spears as arms), than to teach co-operation and to produce shamans (with 'thoughts' as arms).

95

PEACE AND THE DEMARCATION OF 'THE OTHER':
A CONCLUSION

I began this essay by noting that the moral dogma of the Piaroa disallows violence toward anyone who is part of their this-worldly political and social universe. Beings having the sufficient characteristic of 'otherness' to warrant an attack should only be those from other lands or worlds. Indeed, an important aspect of the Piaroa 'complex of peace' is the erasure of most marked divisions among people in the playing out of the social life of the community. Their ideal of endogamy, which treats the marriage exchange as if it were non-existent, is an example of such a mechanism for achieving peace. The Piaroa recognize marriage exchange as an exceedingly dangerous principle to act upon, a lesson they receive from the events of the mythic past which was a time when each marriage alliance between strangers carried in its wake a deadly competition for the poisonous cultural capabilities of predation. Through the endogamous marriage the very notion of marriage exchange, and especially its dangerous mixing of strangers, has been masked (see Overing Kaplan 1972, 1975, 1984).

There is very little idiom through which a Piaroa can demarcate another Piaroa as 'other' than self, and therefore as 'outsider'. Although all Piaroa are considered kinsmen, division does exist, of course: there is the factional politicking of the *ruwatu*; each individual has dangerous affines, even if they are also kin; men have different roles to play from women, and because of their difference in cultural capabilities the genders are dangerous for one another, a difference somewhat marked in ritual. However, unlike the Shavante, whose ritual and rhetoric sets into opposition groups and categories of people, and indeed celebrates separation and opposition, Piaroa institutions downplay, ignore, and mask the principles of separation and opposition, principles they associate with relations of dominance and tyranny (see Overing Kaplan 1981). 'Difference' for the Piaroa always signifies a danger: it can easily lead to violence between individuals and therefore be a deterrent to the possibility of creating the sociality necessary for the creation of community.

Much of the bread and butter of anthropology, the description of elaborate group organization, rites of initiation, networks of marriage exchanges, the hierarchy of groups, and the ranking of men over women are all mechanisms for stressing the 'otherness' among people who daily interact, and, as such, they mark the boundaries within which, and outside of which, daily aggression and domination are played out. Thus, in conclusion, I would like to remark that one reason that descriptions of exceedingly peaceful societies are relatively 'thin on the ground' is most likely because the institutions of such societies are not congruent with the Western (and anthropological) notions of 'the social'. On the other hand, the institutions of the Shavante are but grist for our mill. Their rituals, their rhetoric, their values, and their group organization are familiar to us, while those of the Piaroa are not.

© 1989 Joanna Overing

NOTES

1 An assumption in much of the recent literature on gender is that male obligations give men status, while female obligations constrain women. For example, it is argued that boys in initiation receive esoteric privileged knowledge, but girls only suffer prohibitions and restrictions at puberty (see Bamberger 1974: 277; Ortner 1974: 69). This is an example of what I have labelled a 'Catch 22' clause that is unfortunately very general to interpretations in gender studies.

2 It must be admitted that to a certain extent I am presenting a caricature of the Shavante, if for no other reason than I do not know them as well as the Piaroa. The picture I give, however, is, according to a Bororo expert, Sylvia Caiuby Novaes (personal communication), one to which the Bororo, neighbours of the Shavante, also subscribe. In other words, the image I present of the Shavante is the one they choose to present to the world. However, Aracy Lopes da Silva, who has recently done research with Shavante females, tells me that: (a) Shavante females have considerable strength within the 'domestic arena', and (b) Shavante males are often gentle with women and children when interacting within the domestic field. On the other hand, as Lopes da Silva herself comments (1986a), with the exception of the public bestowal of the 'woman's name' upon the female, women are tied to the domestic, the private, and the individual, while men are associated with the public, the ceremonial, and the political. Also see Lopes da Silva (1986b).

REFERENCES

Bamberger, J. (1974) 'The myth of matriarchy: why men rule in primitive society', in M. Rosaldo and L. Lamphere (eds) *Women, Culture, and Society*, Stanford: University of California Press.

Collier, J. and Rosaldo, M. (1981) 'Politics and gender in simple societies', in S. Ortner and H. Whitehead (eds) *Sexual Meanings*, Cambridge: Cambridge University Press.

Lizot, J. (1985) *Tales of the Yanomami*, Cambridge: Cambridge University Press.

Lopes da Silva, A. (1986a) 'Structural flexibility in Gê-societies of Central Brazil: naming and person among the Shavante'. Unpublished paper.

Lopes da Silva, A. (1986b) *Nomes e Amigos: da prática Xavante a uma reflexao sobre os Je*, Sao Paulo: FFLCH/USP.

Maybury-Lewis, D. (1971) *Akwe-Shavante Society*, Oxford: Clarendon Press.

Meillassoux, C. (1981) *Maidens, Meal and Money: capitalism and the domestic economy*. (First published in French as *Femmes, Greniers et Capitaux* by Librairie François Maspéro, Paris 1975.) Cambridge: Cambridge University Press.

Ortner, S. (1974) 'Is female to male as nature is to culture?', in M. Rosaldo and L. Lamphere (eds) *Women, Culture, and Society*, Stanford: University of California Press.

Overing Kaplan, J. (1972) 'Cognation, endogamy, and teknonymy: the Piaroa example', *SWJA* 28 (3).

Overing Kaplan, J. (1975) *The Piaroa, a People of the Orinoco Basin*, Oxford: Clarendon Press.

Overing Kaplan, J. (1981) 'Review article: Amazonian anthropology', *J.Lat.Amer.Stud.*, 13 (1): 151–64.

Overing Kaplan, J. (1983/4) 'Elementary structures of reciprocity: a comparative note on Guianese, Central Brazilian, and North-West Amazon socio-political thought', in A. B. Colson and H. D. Heinen (eds) *Themes in Political Organization: the Caribs and their neighbours. Anthropologica*, Vols. 59–62. Caracas: Fundacion la Salle.

Overing Kaplan, J. (1984) 'Dualism as an expression of difference and danger: marriage exchange and reciprocity among the Piaroa of Venezuela', in K. Kensinger (ed.) *Marriage Practices in Lowland South America*, Urbana: University of Illinois Press.

Overing, J. (1985) 'There is no end of evil: the guilty innocents and their fallible god', in D. Parkin (ed.) *The Anthropology of Evil*, Oxford: Basil Blackwell.

Overing, J. (1986a) 'Images of cannibalism, death and domination in a non-violent society', *Journal de la Société des Américanistes*, LXXII: 133–56.

Overing, J. (1986b) 'Men control women? The "Catch 22" in the analysis of gender', *International Journal of Moral and Social Studies*, 1 (2): 135–56.

Overing, J. (1988) 'Lessons in wizardry: personal autonomy and the domestication of the self in Piaroa society', in G. Jahoda and I. Lewis (eds) *Acquiring Culture: ethnographic perspectives on cognitive development*, London: Croom Helm.

Overing, J. (in press) 'The shaman as worldmaker: creativity and the end to history', in M. Douglas (ed.) *Coherent Worlds*, Beacon Press.

Rivière, P. (1984) *Individual and Society in Guiana: a comparative study of Amerindian social organization*, Cambridge: Cambridge University Press.

Sanday, P. (1981) *Female Power and Male Dominance: on the origins of sexual inequality*, Cambridge: Cambridge University Press.

Santos Granero, F. (1986) '*The Power of Love: the moral use of love amongst the Amuesha of Central Peru*', Ph.D. thesis: The University of London.

Seeger, A. (1981) *Nature and Society in Central Brazil: the Suya Indians of Mato Grosso*, Cambridge, Mass.: Harvard University Press.

Thomas, D. J. (1982) *Order without Government*. Illinois Studies in Anthropology, No. 13. Urbana: University of Illinois Press.

Chapter Five

PEACE AND VIOLENCE IN BALI:
culture and social organization

L. E. A. HOWE

INTRODUCTION

Culturalism, as a form of analysis, stresses the primacy of ideas and values which inform, generate, or produce social action. As far as it goes this is a reasonable formulation since behaviour is only rendered sensible when interpreted within a framework of inter-subjectively shared meanings. However, it becomes unsatisfactory if little attention is given to the economic, political, and historical conditions within which such shared meanings are socially constructed. Of course, such conditions are themselves conceptualized in terms of existing ideas and values, but changing conditions are also implicated in shaping and modifying the interpretive cultural apparatus (Bourdieu 1977; Giddens 1976).

In a recent essay on the Mbuti, Turnbull argues that the most important factor 'in controlling [aggression], violence and conflict in adult life, is the demonstrably positive value of *ekimi* ('quiet') that the adult has perceived at every stage of his life' (1982: 149). Turnbull (1976), Marshall (1961) on the !Kung, and Dentan (1968) on the Semai, similarly emphasize the role of values in the production of non-violent social activity. While these are very fine pieces of work, it is necessary to point out that the relation between value and practice is not straightforward, but is complex and contingent (Holy and Stuchlik 1983). It may well be that the relatively simple forms of social organization typical of many hunter-gatherer societies (small-scale, pretty much uniform distribution of knowledge and social competence, limited stratification and division of labour, pervasive egalitarianism and autonomy, no durable kin groups, little material property, and constant mobility) provide conditions in which the translation of value into practice is more certain and secure. After all, such a combination of factors produces societies whose cosmologies are rich and complex but equally known and understood by all, whose value systems tend to be self-consistent and equally adhered to by all, whose collective experiences closely match those of particular individuals, and so forth. In short these are societies for which Durkheim's notions of the sacred, of collective representations, of mechanical solidarity are most obviously applicable.

What is clear, however, is that the factors tending to generate the correspondence between representation and action in hunter-gatherer societies are either absent or reversed in larger-scale societies. Such societies are characterized by much larger populations, more complicated divisions of labour, specialist positions, property holding, complex rules of descent, inheritance and succession, unequal distribution of income, wealth and social knowledge, hierarchy or rank systems, and so on. This means that people differentially placed in the socio-economic structure have different perceptions of their society and the way it typically works. Lord and slave, landowner and tenant, employer and employee, rich and poor, cannot be expected to present similar renditions of their society's structure and dynamics. Most important, there is an unequal distribution of power and hence the opportunity for those in positions of influence to impose their definitions of reality on others, as it were to set the cultural and ideological agenda: as Giddens puts it 'what passes for social reality stands in immediate relation to the distribution of power' (1976: 113). In general, then, people in structurally different roles in society may not evaluate belief and action in the same way and, more significantly, the overall value 'system' may not necessarily be self-consistent. Consequently it is unlikely that there will be a concordance between representation and practice.

THE BALINESE

Over two million people inhabit the island of Bali, and the vast majority practise wet-rice agriculture producing two or three crops each year. With the exception of two large and several small towns Balinese live in densely packed villages either on the coastal plains or straddling the ridges radiating out from the central mountainous region. Balinese religion is a syncretic mix of indigenous ancestor cults and imported Hinduism, and their social organization has certain similarities to the Hindu caste system (Howe 1985, in press).

While Balinese social organization and modes of livelihood are very different to those of the Chewong of the Malay peninsula (the subject people of Howell's paper) their ideas about human nature, interpersonal behaviour, and emotional states are in certain respects quite similar. According to Howell the Chewong have a theory of human nature which is an aspect of their general cosmology, and which generates certain forms of interpersonal practice. These are by and large coincident with Chewong verbal statements concerning proper behaviour. The ethnography on which this is predicated relates largely to her close and astute examination of five emotional states which receive considerable cultural elaboration. Two of these are positively valued, and three negatively valued and felt to be characteristic of non-Chewong. The first two are glossed as first shy, timid, and ashamed and second as frightened and fearful; the latter three are glossed as first angry, second quarrelsome, and third brave. In addition the Chewong theory of human nature stresses that the health and well-being of the person is achieved when his being is in balance.

There is abundant evidence that the ideal nature of the Balinese cosmos and the notion of the person is structured by ideas of balance, order, and equilibrium; and that they also experience emotional states similar to the Chewong and valued in the same way. According to Howell, she 'never witnessed a quarrel or an outburst of anger, except among small children' (1984: 37). My experience in Bali was that although social interaction was generally peaceful, quarrels and fights occurred more often than this. If values are so important in the production of social action why then does one encounter in Bali more frequent outbursts of anger, emotional display, and quarrelling than among the Chewong? The argument, crudely, is that the Balinese cannot easily translate their values into practice because of various institutional constraints and because of the (changing) material conditions in which they live and to which they must adapt, both of which generate competition over scarce resources and conflicts over material interests.

I first present some evidence on Balinese concepts concerning emotional equilibrium and on representations of states of mind. I then go on to discuss some historical data and two typical patterns of social relationship which can eventuate in open aggression.

EMOTIONAL EQUILIBRIUM IN BALI

Illness is conceived to be caused in at least three different ways. First, it may be precipitated by accidents, by shocks, or by fainting fits resulting from emotional disturbance. In all of these cases the components of the body and spirit are said to be jumbled up (*madukadukan*) or confused. The remedy is a ritual recognition (*ngulapin anak*) of the components. Second, illness may be an entirely natural matter. Colds, diarrhoea, constipation, headaches, skin infections, and many other ailments are perceived as quite natural, unless they become chronically debilitating, whereupon they can be reclassified as manifestations of spirit interference or witchcraft. Natural maladies are described in terms of the pan-Indonesian distinction between 'hot' and 'cold', the healthy state being 'cool'. Conditions such as colds and diarrhoea, involving excessive excretions, are cold (*nyem*), whilst constipation and skin infections for example are hot (*panes*). Remedies for such complaints are based on the same set of ideas. Thus *nyem* conditions require warming medicines and *panes* ones require cooling medicines, both of which produce the cool state (*tis*).

These terms are also used in a variety of other contexts: marriage preferences; classification of foods; forms of social interaction (unsociable, reticent people are *nyem* and quarrels and fights are *panes*); state of the weather; etc. In short, *panes* and *nyem* indicate conditions of disorder, disturbance, and either inadequate or excessive flow, whereas *tis* connotes conditions of balance, order, and controlled flow.

Finally, illness can also be caused by supernatural agents. These precipitate illness or emotional disturbance for many reasons but most usually because they have been neglected or in some way slighted. The agents most generally implicated are one's ancestors who become angry because a ceremony dedicated to them has either been omitted or performed incorrectly. Once it is recognized that the cause of the illness is not natural it is necessary to visit a medium to obtain a revelation concerning cause and remedy. Typically the cause is one's immediate ancestors who require greater amounts of periodic offerings.

A person becomes ill, not because of some mystical influence emanating from the ancestors, but because an agency enters the mind or body of the person concerned. This agency cannot be the ancestors for these are purified souls of the dead and are too pure to enter mortal people. There are occasions when Balinese are possessed by ancestors or gods but in the village in which I conducted fieldwork this only ever happened to priests and their wives, and only during temple ceremonies and hence in specially purified locations (Howe 1981). Moreover, to be possessed by such, and so go into trance is described as a particularly beautiful experience; such possession is termed *kapangluh*. On a closer inspection the agents which are the immediate instigators of illness are a class of noxious spirits known as the *buta-kala*, and the phrase used in this instance is *kasusupang kala*.

The relationship between ancestors and gods on the one hand and *buta-kala* spirits on the other is complex, but analytically it is based on principles of purity and hierarchy (Howe 1984). Ancestors are purified souls of the dead who gradually become gods as both their purity and distance from the mortal realm increases. But gods are open to temptation and emotional disturbance, and if this is indulged gods cease to be gods. Yielding to impulse, gods metamorphose into *buta-kala*. This transformation involves several changes. Physically gods are quintessentially *alus* (refined, smooth, elegant, oblique) whereas *buta-kala* are *kasar* (crude, rough, coarse, direct); gods are beautiful, ogres are fantastically ugly; gods live in heaven, ogres manifest themselves on earth and especially in marginal places and times; gods are pure, *buta-kala* are polluted (one can eat the remains of offerings to gods but not to the latter).

A further aspect of these spirits is their relation to certain states of mind and emotional feelings. Anyone who is overwhelmed by emotional distress or displays violent feelings or action can be said to be *kasusupang kala* or *kalanan* (in the state of *kala*). Unlike gods, these spirits are named in a very specific fashion: *kala kilang kilung* (bewildered), *kala dangastra* (anger), *kala peteng* (confusion), etc. (Howe 1984: 207). Moreover, the word *kala* counts among its referents a notion of 'time'. *Kali tepet* is mid-day, *sandi kala* is dusk; *kala* is also a common word used to translate 'during', 'while', 'when'. So *kala kilang kilung*, which is the spirit causing confusion, can be glossed, quite properly, as 'when confused' or 'during the time I was confused'. Thus *kala* can be seen either as a concrete external agency or as a manifestation (Hobart 1985: 183). Either way *kala* can be described analytically as a collective representation of socially disjunctive feelings or states of mind. It is worth adding that just as *buta-kala* are transient moods of gods so disvalued emotions such as anger are considered to be transitory states of the human condition (Howe 1984: 208).

More generally it can be argued that those states of mind which the Balinese find most meritorious are externalized or objectified, and taken to be the highly valued, ideal dispositions of high castes, ancestors and gods, while those they most despise are given external, objective representation in the form of noxious spirits (temporary embodiments of negatively valued emotional states) and witches (chronic embodiments of such states).

One major difference between the Balinese and the Chewong is that the latter regard negatively valued inner states as characteristic of non-Chewong people. Such states define a boundary between Chewong and others. The Balinese on the other hand acknowledge that they themselves can at times be assaulted by such feelings. However, in practice they describe themselves much as the Chewong do (fearful, not brave, shy, hesitant, timid, etc.) and tend to foist other dispositions (bravery, directness, aggression, etc.) on to other people (Chinese, Westerners).

There are several methods of controlling the *buta-kala* spirits but the principles involved are identical to those which inform the rite of *ngulapin*. While the latter ritually re-orders a person's mind and body, a *caru* rite, by placating spirits and aiding them to revert to their divine forms, re-orders the cosmos (Howe 1984). In both, a disruption of the normal state of affairs is rectified by rearranging the relations between the gods/spirits concerned and their rightful abodes. There thus exists a close degree of correspondence between the structure of the body/person and that of the larger external world.

At the ideological level, then, the Balinese emphasize notions of balance, order, and equilibrium, and these are desired attributes not only of the cosmos but also of the internal states of people. There is no doubt that, at this general level, such ideas and values have an effect on interpersonal interaction such that the Balinese do not enjoy confrontation, quarrelling, and open disputation of an aggressive kind. Additionally in many social contexts they profess to be timid, fearful, and shy.

Furthermore there are a variety of institutionalized methods by which people can avoid direct interpersonal conflict. Disputes over property (land, water, trees, etc.), over boundaries between houses and between fields, over group membership, over religious matters, etc. can all be adjudicated by one or another village organization or functionary. If the dispute is of a personal nature then the parties to it can simply cease speaking and avoid each other (*puik*). There are also elaborate codes of conduct sanctioned in a variety of ways (fines, expulsion from associations, even from the village, collective wrath of other villagers). All of these mechanisms of dispute settlement and of avoidance of direct confrontation can be analysed as stemming more or less directly from notions concerning the fragility of the internal emotional equilibrium and the desire to maintain this and hence avoid disorientation, illness, and spirit possession. Part of this process involves the positive evaluation of dispositions of shyness, timidity, and diffidence in social interaction and the negative evaluation of confrontation, quarrelling, and aggressive display.

As far as I am aware no one has ever unambiguously described Bali as a purely peaceful society, although a number of authors, Bateson, Mead, Belo and Geertz, have implied as much in certain of their writings. These anthropologists have been very impressed by several of the themes already discussed. For Jane Belo it is notions of balance, bearing, poise, orientation, etc. The Balinese hate to be shocked; they do not enjoy being spatially disoriented; they avoid impulsive movements which would disturb their feelings of well-being; despite the availability of alcoholic drinks they do not get inebriated; they are very patient; they have elaborate forms of politesse and etiquette; and so on (Belo 1970). For Bateson (1970) and Bateson and Mead (1942) the predominant issue is the avoidance of climax and the absence of what Bateson calls schismogenesis. Bateson argues that human beings have a 'tendency to involve themselves in sequences of cumulative interaction' (1970: 391), but that in Bali 'childhood experience trains the child away from seeking climax in personal interaction' and that 'certain positive values — related to balance — recur in the culture and are incorporated into the character structure during childhood' (1970: 401). Geertz (1973a) elaborates the analysis of the absence of climax and in a celebrated essay relates it to what he calls the ceremonialization of conduct, the depersonalization of people, and the detemporalization of time.

The line of argument, sometimes implicit sometimes explicit, is that certain techniques of childrearing together with ideas concerning balance, order, and the ceremoniousness of conduct conspire to dampen or mute hostility, violence, and aggression. My criticism is not so much that these socialization techniques and notions of balance, etc. have been inaccurately described (but on this point, see

Wikan 1987), but rather that the link between these and levels of aggression or peacefulness has not been demonstrated very convincingly, and the nature of the link has not been analysed in detail.

The authors cited base their cases solely on data concerning interpersonal transactions, noting that these are generally peaceful, and structured by rules of etiquette, politesse, shyness, and timidity, and informed by notions of balance and order. However, at more inclusive levels of analysis it becomes less obvious that the Balinese are a relatively peaceful people.

SOME SOCIAL AND HISTORICAL CONDITIONS OF VIOLENCE

During the nineteenth century there were numerous, small-scale wars between rival Balinese kingdoms (Schulte Nordholt 1986: 20), and Balinese slaves (van der Kraan 1983) were considered to make good mercenary soldiers, the Dutch recruiting them at five guilders a head. During the second Dutch expedition to Bali in 1848 (in the Dutch–Balinese war), over 100,000 rounds of ammunition were fired off and whilst the Dutch sustained 264 fatalities the Balinese are estimated to have suffered some 2,000 dead (Hanna 1976: 144). Those social scientists who are more impressed with the later *puputans* (the ritual mass suicides in front of advancing Dutch armies) ignore these earlier very violent conflicts at their peril. In contemporary times Bali was the scene of some of the most appalling carnage and slaughter in 1965–6 when estimates of the numbers killed run as high as 100,000 (Hanna 1976: 116; Legge 1972: 398).

Moreover it should be stressed that Bali is a hierarchical society and in the previous century noble princes and lords commanded the allegiance and services (ritual and military) of the large majority of the peasant population, and even if Geertz is correct in maintaining that such obligations were not always very onerous (1981: 63 passim), it is nevertheless the case that rulers could abduct women for their harems, confiscate property for their own use, and brutally punish low castes for caste-related insults (intentional or accidental). The fact that high castes also espoused common ideals of balance, tranquillity, and order did not stop them having eyes gouged out and hands chopped off (Baum 1973). Additionally, local lords engaged in status conflict which often took the form of competition concerning the size and beauty of palaces, the scope and lavishness of celebrations, the

quality of gamelans, and the virtuosity of dancers. But more significantly such rivalry was also embellished by warfare in which the
contenders, sitting sedately at a safe distance from the main action,
allowed their small armies to confront each other until a few had been
killed (Geertz 1981: 252–4). In these circumstances the individual
internal states of the principal combatants could easily be maintained
in balance since these took no part in the fighting; and the internal
states of those actually doing battle are irrelevant for they were
compelled to fight. Either way given such conditions the emotional
states of particular people have very little to do with the perpetration
of a violent activity. The point is that between those cultural values
emphasizing emotional tranquillity and the individuals who espouse
them there is a variety of social institutions differentiating people
along several axes, and it is these which prevent the direct translation
of value into practice. Social relations of power, domination, and
exploitation which in one form or another are characteristic of most of
the world's societies, now and in the past, will always intrude and
render incomplete analyses founded on purely culturalist assumptions (see Asad 1983).

However, even when rank, status, and relations of power (at the
inter-caste level) are not involved, conflict eventuating in open
aggression and violence can still occur, although the parties to the
dispute espouse values of peaceful interaction. Such situations arise in
Bali with relative frequency and are most usually due to conflicts
between co-residents over material interests broadly defined.

A common form of cleavage involves the relationship between a
mother and her son's wife. If the parents approve of the marriage, if
the girl comes from the same village (and therefore knows the form),
and if she does not have to share a kitchen with her mother-in-law,
then discord is unlikely. If these conditions are not met, however, then
friction is virtually inevitable, and in some cases violent quarrels, in
which the two women hurl insults at one another, are the result. Since
these are personal conflicts within compounds, outsiders should not
interfere. Divorce is a possibility but the presence of young children
(who remain in the compound of birth) makes this problematic.
Should irascibility degenerate into persistent altercation then a
common course of action is to obtain a revelation from a medium concerning the root cause of the strife, and regularly this discloses
ancestral disapproval (manifested by heightened spirit activity causing
emotional blindness) over the omission or incorrect performance of a

ceremony. Further ritual action is the cultural mode of rectifying the state of affairs. However, it is readily acknowledged that this will not necessarily remove the problem, since it is pragmatically recognized that such situations arise because the disputants not only adhere to mutually exclusive values but also because their conflicting interests cannot be easily reconciled without some social rearrangement. In this particular type of case the son asserts his right to marry whom he pleases and the parents assert their right to arrange a marriage with an approved girl. As elopement is common in Bali the son can present his parents with a *fait accompli*, after which they all have to make the best of it; the parents are allowed to complain bitterly but they must not make a meal of it. The ensuing domestic organization is toughest on the two women for they must live and work together, share tasks, allocate responsibilities, and come to some agreement on how things should be done. If there are significant disagreements conflict is unavoidable.

Several points should be made. Because the fractiousness is between co-residents it cannot be referred to any outside authority. Institutional mechanisms such as verbal and physical avoidance, which can be employed to control conflicts between people living in different compounds, are of limited effectiveness in disputes between co-residents, because the relationship demands substantial inter-action. Therefore, despite the fact that everyone espouses cultural values of non-aggression, the material conditions of living and working together may become so intolerable that they nullify any constraining effect these values have. Whilst the rupture is culturally interpreted in terms of ritual incompetence, ancestral wrath, and spirit activity, such explanations are never considered complete for they do not, and cannot, supply the specifics in any particular case. And, of course, the Balinese discuss and gossip about the history of the dispute, the personalities of those involved, and the myriad other contingent factors which are implicated in its genesis and develop-ment. In short, the Balinese recognize that while there are ultimate causes of emotional turmoil and aggression and that these stem from religious forces, they also acknowledge that proximate causes con-cerning material interests are directly involved. However, since these latter are contingent and variable, they do not receive the same degree of cultural elaboration as the former, and so again it is neces-sary to stipulate that cultural values do not translate simply into social practice. Moreover, changing conditions such as, for example, the increasing scarcity of both rice land and compound land create over-crowding, heightened competition for what land remains, and hence new tensions. These and other changes occurring within Balinese society have an effect on typical, culturally informed practices, and thus on the evaluation of social action.

A second typical pattern of conflict is that between co-resident brothers over the allocation of work and rewards. A Balinese compound often houses an extended family: sons bring in wives and daughters marry out. The youngest son becomes the heir to his father's political position in various village associations and to the guardianship of the compound's ancestral temple. Land and its produce, however, are divided equally between all the sons (with one share allotted for the upkeep of the temple and controlled by the heir). Tension and discord occur between brothers if there is disagreement over the day-to-day duties involved in agriculture. Friction can be reduced and even eliminated if partition of produce and land take place early in the developmental cycle. The ideal sequence is that unmarried children work their father's rice plots, contribute to his granary, and eat from their mother's kitchen. On marriage, the son and wife build a kitchen but take rice from the same granary. Later, they can build a new granary and at harvest they take their full share of the crop from individual fields worked communally. The final split occurs when the land itself is separated and each married brother works his own land, stores his crop in his own granary, and eats from his own kitchen. The worst conflicts (which can involve very serious injury) transpire when partition is delayed, and such delay is due to several factors. In general, it is thought desirable to postpone partition because, first, a high value is placed on retaining the unity of the compound for in certain contexts it has to act as a unit; second, it is considered that brothers should co-operate amicably (that is to say, culturally brothers are portrayed as having converging interests, whereas in reality on marriage their interests begin to diverge); and third, early division is thought to undermine the domestic authority of the senior generation. These values receive explicit expression and ritual and social endorsement. However, brothers do not always work together in a friendly and comradely manner and so delayed partition acts as a restricting feature of domestic organization, serving not only to drive a wedge between senior and junior generations, but also setting brothers (and their wives) against each other. The degree to which actual physical aggression breaks out is contingent on a variety of other factors, not least of which concern the personalities of those involved, the status of the in-marrying wives, the frequency of quarrels, and so on.

All such conflicts are handled by ritual and social mechanisms. At the cultural level, the fights are explained by ritual omission, spirit interference, etc. and hence remedied appropriately, that is to say, by visits to a medium, performance of a *caru*, and if necessary a *ngulapin*, and so forth. This can quite easily be interpreted in terms of Geertz's notion of models of and for reality (1966: 7–8). Balinese cultural ideas, beliefs, and values direct attention to the ultimate, religious, causes of friction and thereby provide a conceptual framework for the comprehension and explanation of certain aspects of social reality. At the same time, the same set of beliefs supplies standardized procedures for remedial action. Unfortunately, such solutions do not in themselves rectify these types of conflict, for words have been spoken, deeds perpetrated and relationships permanently soured. To get a grip on these problems pragmatic, contingent solutions are required. Socially, relationships within the compound have to be transformed: a new granary or kitchen is built; the land is partitioned; the senior generation relinquishes its political role of domestic authority by allowing the heir to take over.

At the cultural level there is no disagreement about the interpretation of the causes because these have been revealed from on high. It is true that some people go to more than one medium if the first revelation and related remedy do not work, but this merely postpones the realignment of social relationships that will eventually have to take place. It is true also that in some cases conflicts cannot be solved in the above manner without seriously disrupting the domestic unit. This is the difficulty where discord is the dominant feature of the mother-in-law/daughter-in-law relation when divorce might appear to be the only viable course of action. If this is not taken then the family can either learn to live with the problems and hope that time will smooth things out, or coerce the daughter-in-law into a truly subordinate role. This can be symbolized in a nasty, private ritual in which the girl prostrates herself on the floor of the compound while her mother-in-law treads on her head. The problem with this is that the girl is likely to be further antagonized.

Socially, of course, there is a great deal of variation in the extent to which interested parties agree or disagree about the causes and solutions to disputes within the compound, and much of the talk is quite unrelated to the cultural interpretations. Thus, while a medium may reveal that certain ancestors have been angered by the omission of a ceremony, this says nothing about why the conflict has manifested itself as a quarrel or fight between two brothers rather than, say, a mother and her daughter-in-law, or why the dispute has taken one form rather than another. Only an analysis of all the material and contingent factors prevailing at the time can produce a definitive explanation, and because it is a dispute people protect themselves by invoking self-interested arguments of both a social and cultural sort. In short, cultural explanations are too constant and thus have little power to discriminate; they can only provide the basic conceptual framework. Social practice in a complex and changing society such as Bali can only be understood by analysis of the conceptual and evaluative framework, together with the material conditions within which the former is socially produced.

CONCLUSION

Earlier attention was drawn to the assertion that the purported absence of climax in Balinese interpersonal behaviour noticed by Bateson and further analysed by Geertz was the product of a peculiar method of socializing young children. Typically, a parent stimulates a child in some fashion until the child is very excited, and then abruptly ceases to be interested, thus leaving the child without a focus of attention. Geertz (1973a: 403) argues that the absence of climax is pervasive in Balinese life:

> It amounts to the fact that social activities do not build . . . toward definitive consummation. Quarrels appear and disappear . . . but they hardly ever come to a head. . . . Daily life consists of self-contained, monadic encounters in which something either happens or does not. . . . Artistic performances start, go on . . . and stop. . . . Ritual (consists) largely of getting ready and cleaning up.

I have already criticized aspects of this description elsewhere (Howe 1984: 211 – 12). I would add here that many forms of drama, including the shadow theatre, have a climactic war or fight which resolves the plot; that temple festivals are explicitly perceived as reaching a climax ('peak', 'summit') and that the progression of a festival is likened to the blooming and withering of a flower; and that quarrels, if serious, are either adjudicated or do come to a head more frequently than Geertz would have us believe.

It is the case that Balinese cultural ideas and values, and their socialization methods on the whole do act to constrain the explicit use of aggressive behaviour. But it is also true that they are not completely successful, and in some cases the yoke of culture and socialization is almost totally thrown off. The reasons for this are not difficult to determine. First, as has been consistently argued, ideas and values in a complex and hierarchical society such as Bali do not find easy translation into social practice. Second, the particular technique described by Bateson and Geertz is asked to carry an exceptionally heavy explanatory load. It is well to remember that in the context of a whole childhood such interaction between parent and child is but a small part of a child's total activity. Children do a great many other things (including quarrelling and fighting) often only in the company of other children, and they experience a wide variety of different situations, some of which involve, of course, occasionally seeing their mothers and grandmothers screaming insults at one another, or their fathers fighting each other with fists or weapons. What can be argued is that these ideas and socialization practices, other things being equal, do tend to produce peaceful and reserved human beings. But other things are not equal. Bali is a highly differentiated society and so there is wide variation in the extent and the manner to which culture is assimilated. People in different social positions will learn different things in different ways; Balinese not only learn that order, balance, and harmony are desirable states of mind, they also learn that some people are lazy and others hard working, that if daughters marry into another village they may be in for a hard time, that land is in increasingly short supply, that housing land in some villages is used up, etc. Education and a changing economy are providing new avenues of employment, new forms of patronage, and new scales of status and prestige which combine to complicate existing forms of social ranking. Much of this is a product of rapid social change, and though such changes may be interpreted within established frameworks of meaning, they are also implicated in producing new modes of social practice and new values. The gradual trend in Balinese religion from polytheism to monotheism (Swellengrebel 1960: 71–3; Geertz 1973b), and the now frequently met belligerent stance of young, educated, low caste Balinese towards high castes are two examples of far-reaching changes occurring in Balinese society.

113

The Balinese case is interesting because, despite the fact that, like some hunter-gatherers, they endorse notions of peaceful interaction and positively value timidity and the avoidance of confrontation, violent and aggressive behaviour occurs more frequently. This is because socially produced structures of opportunity and constraint are different for different people, and this circumstance generates competition over scarce resources and conflicts over material interests. In such conditions, complicated by rapid social change, the degree to which cultural values can be translated into social practice is problematic.

Many hunter-gatherer societies are characterized by a simple social organization allowing for relatively great social and economic equality. Under these conditions values, of whatever kind, may more easily be realized in practice.

In highly differentiated societies in which people are locked into social, economic, and political units from which they cannot easily extricate themselves, conflicts are likely to arise more frequently, be more socially disruptive, and hence generate intense emotional states. If people cannot easily escape such situations, the constraining effects of cultural values epousing peaceful interaction will be less powerful. Seen from this perspective, heightened emotional states are just as much a product of social arrangements and material circumstances as they are of values. These states manifest themselves in aggressive and belligerent patterns of behaviour if the conflicts cannot be resolved by institutional means, or if the combatants cannot be physically separated, or if their specific, divergent interests cannot be disentangled. And again the extent to which these resolutions can be implemented depends greatly on factors other than values. In Bali, then, aggressive behaviour occurs despite cultural values which deprecate it and because typical social arrangements and material circumstances provide conditions within which it is likely to erupt.

REFERENCES

Asad, T. (1983) 'Anthropological conceptions of religion: reflections on Geertz', *Man* 18 (2): 237–59.

Bateson, G. (1970) 'Bali: the value system of a steady state', in J. Belo (ed.) *Traditional Balinese Culture*, New York: Columbia University Press.

Bateson, G. and Mead, M. (1942) *Balinese Character: a photographic analysis*,

Special Publication of the New York Academy of Sciences, Vol. II.

Baum, V. (1973) *A Tale from Bali*, Kuala Lumpur: Oxford University Press.

Belo, J. (1970) 'The Balinese temper', in J. Belo (ed.) *Traditional Balinese Culture*, New York: Columbia University Press.

Bourdieu, P. (1977) *Outline of a Theory of Practice*, Cambridge: Cambridge University Press.

Dentan, R. K. (1968) *The Semai, A Nonviolent People of Malaya*, New York: Holt, Rinehart & Winston.

Geertz, C. (1966) 'Religion as a cultural system', in M. Banton (ed.) *Anthropological Approaches to the Study of Religion*, London: Tavistock Publications.

Geertz, C. (1973a) 'Person, time and conduct in Bali', in C. Geertz (ed.) *The Interpretation of Cultures*, London: Hutchinson.

Geertz, C. (1973b) 'Internal conversion in contemporary Bali', in C. Geertz (ed.) *The Interpretation of Cultures*, London: Hutchinson.

Geertz, C. (1981) *Negara, the Theatre State in Nineteenth Century Bali*, Princeton: Princeton University Press.

Giddens, A. (1976) *New Rules of Sociological Method*, London: Hutchinson.

Hanna, W. (1976) *Bali Profile: people, events, circumstances, 1001–1976*, New York: American Universities Field Staff.

Hobart, M. (1985) 'Is God evil?', in D. Parkin (ed.) *The Anthropology of Evil*, Oxford: Basil Blackwell.

Holy, L. and Stuchlik, M. (1983) *Actions, Norms and Representations*, Cambridge: Cambridge University Press.

Howe, L. (1981) 'The social determination of knowledge: Maurice Bloch and Balinese time', *Man* 16 (2): 220–34.

Howe, L. (1984) 'Gods, people, spirits and witches: the Balinese system of person definition', *Bijdragen tot de Taal-, Landen Volkenkunde* 140 (2/3): 193–222.

Howe, L. (1985) 'Caste in India and Bali: levels of comparison', in R. H. Barnes, D. de Coppet and R. J. Parkin (eds) *Contexts and Levels: anthropological essays on hierarchy*, Oxford: Journal of the Anthropological Society of Oxford.

Howe, L. (in press) 'Hierarchy and equality: variations in Balinese social organization', *Bijdragen tot de Taal-, Landen Volkenkunde*.

Howell, S. (1984) *Society and Cosmos: Chewong of peninsular Malaysia*, Oxford: Oxford University Press.

Kraan, A. van der (1983) 'Bali: slavery and slave trade', in A. Reid (ed.) *Slavery, Bondage and Dependency in Southeast Asia*, St Lucia: University of Queensland Press.

Legge, J. D. (1972) *Sukarno: a political biography*, Harmondsworth: Penguin.

Marshall, L. (1961) 'Sharing, talking and giving: relief of social tensions among !Kung Bushmen', *Africa* 31: 231–49.

Schulte Nordholt, H. (1986) *Bali: colonial conceptions and political change, 1700–1940*, Rotterdam: Comparative Asian Studies Programme.

Swellengrebel, J. L. (1960) *Bali: studies in life, thought and ritual*, The Hague: Martinus Nijhoff.

Turnbull, C. (1976) *The Forest People*, London: Pan Books.

Turnbull, C. (1982) 'The ritualization of potential conflict between the sexes among the Mbuti', in E. Leacock and R. Lee (eds) *Politics and History in Band Societies*, Cambridge: Cambridge University Press.

Wikan, U. (1987) 'Public grace and private fears: gaiety, offense and sorcery in northern Bali', *Ethos* 15 (4): 337–65.

Chapter Six

THE NON-VIOLENT ZAPOTEC

CARL W. O'NELL

INTRODUCTION

Whatever it is that we mean by the word peace, as we strive to understand it, that understanding must incorporate within it some appreciation of non-violence as a way of life demonstrated by many of the world's peoples ethnographically described by anthropologists. And, while in my contribution I make no pretence of fully addressing the issue of peace, my purpose is to illustrate a particularistic set of customs, behaviours, and actions contributory to a largely non-violent way of life as I observed it among the residents of 'La Paz', a small community of Zapotec speakers in the Valley of Oaxaca, Mexico.

Phenomena associated with violence have long been of interest to social and behavioural scientists, including anthropologists. As a result, several theories have developed around the question of why people behave violently. It has been only recently that investigators have seriously occupied themselves with the question of why people do not behave in violent ways in response to situations appearing to provoke violence in others. So, while scientific explanations for violence have by no means become closed issues, satisfactory explanations for non-violence have scarcely been articulated. And, regrettably, the issue of peace has barely attracted serious attention.

Confronted as we are by a violent world, one must concede a considerable capacity for violence in human beings, as individuals and in groups. At the same time and as with most other things human, we appear not to arrive at birth biologically 'prepackaged' for violence. While it can to some degree be demonstrated that human beings are born with tendencies toward irritability (largely at the level of the

117

reflex), to react physically and with some degree of vigour to noxious stimuli, evidence is not sufficient to warrant our labelling such reflexive tendencies as violence. It is only when such reflexes become adequately channelled and elaborated through social conditioning that resulting negative or destructive behavioural phenomena merit the classification of violence.

From a scientific point of view it seems quite clear that the burden of understanding violence rests on explanations of how and why human beings develop and exercise an innate capacity for violence. Alternatively, and of primary interest is the task of understanding the development and exercise of non-violence, as a component of peace. This task rests on explanations of how and why human beings can avert developing a potential for violence, developing instead other capacities expressed in socially positive and constructive behaviour. In short, if we are to understand peace, some understanding of non-violence and how it comes about as a cultural phenomenon is imperative.

THE RESEARCH SETTING

I address myself in this paper to various factors explanatory of the relatively non-violent way of life of people in a Zapotec community that I have observed over a number of years (O'Nell 1969, 1972, 1979, 1981). As in other contexts, I refer to the community by the pseudonym La Paz. La Paz is similar to a number of communities in the Valley of Oaxaca, Mexico, giving evidence of being relatively non-violent places. An estimate of violence as indicated by an index of rates of homicide in the mid-1970s suggests a rate about six times greater for the state of Oaxaca as a whole than it was for these non-violent communities. Homicide is not only one of the most serious forms of violence, it provides a reasonably good index for other forms of physical violence occurring in the Oaxacan communities. While only rough estimates can be derived from available statistical data, consistences in these data over time point to wide regional and community differences in levels of violence.

For the forty-year period from 1935 to 1975, ethnographic inquiry yielded information on only two homicides in La Paz, indicating an annual rate of five per year per 100,000 individuals over that time span. This was much lower than the rate estimated for the state of Oaxaca, 73 per 100,000 persons during the mid-1970s, made by Dr

John Paddock, Institute de Estudias Oaxaquenos, University of the Americas (personal communication). Oaxaca has ranked high in homicide rates among the various states in Mexico. In the ten-year period from 1958 to 1968, it ranked second only to Guerrero. While information from the *Anuario Estadistico de los Estados Unidos Mexicanos* provides evidence that homicide rates in Mexico have been comparatively high, it also indicates a consistent decline in average rates for each five-year period beginning in 1935 and leading up to 1975.

VALUES, ATTITUDES, AND SOCIAL IDEALS

Howe, in his chapter on peace and violence in Bali, argues that a close correspondence exists between values and action, particularly in simpler societies, a point well demonstrated by Overing in comparing images of manhood in the Piaroa and Shavante of Brazil in her contribution. Observers of the Oaxacan communities other than myself (Paddock 1975; Hauer 1978; Sumner 1978), voicing a similar point of view, maintain that the clue to the non-violent characteristics of some communities, and the more violent characteristics of yet other communities, rests on decidedly different value orientations and images of the ideal.

I do not in principle disagree with these assessments except to assert that the values in question do not clearly and necessarily explicitly relate to non-violence *per se*. Rather than entertaining a clear concept of what it might mean ideally to be non-violent (or 'anti-violent' in the terminology of these commentators on Oaxaca), community residents in La Paz emphasize values or ideals which in their enactment stand as antithetical to a violent way of life. Furthermore, I maintain that in the implementation of these seemingly more pedestrian values, attitudes and socio-cultural mechanisms have taken shape in the non-violent places which largely preclude violence from becoming incorporated into customary social behaviour. That these mechanisms and the values underlying them often function in largely non-obtrusive and quite subtle ways becomes clear as one examines interpersonal behaviour in La Paz and in many similar communities located in the Valley of Oaxaca.

I believe the values which provide the bias for non-violent modes of interaction and which seem most to guide, if not actually govern, interpersonal behaviour from virtually every perspective are respect, responsibility, and co-operation. These values assume a specificity of meaning in La Paz which renders them uniquely advantageous in minimizing the occurrence of violence.

In referring to themselves and their town, people often use the word *respeto* (respect). While respect is something that can characterize qualities in an individual, in the sense in which it is most often used it applies to valued qualities in social relationships. Among social equals respect relations are both symmetrical and reciprocal, yet respect relations cannot always be symmetrical because of differences in age, sex, and other possible characteristics of persons involved. Respect relationships must, however, always in some sense be reciprocal. The Zapotec insist that respect relationships cannot be one-sided. Respect must 'flow' in both directions or the relationship is considered to be lacking in respect. It is most apparent from this perspective that respect is a characteristic of social relationships rather than a simple mark of esteem for the persons involved. I note here that evidence of being able to show respect to significant others is one of the first expectations parents make of their young children, coming before expectations of obedience or helpfulness to parents (O'Nell 1979).

Although not voiced as frequently as *respeto*, *responsibilidad* (responsibility) is a clearly held value in human relationships. For children it encourages both obedience and helpfulness but it holds other implications as well. Responsibility as a social ideal includes several characteristics, some of which are more obviously personal than is the case for respect. Relative responsibility is a mark of relative maturity (O'Nell 1972). Responsibility connotes not only what one does but what one may be able and willing to do. For present consideration, the core characteristic of responsibility is an alert and responsive sensitivity to both general and situational social expectations. In social situations of whatever kind the truly responsible person knows what is expected of him/her and meets these expectations. For this reason alone no child can be expected to be completely responsible.

Although for the Zapotec responsibility can include the taking of initiative or even the wielding of authority in situations demanding these (the Zapotec are known for their reluctance to assume authority (Nader 1964)), more often than not responsibility implies a social stance more closely allied to dependence on others than to self assertion. Whatever else he/she may be or do, the responsible Zapotec cannot be very independent of others or even convey the illusion of much personal independence.

As a social ideal, *cooperacion* (co-operation) applies more to adults than to children and for adults more to males than to females. Among the more concrete demonstrations of co-operation is the willingness of a person to respond to family or community needs by accepting positions and responsibilities, responding readily to obligations toward others and to calls for community service, offering time, resources, labour, or money to further projects set up to address the common good.

But co-operation as a social virtue goes beyond what can be described here and it has its less tangible characteristics which in their daily implementation shade into respect and responsibility, articulating the social virtues into a pattern meaningful to individuals as a basis for social action. The co-operative individual side-steps delicate and potentially disruptive issues, at least publicly, thereby contributing to an appearance of general harmony so valued by the group of which he/she is a part. The co-operative person underplays individuality in favour of group or community enterprise, not necessarily as an act of self sacrifice but as an act protective of self investment in a social system defining self and community interests as one. Paradoxically, it is through co-operation that the self becomes fully socially defined in granting the status of maturity to the co-operative individual.

Underlying the value system expressed in these social ideals is a strong cultural emphasis on reciprocity in interpersonal dealings which at its most formal level is expressed in the *guelaguetza*, an elaborate system of exchange and reciprocity. As a value, *guelaguetza* has both social and economic implications which have been dealt with extensively in the ethnographic literature on the region (see especially Beals 1970). In the informal ideal system, the ideals of respect, responsibility, and co-operation are reinforced in daily life by people who share in their understanding and acceptance of the formal meaning of the *guelaguetza*.

To be violent toward others is simply and generally incompatible with behaving in ways consistent with the social ideals just outlined. So, in a not very explicit and rather indirect fashion, the ideal system serves to curb hostile and aggressive tendencies generated in social interaction, thus contributing to a generally non-violent way of life.

Ideals are mediated by attitudes and attitudes are to some degree expressed in actual behaviour even to being influenced by such behaviour. In sampling attitudes toward interpersonal violence among twenty-one men in the community I found that nineteen of

121

them felt that violence could under certain circumstances be justified. Justification was most frequently expressed in terms of defence of oneself or another, somewhat less frequently defence of property, and least frequently finding oneself in an irresponsible state, drunkenness or in the throes of any strong emotion such as jealousy or envy. Only two men from the sample contended that violence could never be justified.

Concerning attitudes towards one's mode of recourse toward violence instigated by others, the largest set of responses (fourteen) indicated that if victimized by others, men giving these responses would seek assistance through appeals to the authority system. Only two men indicated they would address the violence themselves and another two said they would either retreat or do nothing (O'Nell 1981). These attitudes appear to demonstrate two things: (1) from one perspective they do not reveal any clearly perceived value of anti-violence; (2) from another perspective they suggest the operation of mechanisms serving to control interpersonal violence.

While values are no doubt important in the maintenance of a non-violent way of life, I believe that it is in understanding the socio-cultural and social psychological mechanisms which come into play in the service of certain of these values that non-violence is to be best understood. This presentation now deals with certain of these mechanisms and the implications they have for the development of the self.

MECHANISMS CONTROLLING INTERPERSONAL VIOLENCE

It has been found that formal mechanisms of social control at the community level are not particularly effective unless bolstered by the activation of informal social control mechanisms (O'Nell 1981; Morrisey 1978). For this reason it is important for me to describe and discuss these informal mechanisms. I refer to one of these two types as 'culturally constituted mechanisms of defence' (following Spiro 1965). The other type I refer to as 'social interaction devices' (O'Nell 1981).

Cultural defence mechanisms

Illness

In the culturally constituted mechanisms of defence it is possible to vent violent dispositions toward others in culturally recognized contexts in La Paz. One context includes behaviours associated with certain kinds of folk illnesses. I use the term 'illness' in the sense in which it is generally used in the social sciences, i.e. in referring to manifestations of debilitating conditions recognized as unhealthy by any given society or within a particular cultural context. In this sense, illness is not to be confused with 'disease', which carries connotations of scientifically determined and biologically specified phenomena. Concerning the issue, for anthropology reference is made to Foster and Anderson (1978); for sociology, to Susser et al. (1984).

Some of the folk illnesses allow one to acknowledge dispositions of hostility, others allow for the recognition of anger and its expression towards others. The most serious of these conditions defines as illness physical violence causing harm to the property or person of another. All of these conditions, from the mildest to most severe forms, require diagnoses and treatments by native curers referred to as ra-uniak in the Zapotecan idiom, or curanderos in Spanish.

The conditions are assumed in all cases by the Zapotec to result from imbalances within the organism of the afflicted person, especially the liver, causing an excessive secretion of bile. In some cases, the problem is believed to be instigated by a malfunctioning of internal organs giving rise to ill humour beyond the control of the patient. In other cases, the problem is seen to arise from provocations to hostility from outside the individual organism. Being maltreated or misunderstood by others, or being a long-standing victim of unfortunate circumstances, are often offered as etiologically relevant explanations for these conditions. Whether or not an exact parallel exists between what I describe here and what Robarchek discusses in his contribution as pehunan is questionable; however, it is interesting to note that a victimized 'self' may express itself actively and in ways normally negatively sanctioned by his or her society, even a society characterized by non-violent ways of life.

With all these conditions noted in La Paz the hostility component is openly acknowledged, sometimes as result other times as cause, but the wilful intent to do violence is categorically denied. The important point to note in these cases is that a person afflicted by any of these conditions is treated as a patient suffering an illness, not as a culprit meriting punishment.

It has been observed (O'Nell 1975) in the most severe forms of these illnesses that patients will quickly develop an additional folk illness found to be strongly associated with self-perceived failure to meet basic role expectations in Zapotecan society (i.e. the 'fright' illness, *susto*). Thus, a failure to be able to maintain respect relationships, and be a truly responsible and co-operative person, even when the failure is looked upon as illness, requires redress in the form of suffering from yet another folk illness.

Alcohol use

Another type of culturally constituted mechanism of defence consists of the periodic mandatory use of alcohol to levels producing at least mild inebriation. It is interesting to examine how this culturally prescribed use of alcohol fits into expressed community values. One who does not participate in ritual drinking and even other social forms of drinking, on occasions calling for these, is looked upon as one who does not co-operate. This type of non-cooperation under certain circumstances may be viewed almost as seriously as a failure to participate in community service and may be an affront to one with whom one is associated in a respect relationship. Yet a stated purpose for drinking and the desirability of heavy drinking on certain occasions is to dull the conscious edge of responsibility and even remove one temporarily from the necessity of attending to normal responsibilities. A few days' respite from discharging normal obligations is expected at the time of celebrating national holidays, religious fiestas and even important family events, weddings, funerals, and the like. The venting of hostility or anger is to some degree tolerated as a result of drinking heavily and the inebriate may be excused from following normal social proprieties under such conditions. Even some forms of physical violence are regarded as being less serious when one is under the condition of reduced responsibility because of drinking. Violence is not, however, a necesary or socially desired result of inebriation.

The limits of reducing responsibility through sanctioned alcohol uses, however, are not precisely drawn and can be exceeded when alcohol use seriously threatens a breach in respect relationships. But it is to be noted that within bounds alcohol use serves as a culturally constituted mechanism of defence in limited expressions of violence wherein the violence is sufficiently contained so that it can be excused by inebriation.

Heavy drinking was customary in much of prehispanic Mexico according to Taylor (1979: 30), to the point where individuals could drink themselves into a stupor 'without shame'. He draws no association between violence and alcohol use. Kearney (1971), on the other hand, describing another present day Zapotecan community, draws some clear connections between heavy and mandatory alcohol use and aggression.

Social interaction devices

Readjustment

Among the social interaction devices serving the control of violence, three stand out as important informal social control mechanisms. I label one of these *readjustment*. Readjustment is largely implemented as a control mechanism through the expressed opinions of others, often the victim or potential victim of violence. Readjustment most directly comes into play through either accusation or threat from a victim. It is effective to the degree that it elicits public sympathy for a victim against an aggressor. Through readjustment the formal and informal mechanisms are sometimes brought together as a deterrent against the escalation of violence. Readjustment can also involve physical defence or retaliation. However, unless it occurs as an immediate provocation to an hostile act, readjustment does not normally serve well as a violence control mechanism.

The fear of retaliation for violence through witchcraft serves as a readjustment mechanism for some in the community. While accusations of witchcraft are almost non-existent, the suspicion of witchcraft occurs, serving most certainly as some restraint to violence. On the other hand, one who is perceived by others as chronically hostile is open to the suspicion of witchcraft.

Needs for reciprocity and co-operation fundamentally serve to inhibit interpersonal violence between people who are ostensibly interdependent. When the possibility of violence arises, continuing interdependence can force some degree of readjustment between the interdependent persons; and cases were observed where tangible signs of interdependence suppressed the expression of hostility between individuals. Individuals can be sharply cognizant of the role interdependence plays in the reduction of potential violence at times. It is apparent in some cases that the inhibition of violence can indeed be rational as well as irrational.

Finally, one of the more important readjustment devices is that of gossip. There is little doubt that gossip in La Paz can serve to deter threats of violence before it occurs and the escalation of violence in early development. At the very least, much gossip about one erodes one's ability to maintain sufficient esteem to function adequately, i.e. within respect relationships, in the community. References in the anthropological literature to the effectiveness of witchcraft, gossip, and social interdependence in the social control of human behaviours are so extensive that they need not be cited. The lifeways of the Zapotec in La Paz constitute but one more example of the effectiveness of these devices.

Avoidance

Avoidance (in one way or another dealt with in several papers in this book) can be one of the more effective of the social interaction devices controlling interpersonal violence, and among the Zapotec it appears to be a commonly used device. Avoidance can assume many behavioural forms but its essence lies in either avoiding or withdrawing from situations with potential to give rise to violence. The general interactive style among people in La Paz tends to be non-confrontational. People tend not to be openly assertive of their personal wants and needs. This does not mean that an individual will not seek to satisfy personal desires but a person who really wants something from another will often be invidious rather than overtly demanding. Important issues will be approached obliquely rather than directly. To withdraw from a situation that might produce unpleasant results is not considered cowardice. Withdrawal and avoidance from a non-violent Zapotecan point of view is looked upon as the better way to address possibly conflictive social issues. Extreme assertions of 'manliness' are rare, *machismo* not forming a part of the Zapotecan value system.

Denial

One of the most effective and extensively used devices to prevent negative dispositions from erupting into interpersonal violence in La Paz is *denial*. A person who feels hostile toward another will often go to great lengths to deny such feelings. Even when an observer from outside the culture such as myself might think an expression of anger to be justified in certain situations one finds that people are still loath to admit to anger. And one must concede that people may in fact not be angry at such times. (As I noted earlier, anger can be taken as a symptom of illness.) Briefly, denial functions in two ways: (1) First of

126

all, it reinforces and publicly supports the ideal system by failing to acknowledge that people are acting in any other way than some respectful, responsible, or co-operative way; (2) Second, it serves to prevent a possible series of disruptive events from developing which in a system served with almost no formal effective control devices can escalate into a dangerous situation threatening the entire system.

In effect, denial stands as an important social interaction device in the control of interpersonal violence in La Paz. It allows the residents to ignore what can be ignored, to redefine what cannot be ignored and, in some cases, to erase from social memory what cannot be redefined. In the redefinition of situations through denial the value system is positively reinforced while the negative aspects of the situation are denied.

FUNCTIONAL ASPECTS OF NON-VIOLENCE

It is probably safe to say that the Zapotecan system of non-violence I described leans more in the direction of being accommodative rather than being absolutely preventive of violence. Yet it is a mistake to regard non-violence within the system as a sham or simply impressionistic to an observer rather than real. The system appears largely to function as a check on incipient violence. The mechanisms redefine incipient violence when possible and generally limit its escalation into more serious forms at times, while at other times they circumscribe the potential numbers of people involved.

One of the effects of the system is that the interplay of the various mechanisms allows and even encourages certain kinds and degrees of violence to occur, up to levels that do not threaten stabilities in basic human relationships as they are defined in La Paz. This is particularly obvious in the operation of the cultural mechanisms of defence in which various folk illnesses permit and positively sanction a certain amount of violence.

To function effectively this largely informal system of control has been heavily dependent on group homogeneity and the stability of cultural forms. The system stresses the significance of primary over secondary social ties. It is not easy to conceive of how such a system could operate in any but small-scale social enclaves. The system is delicately balanced, and, for that reason, fragile. The mechanisms on which the system depends are especially fragile. When any of the mechanisms fail to function, violence erupts precipitously and occasionally with serious consequences.

The violence control mechanisms are most effective at the particularistic (i.e. interpersonal) level of confrontation as one author notes for another valley Zapotecan community (Leslie 1960). If conflict is not controlled at the particularistic level widespread violence may erupt if the issue in conflict is potentially of general concern. One such issue is the question of religion involving the inroads of Evangelical Christianity into areas of traditionally established Roman Catholicism. The point of conflict rarely concerns differences in religious ideals as much as it concerns divisiveness within families which is disruptive of traditional behavioural patterns in the basic social structure. One such breakdown in the violence control mechanisms in La Paz was reported to me in 1960 (O'Nell 1969: 248); another became apparent to me in 1972 (O'Nell 1981: 363).

The informal mechanisms are open to erosion under conditions of social change. And, since there has been little development in the effectiveness of the formal mechanisms of control, there is nothing to offset the rapid deterioration of these mechanisms in the face of rapid change. Given that the residents of La Paz have been prey to periodic outbursts of violence in the past because of the fragility of the informal control mechanisms, it is conceivable that with further change a certain pronounced level of interpersonal violence could become chronic rather than intermittently episodic. Something similar to this in fact may have already transpired in some of the more violent towns, where, it could be hypothesized, erstwhile mechanisms of control have not kept pace in adaptive change with other rapidly changing social conditions.

PERSONALITY FACTORS, THE SOCIAL SYSTEM, AND THE SELF

The socio-cultural system I have in part described in this paper favours the cultivation of personality dispositions that respond positively and dynamically to social psychological contingencies generally occurring in daily life experience. In other words, the system serves to enculturate people who are aware of and responsive to social cues to suppress overt hostility in acquiescence to the meaning of the cues, and to withdraw and deny self interest as seems necessary to facilitate harmonious relationships. Following the lead of certain social learning theorists (principally Bandura and Walters 1963: 135 – 48), I label the dispositions developed in these personalities as *social dependency*.

The significance of social dependency for the non-violent Zapotec in La Paz is paradoxical to say the least (O'Nell 1979: 305 – 18). Initially, children are warmly received into their families. Until they are 3 to 5 years of age they recieve care best described as *affectively nurturant*. Between 3 and 5 years of age affective nurturance gives way to *affectively neutral* care as the warmly attentive parents become 'dry' and withdraw obvious behavioural symbols of deep emotional involvement from the child. This new situation of affective neutrality conveys overtones of emotional rejection which are relatively abrupt and decisive in continuing parent/child relations. It is very important to note, however, that children are not completely rejected with the rather abrupt withdrawal of the warmly accepting symbols. Parents continue to attend to other than the emotional needs of the child as they create a shift from affective to *instrumental nurturance*.

The next stage in the enculturation process occurs as parents continue to wean a child away from emotional dependency towards increasing demands for social dependency. Affective neutrality demonstrated by parents toward the child progressively becomes involved with expectations defining acceptable forms of interpersonal behaviour and task performance characteristic of late childhood and even adult life. Social dependency training is not complete until late adolescence or early adulthood when parents reward their socially dependent children by awarding them symbols indicative of achieving adult status: land for young men, clothing and other gifts for young women, and clear prospects of marriage for both.

Most theoretical constructs of childrearing point to negative and generally antisocial results through the early frustration of emotional dependency. Dependency socialization is theoretically complex but evidence indicates that the severe frustration of children's needs for psychological dependence is conducive to the development of hostile dispositions in children thus frustrated (Freud 1957; Bandura and Walters 1963; Rohner 1975; Stepansky 1977). Hostility in this context is not conceived of as a constantly active drive, the residuals of which can or must be 'siphoned off' either through violence or through socially approved displacement mechanisms. In other words, the 'pressure cooker' analogy does not apply. Rather, the concept of hostility put forward as being more meaningful in this context is one that assumes a readiness to respond with hostile feelings in reaction to significant cues. Thus the personality constant envisioned as being carried over from one time to another implies much more of a cognitive disposition rather than a motivational incentive to act. The cognitive rather than the motivational model of hostility finds support from virtually all aspects of the ethnographic data collected in La Paz, indicated in occurrences of hostility or violence when cognitive disruptions in normally expected behavioural patterns take place. A cognitive compensation appears to occur even in those cases where negative social behaviour tends to be defined as illness rather than culpable hostility (O'Nell 1975).

Fuelling the hostile dispositions cultivated through early childhood training in La Paz are enculturation devices used through middle and late childhood. Chief among these are teasing and ridicule to get children to conform, conditioning children in the fear of others, and deceit, usually related to promises of rewards inconsistently applied (O'Nell 1979: 312–14). That these enculturation devices exert powerful formative influences on the personality dispositions of developing individuals can be little doubted. Teasing and ridicule are conducive to shame, embarrassment, and often anger (Rohner 1975: 150). Learning fear conditions not only the affective dispositions of individuals but also the cognitive interpretations people can make of the social environment (Robarchek 1979). Parental deceit as intermittent reinforcement can play an important role in shaping expectations people make of one another as they become socialized into the system.

In La Paz the enculturative processes lay the groundwork for cultivating dispositions to hostility in the growing child. As one matures the styles of interpersonal interaction one learns are those consistent with one's early training and the styles of social behaviour which will fit one to be a sensitized, socially oriented individual who relies on detecting meaningful and relevant social signals guiding propriety in behaviour. That the overall process is convoluted and paradoxical is obvious and intriguing in its analysis. The very same processes frustrating the need for psychological dependency render an individual susceptible to the development of social dependency. The emotional insecurity initiated in early childhood and aggravated in later development is conducive to the implantation of dispositions to hostility which society circumscribes through mechanisms relying for their implementation on what I have labelled social dependency.

Social dependency should not be thought of as a personality disposition but rather a culturally learned paradigm for social action that in large part defines the self in this society. Self in this context is the nexus between the individual and the society of which he or she is a member.

As we examine the self we encounter a paradox composed of disparate elements theoretically not appearing conducive to integration. On the one hand we have a system which enculturates its members to be psychologically disposed toward hostility. On the other hand the very same system expects its members not to behave in hostile or violent ways. The paradox is further complicated by the fact that the whole system is delicately balanced on mechanisms which do not clearly define the meaning of what it means to be non-violent, certainly not to the degree that one can detect an anti-violent ideal.

There is a dynamic at work within the system which normally sets a balance between what I see as the 'push and pull' of non-violence, as the self is formed and as the self interacts with others in the system throughout life. In the system as I have perceived it in La Paz, I do not see the push for autonomy that Robarchek observes among the Semai. What I do see is the operation of self systems emphasizing the collective but not the individual units. It must not be inferred that a Zapotec individual sees himself or herself in ways similar to those which guide one's own self assessments in societies such as in the United States.

A study of the culture reveals that individual needs are not so much addressed through individual striving but rather in defining one's needs as contingent upon the needs of others. Needs tend to be recognized not as individual but as common needs.

In the process the question asked of the self is not so much, 'Who am I?', but 'How am I a part of something?' The answer appears to be one that creates the cultural climate for a non-violent way of life in a complex and seemingly contradictory system that presents for our consideration but one face of the human condition as we search for the meaning of peace.

REFERENCES

Bandura, A. and Walters, R. H. (1963) *Social Learning and Personality Development*, New York: Holt, Rinehart & Winston.

Beals, R. L. (1970) 'Gifting, reciprocity, savings, and credit in peasant Oaxaca', *Southwestern Journal of Anthropology* 26: 231–41.

Foster, G. M. and Anderson, B. G. (1978) *Medical Anthropology*, New York: John Wiley and Sons.

Freud, S. (1957) *Instincts and Their Vicissitudes*, London: Hogarth Press.

Hauer, R. W. (1978) 'Learning to be violent: psychological contrasts between a violent-prone town and an antiviolent one', *ISRA Biennial Meeting*, Washington, DC.

Kearney, M. (1971) *Los Vientos de Ixtepeji*, Mexico: Instituto Indigenista Interamericano.

Leslie, C. M. (1960) *Now We are Civilized*, Detroit: Wayne State University Press.

Morrissey, E. P. (1978) 'Conflict resolution in an antiviolent town: formal mechanisms and real ones', *ISRA Biennial Meeting*, Washington, DC.

Nader, I. (1964) *Talea and Juquila: a comparison of Zapotec social organization*, Berkeley: University of California Press.

O'Nell, C. W. (1969) *Human Development in a Zapotec Village*, Chicago: University of Chicago, Ph.D. dissertation, unpublished.

O'Nell, C. W. (1972) 'Aging in a Zapotec community', *Human Development* 15: 294–309.

O'Nell, C. W. (1975) 'An investigation of reported "fright" as a factor of etiology of Susto, "Magical Fright" ', *Ethos* 3: 41–63.

O'Nell, C. W. (1979) 'Nonviolence and personality dispositions among the Zapotec', *The Journal of Psychological Anthropology* 2: 301–22.

O'Nell, C. W. (1981) 'Hostility management and the control of aggression in a Zapotec community', *Aggressive Behaviour* 7: 351–66.

Paddock, J. (1975) 'Studies on antiviolent and "normal" communities', *Aggressive Behaviour* 1: 217–33.

Robarchek, C. A. (1979) 'Learning to fear: a case study of emotional conditioning', *American Ethnologist* 6: 585–67.

Rohner, R. P. (1975) *They Love Me, They Love Me Not*, New Haven: HRAF Press.

Spiro, M. (1965) 'Religious systems as culturally constituted defense mechanisms', in M. Spiro (ed.) *Context and Meaning in Cultural Anthropology*, pp. 100–13, New York: Free Press.

Stepansky, P. (1977) 'A history of aggression in Freud', *Psychological Issues*, No. 39, New York: International Universities Press.

Sumner, M. L. (1978) 'The social face of antiviolence: structure and control', *ISRA Biennial Meeting*, Washington, DC.

Susser, M. W., Watson, W. and Hopper, K. (1984) *Sociology in Medicine* (3rd edn), New York: Oxford University Press.

Taylor, W. B. (1979) *Drinking, Homicide and Rebellion in Colonial Mexican Villages*, Stanford: Stanford University Press.

Chapter Seven

THE 'PEACE PUZZLE' IN UFIPA

ROY WILLIS

In communicating one spies, and is spied upon. — *Fipa proverb*

The problem I wish to consider may be formulated thus: Why is it that from the beginning of their recorded history the people inhabiting the Fipa plateau in southwest Tanzania have been described by a succession of observers of varying ethnic and cultural backgrounds as remarkably peaceful and orderly? The problem is made more acute because of convincing evidence that Fipa territory was the site of endemic armed conflict between rival groups during a period that ended not long before European contact began in the later nineteenth century. What happened, and how?

The country of the Fipa, which is called Ufipa, mainly consists of a high and almost treeless plateau, flanked by the Lake Tanganyika shore on the west and the Rukwa valley and lake on the east. The whole territory covers more than 25,000 square miles and the present population is about 150,000, of whom about one-third are non-Fipa. In the late pre-colonial period with which we are principally concerned the population would have been considerably less, and probably numbered between 30,000 and 50,000.

The inhabitants of Ufipa are predominantly Bantu-speaking cultivators, with finger millet (*Eleusine corocana*) as the staple crop. Livestock, especially cattle, goats, sheep, chickens, and pigeons, are kept in considerable numbers. Possession of cattle is a mark of wealth and status, and in pre-colonial times is said to have been restricted to members of the royal dynasty called *Twa*. Hunting and trapping of small game, and fishing in the rivers and lakes, are and have been commonly practised.

The virtual absence of forest cover over most of the Fipa plateau has precluded the possibility of swidden or 'slash and burn' cultivation such as is the custom among the neighbouring peoples who inhabit lower-lying scrubland. Instead, the Fipa have developed a distinctive method of cultivation using compost mounds. The technique has the advantage of being vastly more efficient in economic terms than the swidden method, being more than six times as productive. An important consequence has been that Fipa villages are virtually sedentary and long-enduring, so making possible the culture of intense sociability here to be described.

Archaeological evidence shows that the territory of the Fipa has formed part of a wider network of regional economic exchange for many centuries. The plateau itself forms a natural corridor linking East and Central Africa. In the late pre-colonial period this geographically strategic position meant that Ufipa served as a junction and crossroads for the trans-continental trade routes channelling ivory, slaves, and manufactured goods. As well as participating in this lucrative trade, Ufipa produced and sold on both internal and external markets substantial quantities of ironwork, cotton cloth, woodcraft, grain, and dried fish. By reason therefore of both its superior agricultural technology and its advantageous geographical situation for participating in long-distance trade, late pre-colonial Ufipa was a good place to do business. Small wonder that the first European visitors remarked on the apparent prosperity, and evident industry, of the people. The English missionary E. C. Hore, who visited Ufipa in 1880, called it 'the land of plenty' (Hore 1880).

TROUBLE AND STRIFE

It had not always been thus. The copious oral-traditional histories of the Fipa record what seems to have been a long period, spanning many generations, of political conflict and warfare between two rival factions of the Twa dynasty who were both striving for domination of Ufipa's human and material resources. The oral chronicles vividly depict duplicity, murder, and devastation. A brief excerpt typifies the content of these narratives:

Soon after the building of Ilembo there was a great famine in Lyangalile [one of the two indigenous states into which Ufipa became divided]. When the aKansi [the people of Nkansi, the other state] heard about this the king of Nkansi got an army together, including a great number of aTwa [members of the royal family], and told them: 'Go and strike them now, while they are weak with hunger!'

The aKansi thereupon invaded Lyangalile and began attacking the aLyangalile. But they did not know that the king Nguwa had brought back with him from Umambwe [a neighbouring country in which he had taken refuge from an earlier defeat] knowledge of the technique of using arrows in warfare. The aKansi began the battle by throwing their spears, and suddenly their bodies were pierced by arrows, which they were unable to extract. Not having encountered such a thing before, they fled in confusion. The fleeing aKansi were pursued by the aLyangalile, who slaughtered them in great numbers. (Willis 1981: 73)

What historical value can be ascribed to these narratives? Since not only the royal village of Ilembo but forty other abandoned village sites can be identified with villages mentioned in the oral narratives concerned with this period of war and disaster, it has seemed to me that the main pattern of events described in the oral traditions is likely to reflect a real historical process. It is also significant that all these ancient sites exhibit visible remains of having been surrounded by a circular earthworks which would have been surmounted by a defensive pallisade (*iliinga*). The historical process I have referred to culminated in the 1850s with the definitive establishment of twin Fipa states, Nkansi and Lyangalile. Notwithstanding their traditions of mutual hostility, these new states thereafter pursued policies of peace in relation both to each other and to the external world.

Certainly by 1880 the Fipa had acquired the reputation, as the Scots explorer Joseph Thomson put it, of being the most peaceable race in Central Africa (Thomson 1881 II: 221): '[They were] more of a purely agricultural race than any other tribe I have seen. To the cultivation of their fields they devote themselves entirely. They never engage in war, though they will, of course, defend themselves' (ibid.: 222). In the same year Hore, after noting that most Fipa villages had been fortified, observed that the pallisades had been allowed to fall into disrepair, and 'it looks as if the necessity for them was past' (Hore 1880).

With peace, there had evidently also come prosperity. Elsewhere, Hore refers to the 'many rich and populous villages' of the Fipa (Hore 1883: 18). He further describes Ufipa as a rich, well-wooded country, ruled over by an influential chief, Kapuufi [Kapuufi I, king of the territorially more extensive Fipa state of Nkansi] and a fairly complete organization of local sub-chiefs. The order and strength thus maintained, the natural advantages of the country, and busy energy of the people, secure a good measure of peace and prosperity to the Wafipa. (Hore 1892: 157)

The German explorer Paul Reichard, who also visited Ufipa in 1880 but seems not to have met either Thomson or Hore, none the less recorded essentially similar impressions of the country and the people: 'Ufipa possesses a tolerably well managed state, within the borders of which reign calm, peace and order . . . His [Kapuufi's] rule is generally, *energetic, but nevertheless mild*' (Reichard 1892: 400; emphasis added). The seeming contradiction in that last sentence of Reichard's (*'Er führt überhaupt ein energisches, aber dennoch mildes Regiment'*) hints at what we began by calling the 'peace puzzle' in Ufipa. How can a social regime be both 'mild' and 'energetic'? One senses a similar awareness of some underlying mystery in Thomson's statement that Kapuufi is looked up to as being 'not only nominally but practically the leader and chief of the people throughout the whole of Fipa. He is greatly respected and reverenced. He wields an actual power of government, so that his orders are respected everywhere' (Thomson 1881 II: 223).

Yet this orderliness and respectful obedience to higher authority also appeared to Thomson to have been achieved without resort by the indigenous state to overt repression. Thomson even gained the impression, which was almost certainly mistaken (the Twa states maintained official executioners), that capital punishment was unknown in Ufipa: 'The only punishments are flogging, fining and imprisonment. Adultery is punished by fines; murder by the culprit being tied for a certain period to a post, and all his goods confiscated' (Thomson 1881 II: 222). The same rather puzzling impression of uncoerced docility recurs in the mission reports of the Roman Catholic White Fathers, who entrenched themselves in Ufipa with the beginning of German colonial rule in 1890. The Fipa population of the Rukwa valley are described as 'gentle people, used to obeying their *powerful but pacific* kings of Kapuufi's dynasty' (*Chroniques Trimestrielles* n.d. 82: 233, emphasis added). The annual reports of the British colonial administration which succeeded German rule in 1919 (it is unfortunate that the German colonial reports appear to have been lost during the fighting in Ufipa in 1916) paint a similar picture of tranquillity. Violent crime appears to have been virtually absent among the people. An unmistakable note of boredom pervades this typical comment by a British district officer: '1938 has been marked by nothing especially noteworthy in Ufipa. The District has maintained its usual placid, even tenor, undisturbed by the outer world' (British Colonial Reports 1938–39–40). What sort of personality does this unusually peaceable society and culture produce? Here again there is a remarkable consistency and continuity in comments by outside observers and again a suggestion of a somewhat puzzling juxtaposition of qualities. The typical Fipa, it appears, is an engaging person, honest and cheerful of countenance, who loves to talk, especially with strangers; but he or she is also, it is repeatedly said, notably energetic and industrious. The English missionary Hore, who visited the Lake Tanganyika settlements of the Fipa in 1880, found the people not only prosperous and evidently hard-working (he noted 'vast fields' of various crops) but also surprisingly friendly and self-possessed: 'Here in Fipa more than anywhere else the people most wonderfully disguised their surprise on seeing me. One would think white men were as common as black among some whom I knew had never seen one before' (Hore 1880).

The Fipa, writes a missionary priest, are *'d'un esprit gai et causeur'* ('of a cheerful and talkative character', *Kala Mission Diary*, 1890). The Frenchman's comment is similar to that of an anonymous contributor (probably Paul Reichard) to the *Deutsche Kolonial Lexikon*, who reported the Fipa as being of agreeable appearance, 'goodhearted and outgoing' (*'gutmuttig und freiwillig'*) (Reichard 1919: 213).

To summarize the account so far, we have a picture of a people who in the middle of the nineteenth century emerged from a period of conflict and civil war to construct a peaceful, orderly, and prosperous society, the members of which consistently impressed visiting strangers as engagingly spirited, spontaneous, and outgoing. We must now consider how it was done.

POWERFUL AND PACIFIC

The people of late pre-colonial Ufipa, as we have already seen, were well placed to participate in and profit from the commercial boom that accompanied the beginnings of Western capitalist penetration into the African interior. Where other groups, like the Bemba or the

Nyamwezi, reacted to the new commercial opportunities by organizing war and slave-raiding, the Fipa devoted themselves to peaceful production and exchange. Instead of preying on their neighbours, they welcomed immigrants and visitors, especially foreign merchants, as Richard Burton had already reported in 1860 (Burton 1860: 153). Reichard reported that he and his caravan were not allowed to pay for anything during their visit in 1880, such was the honour the Fipa felt was due to a guest of their king Kapuufi (Reichard 1892: 400). Thomson also reports this custom, which he apparently found somewhat puzzling: 'It appears that it is his [Kapuufi's] custom, when he takes a fancy to any trader, to empower him to levy whatever he wants from the different villages without payment; and curiously, this exaction is not resisted' (Thomson 1881: 229). Curious indeed, given the lack of overt repression which distinguished Kapuufi's 'energetic but mild' regime. But this seeming docility, and the uniform respect accorded to the indigenous government, become easier to understand when we know that in late pre-colonial Ufipa all the offices of government, with the exception of the kingship and a few other royal officiants, formed part of the same commercial network that animated the country and people as a whole, being perpetually open to the highest bidder according to a custom the Fipa called 'dissolving rank' (Willis 1981: 169–70). This hierarchy of biddable offices that includes civil and military governorships and a number of executive posts at the Twa royal court, and which is a system predominately run by wealthier male householders, is paralleled by a judicial and punitive system staffed by women. These female magistrates are explicitly concerned with the maintenance of public order at village level. It is their duty to repress what are called 'sexual' offences, a category which is broadly interpreted to include the public use of obscene language, and they are empowered to impose heavy fines on offenders. But powerful as they are, these female office-holders are still under the authority of the village headman, whose appointees they are. This dualistic but unequal structure replicates at the level of state organization a hierarchic dualism that relates the Twa dynasties, mythologically descended from intrusive stranger-women who were symbolically associated with Earth, to the aboriginal source of kingship in Ufipa, the ruler of Milansi, the 'Eternal Village' in the centre of the country, whose primal ancestor was a man who fell from the sky at the beginning of time.

This pervasive, cosmological image that juxtaposes Settler and

Stranger in a continuing relation of both polarity and hierarchic imbalance is also formally recurrent in the relation between the sedentary Fipa village community and the surrounding bush (domain of Nature, wildness, source of energy and incoming strangers) and the country itself, ever ready to welcome and incorporate people from outside. At the other extreme of social organization the fluid, competing Fipa kindreds whose changing memberships both crosscut village membership and link villages together, are polarized between relations through the wealth-providing senior males and relations through the incoming wives.

Finally, the Fipa concept of the 'person', *unntu*, provides a further instance of the cosmological image, being polarized between the 'head' (*unntwe*), associated with fixity, humanity, seniority, intellectual control and communication, sociability, superordination, and maleness, and the 'loins' (*unnsana*), associated with energy and movement, juniority, sexuality, animality and fertility, and femaleness. Overturning of this proper hierarchic relation between personal 'head' and 'loins' is associated with sickness and madness, with animality, with relapse into non-humanity (cf. Willis 1978b). We hypothesize, therefore, that it is the operation of this self-governing 'inner cosmos' that constitutes the Fipa person, which is reflected in the persistent observations of outsiders, suggesting that the Fipa are abnormally peaceful, docile, well behaved, and so on.

Moreover, the generalization of that cosmological model of the person to embrace the organization of the kindred (in which relations through males are called 'head' and relations through females 'loins'), the whole country in relation to the external world, and finally the intricate structure of governance, coincided, we suggest, with the transition from the period of conflict, destruction, and war to the regime of peace, order, and prosperity.

It may have occurred to the reader that I have thus far refrained from describing my own impressions of the Fipa, as a field anthropologist. Looking back on that experience, I certainly could not disagree with all those witnesses who have, during a period of 100 years, recorded descriptions of a peaceful and orderly society and an eminently 'sociable' people. Yet I would also find such labels irritatingly superficial in relation to what, in my memory, it actually felt like to live in and among that people. Yes, they *did* smile a lot, and lively talk was almost incessant during waking hours. During nearly two years' residence in Ufipa I never saw anyone fighting, even children, except in play. But I fancy that I also must have smiled quite a bit, just as, I suspect, did Thomson, Hore, and Reichard and a succession of missionaries and colonial administrators, despite the stern implications of their respective callings.

Why can't I remember whether or not I smiled? Because it was my business, as I understood it, to make out what the Fipa were saying. Out of that continuing effort I was eventually able to construct an account of what I have here called the Fipa cosmology. Early in that endeavour my attention was drawn, by my Fipa friends, to the interesting fact that there was an apparent contradiction in the relation between the two fundamental principles of that cosmology, invoked at the social level by the terms Settler and Stranger, and in the domain of personhood, and also of kinship, and descent, by the terms Head and Loins. Strangerhood was powerful, bringing wealth, energy, increase, but only insofar as the Stranger, mythologically represented as an invasive woman, was incorporated into Fipa society under the pacific control of already established authority. This was a continuing process, by which Strangerhood was all the time being converted into Settlerhood.

Similarly, the 'energetic but mild' regime recorded by Reichard, and the 'pacific' and 'powerful' indigenous government remarked on by a missionary priest, mirror, in terms of political and social organization, the symbolic oppositions of Settler and Stranger, of Head and Loins, that Fipa describe as structuring their world. The same surprising 'fit' is apparent, at the personal level, between the contradictory yet complementary attributes of the polarized and hierarchic cosmology, and the relaxed, engaging, yet industrious people described in the documentary sources.

It seems to me that these two apparent facts, the uniformity in 'objective' descriptions of Fipa society and people delivered by different observers, and the formal similarity between that common description and the basic structure of Fipa cosmology is rather strong evidence for the innate intersubjectivity posited for the human species by Trevarthen and Logotheti (in this volume), and for the innate 'sociality' proposed by Carrithers (also in this volume).

'US' AND 'THEM'

A further, distinctive characteristic of Fipa culture became fully apparent to me only in discussion of this paper with Signe Howell, who asked me how the Fipa 'saw themselves'. I then realized that in fact 'the Fipa' do not see 'themselves' as an Us opposed to a Them, which is what the question implies. The term 'Fipa' as denoting the inhabitants of the Fipa plateau appears to have been a late nineteenth-century neologism invented by incoming Zanzibari traders. The root *-ipa* means 'cliff' or 'escarpment' and refers to the geographical fact that the Fipa plateau is a raised block or *horst*, access to which requires, on three of its four 'sides', a steep ascent of between 2,000 and 3,000 feet. The concept of 'the Fipa' as a solitary group distinct from other groups, invented by foreign traders, became institutionalized by two successive colonial administrations, German and British, and was inherited by the government of independent Tanganyika (now Tanzania). The term has also been employed, as convenient shorthand for 'inhabitants of the Fipa plateau and adjoining Tanganyika and Rukwa valleys', by this anthropologist.

In reality 'the Fipa', unless influenced by social-scientific ways of thought, rarely if ever talk about 'themselves' in such reifying terms. Nor does Fipa culture include a concept of a 'Self' at all similar to our modern idea of an atomistic human essence inherent in each individual, an idea which would seem to have emerged with the rise of the capitalist bourgeoisie in Europe. There is in the Fipa language a suffix *-kola*, applicable both to animate beings and to things, which conveys the meanings of specificity and particularity. But the distinctive characteristic of the human being or person, *unntu*, is definition in relation to others who participate in the same abstract quality of personhood or humanity (*uunntu*). This relative nature of the person is given ideological expression in numerous proverbial sayings (*imiluumbe*) which are primarily used to instruct children in Fipa cultural values. A quarter of the 200 proverbs I collected in Ufipa are of this kind. A typical example is 'Clever person, can't cut his/her own hair' (*'Unntu unnceenjesu, ataaipeele'*), the meaning of which is obvious. The same model of dynamic complementarity, this time in the domain of cognition, informs the Fipa proverb that stands as epigraph to this chapter: 'In communicating one spies, and is spied upon' (*'Amalaango yano yal' ukuneengula, ayali yali n'ukuneengulwa'*). And note the military metaphor used to characterize a pacific situation!

Personhood and selfhood are therefore, for Fipa, imbued with implications of a complementarity which formally resembles the pervasive cosmological dualism described earlier. This 'Self/Other' concept (as it might more accurately be termed) stands, moreover, in a relation of hierarchic superiority and inclusion to the analogous distinction, and complementary opposition, of gender and sex. For not only are the distinctions of 'man' (*umoosi*) and 'woman' (*umwaanaci*) merged in the concept of 'person' (*unntu*), but every Fipa person, male or female, participates symbolically and equally in the complementarity of male and female attributes which is part of the cosmological dualism that unites bodily 'head' and 'loins' in dynamic and reciprocal opposition.

Such being the case, it would seem logical to expect to find in Ufipa a measure of social equality between men and women, males and females, that is qualitatively distinct from that found in some other cultures where sex and gender differentiation serve as symbolic models for hostility towards the strange Other. And indeed, outside certain ritual contexts in which organized female violence against males was (formerly) institutionalized (Willis 1980), social relations between the sexes in Ufipa appear in comparative perspective as remarkably egalitarian. Of particular note is the Fipa custom of male – female commensality, the twice-daily sharing of food and conversation between males and females, including adults. Such commensality, of which Robertson Smith was the first to note the implications of equality and comradeship, is most unusual in Africa, where sexual segregation at meals is the general rule (see Goody 1982: 86; and Willis, in press). A similarly atypical instance is the playing by and between members of both sexes in Ufipa of the board-game *isuumbi*, a variant of the well-known *mancala* game, which elsewhere in Africa is the prerogative of one sex only, most usually males (Willis 1983).

The behavioural norms observed by properly socialized Fipa accentuate the social skills of oral communication and agreeable self-presentation. The cultural preoccupation with the exchange of words is evidenced in the existence of at least sixty verbs referring to different ways of talking and speaking. To possess *ufukusu*, good and — above all — pleasing manners is the most prized social quality. Conversely, the overt expression of socially unpleasing emotions such as anger and hatred and, *a fortiori*, the use of physical violence between persons, are rigidly suppressed by the Fipa. The cultural climate so engendered is not one that lends itself to the construction of 'Us/Them' social oppositions.

Such a cultural climate is not easy for us to understand, doubly conditioned as we are by the objectifying language of social science and the confrontational rhetoric of nation-statehood. But the evidence suggests that these people did manage to transform their society from one riven by division and violent conflict to one that combined energy and order into a novel and enigmatic balance.

I would now like to return to the 'problem' posed at the beginning of this chapter, of how a society, that suffered from conflict and violence, was able to transform itself, during what appears to have been a remarkably short period of time, into a seeming paragon of peace and prosperity. Part of the answer has already been outlined. In terms of the economic, technological, and social environment of mid-nineteenth-century Ufipa, repression of personal and collective violence and channelling of human energies into productive action suddenly 'made sense' for a people newly provided, in the structures of indigenous statehood, with the political means of activating and enforcing a collective will. Constructed out of the exigencies of factional conflict and civil war, the new states were also moulded, with their opposed and complementary 'male' and 'female' administrative systems, in the image of the pervasive dualist cosmology that constituted the principles of peace and order in control of energy.

But part of the 'puzzle' presented to us, as observers and interpreters of a change from bellicose to pacific, might well be an artifact of our own categories. Our use of the term 'aggression' to denote behaviour that is inherently, and often actually, violent and destructive and always morally 'bad', a usage recently reinforced by sociobiological theory, is symptomatic of a dichotomy that may be peculiar to our own worldview. As Erich Fromm reminds us, the word 'aggression' is derived from Latin terms meaning 'to move towards' (Fromm 1973). In its original sense, therefore, 'to aggress' may equally well imply welcoming, friendly, and constructive behaviour as hostile and destructive. The use we have come to make of the basically neutral term 'aggression' is part of a complex of attitudes ingrained in our existing Western value system, that equates 'peace' and 'non-violence' with spineless passivity.

Viewed through the lens of that value system, it is difficult to understand how a people so evidently peaceful and orderly could also be not only energetic but also, as I learned during fieldwork, passionately competitive (Willis 1981, 1985). But if, modifying our simplistic and absolutist use of the term, we admit that human 'aggression' may manifest equally in the form of affiliative, constructive, and 'peaceful' action, as it may also be destructive and warlike, the 'peace puzzle' in Ufipa becomes less puzzling. For not only can we more easily comprehend the 'peaceful' society that first came into being more than a century ago, we can also envisage the transition from 'war' to 'peace', not as a contrast of incompatible conditions, but as a rather less fundamental change: from a state of 'negative' to one of 'positive' aggression.

We need not suppose that the emotional experience of anger, of hatred and of violence is absent from this latterly 'peaceful' Fipa society, despite lack of overt expression. One indicator that such negative emotions do indeed flourish is the prevalence of fears and rumours centred on witchcraft and 'poisoning' (Willis 1968). And another is the commonly told traditional stories (*ifilaayi*), which are replete with incidents involving treachery, cruelty, and murder, often arbitrary and unmotivated. These stories provide good evidence that Fipa, like ourselves, enjoy committing in fantasy acts they would never think of perpetrating in actuality. In the perspicacious observation of the moral philosopher Mary Midgley:

> There are not (as used to be supposed) any non-aggressive human societies. Opposition is an essential element in human life: aggression is part of the emotional equipment for making it work. Societies which keep it within reasonable bounds (unlike our own) are doing something much harder and more interesting than merely never feeling it in the first place (1984: 92).

© 1989 Roy Willis

REFERENCES

British Colonial Reports (BCR), Ufipa (1919–1940) Dar es Salaam: Tanzania National Archives.

Burton, R. F. (1860) *The Lake Regions of Central Africa: a picture of explorations*, London: Longman, Green.

Chroniques Trimestrielles, Journal of the White Fathers' Missionary Society. Rome: archives of the White Fathers (Padiri Bianchi).

Deutsche Kolonial Lexikon (1919) Leipzig: Spamer.

Fromm, E. (1973) *The Anatomy of Human Destructiveness*, New York: Holt, Rinehart & Winston.

Goody, J. (1982) *Cooking, Cuisine and Class*, Cambridge: Cambridge University Press.

Hore, E. C. (1880) *Journey to the South End of Lake Tanganyika*. Unpublished letter in the Archives of the London Missionary Society.

Hore, E. C. (1883) 'On the twelve tribes of Tanganyika', *Journal of the Royal Anthropological Institute*, III: 1–2.

Hore, E. C. (1892) *Tanganyika: eleven years in Central Africa*, London: Stanford.

Kala Mission Diary, Ufipa (1890) Archives of the White Fathers, Rome.

Midgley, M. (1984) *Wickedness: a philosophical essay*, London: Routledge & Kegan Paul.

Reichard, P. (1892) *Deutsch Ostafrika: das Land und seine Bewohner*. Leipzig: Spamer.

Thomson, J. (1881) *To the Central African Lakes and Back*, 2 vols. London: Cass.

Willis, R. G. (1968) 'Changes in mystical concepts and practices among the Fipa', *Ethnology*, VII (2): 139–57.

Willis, R. G. (1978a) *There was a Certain Man: spoken art of the Fipa*, Oxford: Clarendon Press.

Willis, R. G. (1978b) ' "Magic" and "medicine" in Ufipa', in P. Morley and R. Willis (eds) *Culture and Curing*, Pittsburgh: Pennsylvania University Press.

Willis, R. G. (1980) 'Executive women and the emergence of female class consciousness', *Anthropology*, IV (1): 1–10.

Willis, R. G. (1981) *A State in the Making: myth, history, and social transformation in pre-colonial Ufipa*, Bloomington: Indiana University Press.

Willis, R. G. (1983) 'Isuumbi: a Fipa boardgame', *Anthropology*, VII, 2: 1–12.

Willis, R. G. (1985) 'Do the Fipa have a word for it?' in D. J. Parkin (ed.) *The Anthropology of Evil*, Oxford: Blackwell, pp. 209–23.

Willis, R. G. (in press) 'Power begins at home: the politics of male–female commensality in Ufipa', in W. Arens and I. Karp (eds) *The Symbolism of Power Relations*.

Chapter Eight

'YOU ONLY *LIVE* IN YOUR BODY':

peace, exchange and the siege mentality in Ulster[1]

ANTHONY D. BUCKLEY

In Northern Ireland, some districts are visibly more peaceful than others. Concentrating upon one such peaceful area, the 'Upper Tullagh', I shall argue that different circumstances encourage people to adopt different moralities, some which permit, and others which preclude, violent action.[2] Paradigms employed in the definition of both self and society are sufficiently flexible to permit Ulster people to be either gentle or violent, generous or self-seeking, as their predilections or circumstances require.

In Ulster, as elsewhere in Europe, there is no single shared image either of society or of the self. There are several commonly occurring ideas about such entities as 'body', 'soul', 'spirit', 'mind', 'thoughts', 'feelings' and the like, together with some commonly used principles. These are used to construct sometimes mutually inconsistent versions of what the self typically is. The general principles used to build ideas about the self are also used in descriptions of social institutions. They commonly focus upon ideas of fighting, among which a major archetype is the image of the siege (see also Buckley 1984).

Despite the pre-eminence of fighting as a metaphor for the self and society, this image is only indirectly related to whether people do in practice fight. It does not enslave them so that they are doomed mindlessly to kill each other. The image of war is both complex and dynamic and includes a sense of dramatic process. Even in abstraction, active fighting is only one, albeit important, feature of warfare. Because of this, the siege metaphor in Ulster can be used in a variety of different ways. It can be used, for example, to give meaning not only to bloody forms of conflict, but also to the ones which are comparatively restrained. And similarly the siege gives definition not only

146

to conflict itself, but also to its precursor and its aftermath, the state of peace.

Sahlins has differentiated between 'assistance freely given, the small currency of everyday kinship, friendship and neighbourly relations', and 'self-interested seizure, appropriation by chicanery or force' (Sahlins 1974: 191). In Ulster, people have become rather famous for this latter form of interaction which Sahlins calls 'negative reciprocity'. I wish to suggest, however, that there exists in Northern Ireland a gamut of systems of reciprocity and exchange, embracing the 'generalized reciprocity' of motherly love and good neighbourliness on the one side, through the 'balanced reciprocity' of much economic life, to the 'negative reciprocity' of bombings, murders, and 'kneecappings', on the other.

A major reason for using Sahlins's threefold distinction between types of exchange is that it corresponds closely to idealizations made by people in the Upper Tullagh. In general, people here claim to approve of generalized reciprocity which they often describe in glowing terms. In contrast, they disapprove when balanced reciprocity, and, even more, negative reciprocity, disrupts relationships based upon generalized exchange.

It would be unwise, however, to become trapped by Sahlins's triad. Sahlins himself writes that 'the actual kinds of reciprocity are many' (Sahlins 1974: 192), and not all of these fit comfortably into his continuum. Moralities, like political systems (Barth 1959), arise from individual choices. In relationships, there is a continual negotiation, which determines what sorts of actions and objects may be exchanged (Buckley 1983a; Haley 1959a, 1959b). My supposition is that individuals seek to optimize the satisfaction of their desires but that there are different sorts of advantages attached to different systems of morality. For example, there is often an advantage in power or prestige to be gained from being kindly or generous, whether to specific people (e.g. one's wife and children), or to people in general (Homans 1958; Blau 1967). Cashdan (1985) has further argued that generalized exchange is often comparable to insurance. By giving to the needy, one gains the right to claim in turn from others. I have, for example, shown how this principle operated in an Ulster village early this century. For the farm-workers, good neighbourliness could be considered to be a 'rational' stratagem, while, for their employers, the farmers, it was not (Buckley 1983a).

It seems that morality is involved in all sorts of interaction, from selfless kindliness, through trading, to street fighting, and war itself. Studies of street and football terrace violence (e.g. Buckley and Kenney forthcoming; Gill 1977; Marsh 1978; Marsh *et al.* 1978) indicate that fighting is seldom 'unbridled'. When individuals or groups compete for mutually incompatible goals, rules of conduct are usually implied. Frequently at issue in the negotiation of such rules are questions of whether, and to what extent, an individual should sacrifice his own interests for the sake of others, or may further his own purposes at other people's expense. At issue too are the means which he may use to achieve his ends. May he act independently, or must he consult? Must he remain honest, or may he deceive? Should he just talk, or may he shout, use fists, knives, guns? One constraint upon action is often that, when one person does something, the other may take this as a sign that he may reciprocate with an equivalent type of action. Thus if, in a discussion, one participant draws a knife, he risks that his opponent may also use equivalent force. The other may feel that he is *entitled* so to do. The drawing of the knife would have given him *permission*. There is often here a species of reciprocity, a meta-morality, which may be broadly stated as 'I am allowed to do whatever you are allowed to do'. This reciprocity of rules is not always present in a relationship and it may itself be subject to negotiation. Nevertheless, it is often a factor in the continuing transformation of the conduct permissible between individuals.

In Ulster there are places where, by an agreed morality, the population largely declines to use violence to achieve individual or collective ends. In other districts there are moralities in which individuals, often claiming to act in defence of their 'community', are sometimes permitted to use force. My argument is that the range of moralities found in any area depends largely upon local circumstances and upon whether the balance of advantage for different individuals comes from adopting one system of morality or exchange over another.

The different forms of exchange found in Northern Ireland, and particularly the contrast between 'selfless' giving and self-seeking or violent behaviour, are drawn together ideologically by metaphors of war and siege, used in the description of both self and society. All these different types of exchange participate in the dynamics inherent in the specific rules of each emergent system. They also exist in response to concrete circumstances. It is these metaphors for self and society, intertwined with ideas of reciprocity and exchange, which I wish here to explore.

THE SELF AND SOCIETY UNDER SIEGE

Let us start with the physical body. In Europe, and here Ulster is no exception, the physical body is said to be liable to illnesses caused by tiny organisms, known loosely as 'germs', and typically said to be lurking in air, water supply or food, outside the body. These have the propensity to invade the body, particularly when the body's defences are weak. It is these which cause illness.

This 'germ' theory may be highlighted by means of a comparison with ideas expressed to me by Yoruba herbalists in western Nigeria (Buckley 1985). These men also believed that illnesses were caused by organisms (*Kòkòrò*) which, in this context, I translated as 'germs'. These germs, however, were not to be found *outside* the body trying to get *in*. In contrast to European germ theory, Yoruba herbalists argued that germs were located 'where God has placed them', in tiny bags inside the body, fulfilling functions beneficial to health. When, however, a person over-indulged, for example, in food or wine, the germs would grow and multiply and overflow their hiding place. Thus they would spill out and cause illness. The Yoruba germs are therefore *inside* and in danger of getting *out*.

Despite superficial similarities, these two theories are based upon radically different paradigms. In the one, evil (in this case disease) is defined as overflowing a hiding place; in the other, evil is an invasion. In the Yoruba case, evil is the revelation of whatever is hidden; in the European, what is hidden is precious and yet vulnerable to harmful forces without. European approaches to evil, as exemplified by germ theory, are therefore based on the idea of the siege.

Europeans do not, of course, restrict their ideas of the self merely to physiological descriptions, for the body is also differentiated from such entities as thoughts, emotions, etc. Nevertheless, popular ideas about spirituality, intellect, feeling, and so forth, though sometimes used with considerable rhetorical force, are frequently vague and ill defined. Pervading discussions of such matters is often an imprecise Cartesianism, a 'ghost-in-the-machine' psychology. According to this view, a person's intellect, emotion, and spirituality form part of his 'inner life' which is somehow distinguishable from his body.

One expression of this imagery, clearer than many others but not shared by everyone, is the Christian notion of the soul. Here, it is asserted, there is an immortal soul contained within the body, but detachable at death. In Ulster, this notion is commonly used in the context of bereavement. It is consonant with an idea of the body as merely a place of habitation, occupied by the 'real' self. I recall hearing, for example, one variant of this hypothesis used by a man to comfort someone following the death of a relative. He said, 'you only *live* in your body'.

That which belongs to a person's 'inner life' is often thought to be sacred. Sometimes, Christian thought articulates this in the image of the body as a 'temple', for, it is said, Christ may 'come into our hearts'. Even apart from religion, however, when people speak of their 'innermost' thoughts or feelings, they are indicating that these experiences have some importance. Closely related to such notions is the idea that what is private and sacred is also vulnerable. Again a useful contrast may be drawn with the Yoruba. For them, thoughts which are hidden in the body are not so much vulnerable to outside attack, as dangerous forms of power which need to be kept locked up. For both Europeans and the Yoruba, the sacred is to be hidden away. But whereas for the Yoruba the hiding is to prevent dangerous inner forces from causing havoc (Buckley 1985), European hiding is to safeguard a person's most vulnerable thoughts and actions for fear they may be damaged, perhaps only by a mocking glance.

I do not pretend that the siege metaphor exhausts the imagery available in Ulster for the description of the self. Sometimes the self is compared to an engine whose 'internal pressures' need a 'safety valve'. Another idea is that we have 'higher' and 'lower' faculties. These correspond in physiological imagery to the head and genitals (see Willis 1967, 1972, 1978), for the 'higher' faculties are often supposed to be rational and cerebral, while the lower are passionate and erotic. Useful studies of metaphor have been made by Lakoff and Johnson (1980) and Ortony (1979) (see also Kuhn 1962), but a glance at Roget's *Thesaurus* will indicate the wealth of imagery available to English speakers for the definition of the self. Despite this complexity, however, some images are undoubtedly more important than others, and the siege is one of these 'root metaphors' (Turner 1974).

The bodily metaphor of the siege also has directly social implications. A person's intimate thoughts are generally concerned with his intimate relationships and they are therefore shared only with his most intimate acquaintances. Social institutions are similarly understood to be bounded entities, from which, ideally, wicked people or evil influences should be excluded. I have suggested elsewhere that such 'corporate groups' as families, farms, communities, churches, and secret societies are typically described by Ulster people in inherently the same manner as the body itself (Buckley 1984). Within the bounds of such institutions, the spiritual and the good are supposed to be able to live in brotherhood, simplicity, and peace. It is supposedly outside such an institution that one encounters self-seeking, 'materialism', and fighting.

In Northern Ireland, as is well known, there are two endogamous sets of people defined by religious affiliation (Protestant and Catholic), and by identification with different nation-states (the United Kingdom and the Republic of Ireland). Each of these so-called 'communities' has its own characteristic myth which also provides an important basis for the definition of their present-day interactions. Each story contains an image of a siege and of invasion similar to that found in the ideas of the self which transcend both communities.

In the first of these stories, the Plantation of Ulster, the native Irishman was living a life of democracy, peace, and spiritual reflection. Successive invasions, however, by Danes, Normans, and finally the Scots and English deprived him of his heritage, prohibited his religious practices, and turfed him off his land. In Ulster, where this plantation was most vigorously pursued, the Gael was deprived of the good sweet land and allowed to live only on mountainy hill-farms where he had to content himself with poverty and the beautiful view. His new Protestant neighbour in the lowlands, supported by an alien government, was comparatively wealthy.

The Protestant story which corresponds to this (see, for example, Heslinga 1962: 66) is that of the Siege of Derry. This story has remarkably similar elements, except that the heroes, in this case the Protestants, were successful in repelling the invaders. Inside the walls of the city were the virtuous Protestants living lives of political freedom, sobriety, frugality, and religious zeal. Outside the walls were the Catholic armies of King James, who threatened their political and religious liberties.

The similarities between these two images are quite substantial. For example, there is the question of gender. Ireland has, not infrequently in patriotic literature, been described as 'Mother Ireland'. Londonderry, by a similar image, is 'The Maiden City, wooed but never won'. Here, the crimson displayed in the much-used flag of the city and on the collarettes of the 'Apprentice Boys of Derry' who twice annually celebrate the siege, has a clear association with the city's virginity. Those who threaten to invade are most emphatically men, as indeed are those who do the defending. The myths of both sides, therefore, are able to define modern conflicts as a siege. For the one side, it is the invading Briton who must be repelled. For the other, it is the invading Catholic. For both, however, images of rape and personal violation intertwine with territoriality to create a scenario in which defender confronts violator.

Although this imagery has obvious relevance to situations in which there is actual violence, it also has a place in the definition of more peaceful situations. In Northern Ireland, except in comparatively few localities, violence is something to be read about in the newspapers, or watched on television. Despite many years of living in Ulster, except when I have set out to find it, only once have I seen physical force actually being used. True, if one wishes to find violence, it is not difficult. I have, for example, attended a number of riots. These, however, were 'advertised' in newspaper articles which, sometimes implicitly, explained that rioting was to happen. One could, if one wished, turn up and watch. In general, violence is highly localized and confined to specific groups in society. This, however, is not to say that violence is unimportant in Ulster. It has, for everybody, important political implications, since it has real costs in lives, misery, and money. Even those not directly involved use its existence to exert political pressure on others.

In a more general way, images of violence and more specific images of the siege have symbolic significance. There is, for example, television drama and the news itself. Here, virtually every aspect of life is portrayed as a form of 'conflict'. By its very nature, even the most innocuous dramatic presentation involves a 'conflict' between people which is either resolved or else dissolved in calamity or schism. Turner argues that fictional dramas have their counterpart in real-life 'social dramas' (Turner 1982: 61ff). Whether or not he is correct in regarding this dramatic form as inevitable and universal, it is indeed to be found in Europe, not only in art, but in everyday life. Throughout Europe, even peaceful existence is modelled upon violent existence, and one of the most striking images of violence is the idea of the siege. For Europeans, violence and the siege are, quite simply, *bons à penser* (Lévi-Strauss, 1962).

A PEACEFUL COMMUNITY IN ULSTER

It is somewhat hazardous to speak of 'peaceful societies' in Ulster, since nobody in the province can remain immune from the 'troubles'. Localities can sometimes change quickly and drastically. This article refers to the Upper Tullagh of 1975–6, before the IRA hunger strikes, the recession of the 1980s, the opposition to the Anglo-Irish Agreement, and other significant developments. I gather that, since my fieldwork, relations in the area have become more strained. When my fieldwork was undertaken, however, the people of the Upper Tullagh were proud that theirs was a peaceful community. What I hope to illustrate is that even this peacefulness was nevertheless given definition by images of war in the so-called siege mentality.

The topic of peacefulness is consistently related by the people of the Upper Tullagh to that of 'good neighbourliness'. Violence, they say, is found outside, in Belfast, Londonderry, and elsewhere, where people are self-seeking and not at all neighbourly. This opinion, it will be noted, differs sharply from that of the peoples described in this volume by Gibson, Howell, Overing, and Robarchek, for whom peacefulness is associated with an extreme degree of personal autonomy. Good neighbourliness in the Upper Tullagh is said to be exemplified when somebody is sick or otherwise in difficulties and has no relation to take care of him. Then a neighbour, often a woman, will make his tea, clean his house, do the shopping, collect his pension, or in other ways be useful. Among farmers there is also a practice of giving aid to a neighbour at busy times or when there are other difficulties (Bell 1978). Although this is often virtually a commercial relationship, it is often said to typify Upper Tullagh good neighbourliness.

It is of course untrue to suggest that all of the relationships between the people of the Upper Tullagh are of this generalized type. Even within a context of generalized exchanges, people only give 'what they can', balancing their own interests against those of other people. It is tacitly acknowledged that people must usually pursue their own interests. Nevertheless, there is a perceived divergence between the pursuit of one's own needs, archetypically the quest for wealth and position, and the cultivation of proper relationships with kin and neighbours. The basis for much antagonistic gossip is that the other person has 'cut himself off' or is 'stuck up', and this is often identified with the person's alleged desire to make money. Cautionary tales are told of the 'past' — the period between the wars — when grasping farmers exploited the poor in pursuit of their own selfish interests. There is thus a perceived tension between generalized forms of exchange appropriate between kin and neighbours, and more self-seeking ethics which permit someone to look after his or her own interests. This latter form of morality is popularly typified with reference to commercial transactions.

Significantly there seems to be only one sphere where it is universally and vociferously agreed to be permissible to strive to win. This is on the hurley field. Here, the teams representing the three Catholic parishes which constitute the Upper Tullagh regularly engage in this dangerous game in which the periodic battles are described in explicit metaphors evoking warfare. Here the participants represent well-defined territories and what is at stake is the victory of one geographical area over another.

RELATIONS BETWEEN INDIVIDUALS, GROUPS, AND TERRITORIES

Largely because of the rule of endogamy, the two 'sides' in Ulster often relate to each other as corporate groups. This is further enhanced by a tendency of specific districts to become populated by members of one group or the other. Many of the violent occurrences which constitute 'the troubles' of Ulster are concerned with territory simultaneously at two levels. The macro-territorial question of whether Ulster should become part of the Republic of Ireland or remain in the United Kingdom is made to coincide with issues of defining and protecting nationalist and loyalist territories in a comparatively small locality.

Examples of violent occurrences over questions of territory are legion. In 1985, M. C. Kenney and I witnessed riots in Cookstown, Portadown, Belfast, and elsewhere at which police were attacked with missiles. In each case, the issue had to do with the macro-question of 'the border', and in each there was also at stake a local territorial conflict. In Cookstown, on two occasions, loyalist processions were observed challenging a police ban on loyalist marches through a 'Catholic' street. In Portadown, a larger but similar disturbance arose over a similar re-routing, this time of the annual Twelfth of July procession. In both places, loyalists complained that they had been prevented from following their 'traditional' routes through what was, in reality, a disputed territory. In Belfast, the nationalist St Patrick's Day parade provided the occasion for an assault upon the formidable Andersonstown police station, a symbol of intrusive British power in a recognized Catholic area. This was followed by a battle with stones, bottles, and petrol bombs. In Belfast's Catholic Ardoyne area, later in the year, the intrusion of police upon a celebratory bonfire led to stone and petrol bomb attacks upon their convoy (Buckley and Kenney, forthcoming).

Darby (forthcoming) tells of even more serious events in 'Kileen' in Belfast in the early 1970s. Here a rapid shift in the religious composition of a hitherto harmonious and 'mixed' urban area produced a situation where a 'wedge' of Protestant houses intruded into what was now a Catholic housing estate where the IRA were active. Despite or perhaps because of a 'peace line' manned by soldiers Protestants were, house by house, intimidated into leaving their houses in the first of the streets in the area. These were then occupied by Catholic families. The peace line now being useless, it was removed and re-erected in another street. This Catholic progress was repeated several times despite resistance by both soldiers and loyalist mobs until the intrusive Protestant wedge had disappeared. This gradual Catholic advance was more than superficially similar to the trench-warfare in the Great War. Individuals on both sides described it in terms of military strategy and territorial advance.

In cases of this sort, the individuals who actively fight are, in the popular cliché, 'a small minority'. Often they are defined as 'outsiders'. In the riots which Buckley and Kenney observed, they were often young men of the lower working class, and included 'hard men' or simply men identifiable as 'rough' (Buckley 1984; Buckley and Kenney, forthcoming). Many such youths are merely looking for excitement. Their actions, however, are given prominence because, in specific circumstances, ordinary respectable people cannot bring themselves to disapprove of or prevent what they are doing. A similar pattern arises in football violence (Marsh *et al.* 1978). Here a comparatively few individuals engage in 'aggro' (Marsh 1978) or outright fighting, often in defence of only a small territory of football terrace. Here too they are buoyed up by other, non-violent sections of the crowd who enjoy the excitement and entertainment they provide. In another description of urban violence (Gill 1977: 160–8), the support of non-violent onlookers was enhanced by the supposed moral justice of the fighters' case.

In discussing territories in Ulster, much depends upon conditions which are wholly local. One factor, however, does seem to be that peaceful conditions often exist where there is no local predominance of one 'side' over the other (Poole 1983). The Upper Tullagh has precisely this structure. It is predominantly Catholic overall with less than a quarter of the population Protestant, but there are not, *within* the district, any distinctively Protestant or Catholic areas. Here Protestant lives side by side with Catholic, and the area as a whole has roughly the same proportion of Catholics and Protestants throughout. Catholic dominance overall is widely accepted by Protestants, but this acceptance is more a matter of social geography than personal choice. For, given their numbers, there is no likelihood that Protestants could ever predominate in the foreseeable future.

I have suggested that there are different sorts of advantage to be gained by individuals who adhere to different moralities. There are, of course, advantages to be gained from being at peace — not least, that it increases one's chances of living to a healthy old age. In a situation in which the dominant group has nothing immediately to gain, where there is a long-standing ethos of peaceful relationships, and where the minority presents little of a threat, it is in everybody's interests to adopt an easy-going and peaceful lifestyle.

There are, of course, costs in such a course. Individuals on each side readily identify themselves with participants in the province-wide conflict. In this, each side has suffered defeats, and each has won but scant victories. It is difficult sometimes to resist the temptation to blame neighbours for the actions of their co-religionists. Nevertheless, since in the Upper Tullagh neither side wants violence, both sides make the effort to be peaceful.

One aspect of this effort has been the deliberate cultivation of links across the 'sectarian divide'. In the Upper Tullagh, important church-based activities continue to divide the community. The all-important rule of endogamy also remains intact, despite protestations that 'people should be allowed to marry who they like'. Nevertheless, there are many voluntary associations, Women's Institute, Historical Society, Lion's Club, and others which are recruited on non-sectarian lines. There are contacts between the main churches, and the good personal relationships between Protestant and Catholic clergy are noted and approved. Above all, generalized exchange between neighbours is cultivated irrespective of denominational affiliation. This extends far beyond the reciprocal attendance at funerals found in nearly all parts of Ulster, to ties of personal friend-ship. I have found, for example, several instances where Catholic and Protestant farmers share machinery as part of a semi-formal 'neigh-bouring' relationship, requiring a high degree of mutual trust.

Another aspect, moreover, has been the deliberate enforcement of peaceful relationships. In the same way as certain types of generalized reciprocity draw upon a pool of ill-defined indebtedness, calling forth further acts of generosity (where 'a' gives to 'b'; 'b' gives to 'c'; and 'c' to 'd' and so forth), so also can this have a counterpart in negative forms of generalized exchange. Here may exist a sub-culture not of good neighbourliness but of generalized aggression, where 'a' is aggressive to 'b'; 'b' aggressive to 'c', and so forth, evoking not grati-tude and generosity, but resentment, needing cathartic expression in further aggressive behaviour (see Heelas 1983). In the still optimistic climate of the mid 1970s where, in the Upper Tullagh, unemploy-ment was still comparatively low, such generalized resentment seemed rare. Nevertheless, in the Upper Tullagh, as elsewhere, there exist individuals, especially youths, who are prone to delinquency, and these present problems of control.

In riots, and especially in the more warlike conflict described by Darby in Kileen, where a population became seriously threatened by 'the other side', respectable people were willing to tolerate aggressive action, identifying it as a defence of their 'community'. In the calm of the Upper Tullagh, however, they are not. Here, as indeed in the ill-fated Kileen before their 'mixed' community was divided, there were, in the early days of the troubles, vigilante patrols organized jointly by both Catholics and Protestants. When these had outlived their usefulness, informal vigilance against teenage misbehaviour was maintained. In particular, there has been a steady informal resistance to the daubing of graffiti which, commonly in Ulster, are used, not only to assert rebellious youthfulness, but also to provide territories with sectarian identities. With the single exception of the public toilets, graffiti in the Upper Tullagh are virtually unknown.

This resistance to 'trouble' reaches an occasional if tragic peak when there is an act of terrorism in the area. There have been several bombs in the Upper Tullagh, one of which killed a young man out-right. The response of the community to such outrages has been strenuously to avoid recriminations across 'the sectarian divide'. Since it was a Catholic who died, the Protestant 'community' all trooped to the funeral ('you couldn't get into the chapel for

Protestants'). And above all, there was a determined tendency to regard such trouble as the work of 'outsiders'.

OUTSIDERS: KEEPING OUT THE BAD

In the metaphor of the siege, 'outsiders' of whatever kind have a crucial role. The Upper Tullagh is something of an enclave, surrounded by, but socially isolated from, an area which is largely Protestant. Despite the contrast between these adjacent areas, relations between their inhabitants are largely peaceful. One reason for this is their lack of interaction caused, not so much by mutual avoidance, as by the convenience of social geography. Most of the everyday shopping and entertainment needs of the people of the Upper Tullagh are provided within their own village of Kilbeg. When Kilbeg shops prove inadequate, a person will tend to travel to Belfast or to another of the more distant large towns. There are many visitors to the Upper Tullagh from outside. These, however, are largely day trippers, intent on a quiet family outing, and coming often from far afield. On Saturday nights, there is something of an influx of young people from the surrounding villages and countryside. Even here, however, there is no very systematic invasion.

Several points of a territorial nature may be made in this context. The first is that one of the nearest villages lying immediately outside the Upper Tullagh has a 'mixed' population, and so people who come to Kilbeg from outside are as likely to be Catholic as Protestant. Second, however, even those Protestants who come to Kilbeg from outside constitute only a slight Saturday night threat to the overall territorial supremacy of Catholics. More than this, Protestant youths are unlikely to erode the fundamental supremacy of Catholics at the territorial boundaries of the Upper Tullagh. The reason for this is, once more, local geography. The effective border around the area is composed not of a highly mobile urban-style population which can be readily displaced, but of settled farms. Territorial patterns here could not be threatened by marauding Saturday night youth, but only by long-term shifts in land-occupation by farmers.

In the Upper Tullagh, a more substantial fear is of the violent men from Belfast. There is a suspicion that terrorist groups might infiltrate the area and overthrow the Upper Tullagh's quiet ways: 'They hate us down here.' In particular, there has been mistrust of newcomers, mainly from Belfast, who now occupy a housing estate. This estate, known as 'Ballymurphy' in echo of the more notoriously violent republican area of Belfast, is supposed by many to be a source of trouble. It is feared that the youth of 'Ballymurphy' will corrupt the more peaceful youth of Kilbeg into causing trouble.

This 'invasion' of Belfast people is, however, part of a more general source of tension throughout Northern Ireland, the problem of housing allocation. In Londonderry, where it was related to questions of gerrymandered elections, this was perhaps the central issue of the 'Civil Rights' protests which began the current troubles. In the Kileen of Darby's (forthcoming) description, and this case is not unusual, there was a forceful 'reallocation' of property by intimidating mobs. And I have found it to have been a major preoccupation in Listymore, in north Ulster, which is another (more or less) peaceful area where I have undertaken fieldwork (Buckley 1983b, 1984).

In this context, the influx of outsiders into both Listymore and the Upper Tullagh is blamed upon the Northern Ireland Housing Executive. Until 1971–2, local authorities exercised control over the allocation of public housing. The NIHE was established, at least in part, to remove this local control and thus to prevent discrimination. In both Listymore, where Protestants predominate, and in the Upper Tullagh, where Catholics have a majority, I heard the same complaint. Since the NIHE took over, it was said, outsiders were coming in, and when they came they brought trouble. In Listymore, I did rather suspect that, included in the complaints against 'outsiders', was another complaint that the once almost exclusively Protestant complexion of one of the Listymore villages (Long Stone) was being diluted by Catholics. The opposite complaint was not appropriate in the Upper Tullagh since most of the incomers on the new Kilbeg estate were, like the rest of Kilbeg, predominantly Catholic. Even in Listymore, however, sectarianism was not the central issue. The main point was that those who should be allowed to settle in one's own area should be 'people that we know'. These are what Donnan and McFarlane (1986) call 'your own' people, not only in a sectarian sense, but more generally. In Kilbeg, objections are made to the incomers, not because of their religion, but because they are 'not of our own kind' because of their allegedly brutal urban ways.

I am arguing that an imagery which suggests that a community is besieged by hostile external forces is by no means one that involves only ideas of bloodletting. First of all, as in the rest of Europe, there are held to be different degrees of 'conflict', from minor disagreements to outright bloody warfare. Second, conflict — especially the repulsion of invaders — is only one moment in the drama evoked by the idea of the siege. In the image lies the possibility, as indeed is said to exist in the Upper Tullagh, that the forces of evil may be held at bay. When this is the case, peace and tranquillity may exist within the community's boundaries.

The implication of this is that whether or not violence exists is not inherently a function of the siege metaphor. Rather, the metaphor provides a means of articulating social relationships into categories. These include not only good and evil, friend and foe, defender and invader, but a much wider range of roles and attitudes which cannot be discussed here, among them traitors, rescuers, peace makers, diplomatists, and others, all of which have a place in images of siege and war. The siege metaphor does, of course, shape human relationships, not least by translating divergences of personal and group interest into ideas of territorial conflict and into notions that conflict is in defence of 'community', 'principle', 'religion', 'ideology', 'culture', 'way of life', or 'belief'. But whether or not individuals actually fight in pursuit of their goals is a matter of their practical inter-relationships on the ground. Here arise wholly local questions of the balance of power between individuals and between groups. These in turn lead to calculations of the usefulness of becoming involved in one or other type of morality or system of exchange. The siege metaphor provides the means for the definition of different sorts of exchange, in a manner which is close to Sahlins's (1974) analytical categories. It also defines the manner in which certain types of exchange can be put into practice. In Ulster, where there exists a siege mentality, there are to be found places where an albeit fragile peacefulness can be found. In the last resort, however, such issues of peace and war depend less upon idioms of expression, and more upon day-to-day interactions of individuals and groups in pursuit of prestige, power, and safety in their own immediate environments.

© 1989 Anthony D. Buckley

NOTES

1 I wish to thank Miss Hilary Smyth for her efforts at the typewriter in the preparation of this chapter, and the people of 'Upper Tullagh' for their many kindnesses in the course of my fieldwork.

2 'Upper Tullagh' and most other proper names here are pseudonyms. The chapter is an attempt to place in broader context the findings of an earlier study (Buckley 1982).

REFERENCES

Barth, F. (1959) *Political Leadership Among the Swat Pathans*, London: Athlone.

Bell, J. (1978) 'Relations of mutual help between Ulster farmers', *Ulster Folklife* 24: 48–58.

Blau, P. (1967) *Exchange and Power in Social Life*, New York: Wiley.

Buckley, A. D. (1982) *A Gentle People: a study of a peaceful community in Northern Ireland*, Cultra: Ulster Folk and Transport Museum.

Buckley, A. D. (1983a) 'Neighbourliness: myth and history', *Oral History* 11: 44–51.

Buckley, A. D. (1983b) 'Playful rebellion: social control and the framing of experience in an Ulster community', *Man* (NS) 18: 383–95.

Buckley, A. D. (1984) 'Walls within walls: religion and rough behaviour in an Ulster community', *Sociology* 18: 19–32.

Buckley, A. D. (1985) *Yoruba Medicine*, Oxford: Oxford University Press.

Buckley, A. D. and Kenney, M. C. (forthcoming) 'Fighting and fun: stone throwers and spectators in Ulster riots'.

Cashdan, E. A. (1985) 'Coping with risks: reciprocity among the Basarwa of Northern Botswana', *Man* (NS) 454–74.

Darby, J. (forthcoming) 'Intimidation and interactions in a small community: the water and the fish', in J. Darby, W. Dodge, and A. C. Hepburn (eds) *Political Violence*, Belfast: Appletree Press.

Donnan, H. and McFarlane, G. (1986) ' "You get on better with your own": social community and change in rural Northern Ireland', in P. Clancy, S. Drury, K. Lynch and L. O'Dowd (eds) *Ireland, a Sociological Profile*, Dublin: Institute of Public Administration.

Gill, O. (1977) *Luke Street: housing policy, conflict, and the creation of the delinquent area*, London: Macmillan.

Haley, J. (1959a) 'An interactional description of schizophrenia', *Psychiatry* 22 (4): 321–2.

Haley, J. (1959b) 'The family of a schizophrenic: a model system', *Journal of Nervous and Mental Disorders* 129: 357–74.

Heelas, P. (1983) 'Anthropological perspectives on violence: universals and particulars', *Zygon* 18: 375–403.

Heslinga, M. W. (1962) *The Irish Border as a Cultural Divide*, N.V. Van Gorcum.

Homans, G. C. (1958) 'Social behaviour as exchange', *American Journal of Sociology* 63: 597–606.

Kuhn, T. S. (1962) *The Structure of Scientific Revolutions*, Chicago: University of Chicago Press.

Lakoff, G. and Johnson, M. (1980) *Metaphors We Live By*, Chicago: University of Chicago Press.

Lévi-Strauss, C. (1962) *Le totemisme aujourd'hui*, Paris: Presses Universitaires de France.

Marsh, P. (1978) *Aggro: the illusion of violence*, London: Dent.

Marsh, P., Rosser, E. and Harré, R. (1978) *The Rules of Disorder*, London: Routledge & Kegan Paul.

Ortony, A. (ed.) (1979) *Metaphor and Thought*, Cambridge: Cambridge University Press.

Poole, M. (1983) 'The demography of violence', in J. Darby (ed.) *Northern Ireland: the background to the conflict*, Belfast: Appletree Press; New York: Syracuse University Press.

Sahlins, M. (1974) *Stone Age Economics*, London: Tavistock.

Turner, V. W. (1974) *Dramas, Fields and Metaphors: symbolic action in human society*, Ithaca: Cornell University Press.

Turner, V. W. (1982) *From Ritual to Theatre: the human seriousness of play*, New York: Performing Arts Journal Publication.

Willis, R. G. (1967) 'The head and the loins: Lévi-Strauss and beyond', *Man* (NS) 2, 519–34.

Willis, R. G. (1972) 'Pollution and paradigms', *Man* (NS) 7: 369–86.

Willis, R. G. (1978) ' "Magic" and "medicine" in Ufipa', in P. Morley and R. Wallis (eds) *Culture and Curing — anthropological perspectives on traditional medical beliefs and practices*, London: Peter Owen.

Part Two

SOCIALITY AS INNATE CAPACITY

Chapter Nine

CHILD IN SOCIETY, AND SOCIETY IN CHILDREN:
the nature of basic trust

COLWYN TREVARTHEN
AND KATERINA LOGOTHETI

THE TASK BEFORE US — TO MAKE THE ORIGINS AND PURPOSE OF HUMAN MOTIVATION CLEARER

Some anthropologists, we understand, feel that simple zoological theories about the inherent drives, especially the aggressiveness, of human beings are 'wrong' — both 'untrue' and morally 'bad'. It is suggested that human nature has been underrated by ethologists, socio-biologists, and evolutionary theorists, and that the potential for goodness in people, in the sense of a desire to live in peace with other humans, is greater than has been surmised.

It seems to us that in facing the above problems anthropologists are being distracted by a dichotomy that has also troubled sociology and psychology: the division separating learned and sophisticated, rather literary 'goodness' on the one hand from inherited, primordial 'badness', or at least 'wickedness' on the other. The same forced choice appears in the Cartesian mind/body split, and in the ancient Manichean division between good and evil. Both of these place undue responsibility on the actions and thoughts of the rational and authoritative individual (philosopher or king), lifted out of affectionate relation to other persons, except in conscience — or, rather, in anxiety and guilt. We share with Mary Midgley, the moral philosopher, the belief that goodness and wickedness are inseparable sides of the human spirit and that this will be clear if we consider human life in community (Midgley 1984).

We shall take the view that faith in humanity can be restored if one looks as an honest naturalist at the roots of human 'communitas' in infancy and childhood. The trusting optimism of children is vindicated by their great skill in communicating. This basic skill adults must strive to retain, alongside the necessary exercise of their much greater sophistication, power, and responsibility in action. In a child's unreflective innocence, the other side of the complexity of human motivation is also revealed, that which gives a place to human wickedness. Children are capable of fear and anger with people they mistrust or who they feel oppose them. The potential for evil of these emotions is limited only by the child's immaturity and weakness.

Human evil, is, we believe, to be interpreted with understanding what human minds try to achieve in co-operation, and the difficulties that have to be overcome. We have to perceive the collective psychological effort that goes into keeping a culture going; what communicative powers, and alliances, individuals must use to link up with the minds of others in the past, the present, and the future. Psychological theories based only on experiments with the motivations, perceptions, thinking, and learning of individuals in unsocial situations, in which communication is poor, cannot be sufficient. We must begin with a theory of a communal intelligence capable of generating a collective consciousness.

Infants and children are avid and effective communicators before they think about the problems of dealing with practical reality on their own; they begin with a commitment to share. The living frame of emotions that defines human social needs and gives values to human understanding can be brought to light by watching the efforts of infants to enter into communication with other people's minds. We see young children take steps to estimate experiences in direct empathy with affectionate adults. They actively use their inherited human motives to find a path for learning the ancestral culture and its symbols, and openly invite adults to accompany them.

THE NEW PSYCHOLOGY OF INFANTS

In the past twenty-five years developmental psychologists, working like archaeologists of mental evolution, have uncovered motivations in infants that have revolutionary implications for the human sciences. Received opinion, disregarding Darwin's remarkably accurate observations of children (Darwin 1872, 1877), and misinterpreting his evolutionary theory, had been that the essential motives of humans in society and in relation to culture must be learned additions to what an infant had inherited; constructions transforming inherited drives, the latter being evolved to provide reflexive controls for survival of the individual. This theory left imitative and co-operative skills of children a total mystery.

Now we possess evidence that the newborn can imitate expressions of persons and enter into an exchange of feelings. One year later the baby shows a specific need to share purposes and meanings and to learn how to denote common ideas by means of symbolic expressions. Human cultural intelligence is seen to be founded on a level of engagement of minds, or intersubjectivity, such as no other species has or can acquire.

Infant communication appears to be regulated by the same emotions that make or break contacts and relationships between mutually aware adults, and that either assist them to find common rules for social conduct and common evaluations for a world of artifacts, or set them apart in miscomprehension and enmity. Why should there be such a precocious complexity of interpersonal motives at this most dependent, unspeaking stage of life? Evidently an organized field of motives for communication has to be set up from the start, to regulate the growth of rational consciousness in relation to shared feelings and interests.

DEVELOPMENT TOWARDS SOCIAL RESPONSIBILITY IN RESPONSIVENESS

Steps in early psychological development, while adjustable to different styles of upbringing that convey different social and moral principles, reveal universal powers and needs for emotion and communication that are essential to normal 'socialization' and to normal 'cognitive growth'.

The first year

1. Newborns, even 10 weeks premature, can achieve direct engagement through hearing and seeing an affectionate 'other', and by feeling body contact and gentle movements (Sander 1983; Brazelton 1985; Stern 1985). The infant makes orientations, expressions, and gestures and moves in concert with the sympathetic partner. Eye contact is sought and the baby can imitate movements of the eyes and mouth (Field et al. 1982; Meltzoff 1985). This is primary intersubjectivity or basic person–person awareness (Trevarthen 1979). Development of the baby's brain may benefit from emotions generated in

such communication, the existence of which proves that the baby has a dual 'self + other' organization in its mind, ready for contact with the expressed feelings of a real partner.

The mother recognizes an awakening to her regard and smile at 46 weeks' gestational age, and thereafter protoconversational exchanges are set up on a common beat of moving modulated by emotions, which are expressed in the face, the voice, the hands, and the posture of the body by both mother and baby.

2. The infant quickly identifies the most protective, most constant and most affectionate partner who is responded to preferentially with expressions of attentiveness, happiness, and an eagerness to make 'utterances'. In contrast, unknown persons tend to be regarded with unsmiling suspicion and expressions of fear and withdrawal (Trevarthen 1984, 1985, 1986b). Thus, the first stage of human intersubjectivity is marked by affectionate attachment with a caretaker. The infant seeks direct engagement in a dialogue exchange of expressions with this responsive person, showing little interest in the still remote impersonal world. Rejection or withdrawal of affection by the principal caretaker causes the baby acute distress (Fraiberg 1982; Murray and Trevarthen 1985).

3. Three months after birth, the infant shows more curiosity and exploration, looking up and reaching more and more away from the mother towards physical 'things' that cannot smile or speak (Trevarthen 1980, 1983). Rational awareness is shown by persistent efforts to solve problems that arise when the baby moves to test experiences of body movement, or of objects in the outside world (Papousek and Papousek 1984). The child is also beginning to show clear autonomy of reason and purpose, and may defy or attack a partner in play with an expression of aggressive determination. If the child's will is thwarted, it can protest strongly.

4. At this age, when the infant's emotions defend individuality in companionship, the sharing of pleasure in playful combat takes ritual socio-dramatic, musical, or poetic forms (Stern 1985; Trevarthen 1983, 1988a; Trevarthen and Marwick 1986). Mothers sing traditional nursery songs that bring out clearly the universal beat and rhythms of interaction and the qualities of voice that signal feelings. The songs and poems excite the infant to share in the development of

the melody or action game, stimulating the infant's body-awareness and reinforcing musical qualities of communicative movement. In different cultures, the same standards of beat, rhythm, melody, and rhyming of 'baby music' are favoured for joint control of mood and moving in sympathy. Infants show acute joy in this play, at the same time as they assert increasing individuality of purpose within the companionship they experience through play.

5. Before they can manipulate objects well, infants become aware of others' hands, and of the vocalizations others make, while they act on things or present them. This awareness is provoked in imitation tests (Trevarthen 1986b). Three-month-olds watch the trusted other's interest and handling of things, while the baby's control of his or her own manipulations is immature and ineffective.

6. At 6 to 9 months, self-consciousness and self-display show themselves clearly, as the child develops a mastery of intended activities that arise in independence of others' wills, but that acknowledge others' interest and approval or disapproval (Bruner 1981; Rogoff 1984; Trevarthen 1984, 1986b; Trevarthen and Marwick 1986). The child is now sensitive to the 'affect attunement' (Stern 1985) that a mother, or other familiar playmate, unconsciously gives to 'gloss' the infant's interest and actions. Infants begin to 'show off' and act comical, with evident awareness of the praise of an audience, and they can start a game to amuse themselves and others. They may become angry when other people try to block their purposes. They begin to join in imitative play with a sibling or a friend, but often show rivalry or jealousy, and may fight over a toy. Many infants show an intensified suspicion or fear of strange people and strange places or objects at this age. They defend their attachment to the mother, or her substitute, with 'fierce intensity' (Bowlby 1969). If separated from the affectionate caretaker, they become depressed and withdrawn and they may show the anger of resentment at rejection (Bowlby 1973). To strangers they may offer favourite 'tricks' as if performing a 'magic' form of communication (Trevarthen 1986b). These first performances are part of each child's germinating social identity — understood by family and friends, but baffling to strangers. They function as protosymbols, but their conventional acceptance is limited to a small family circle.

7. There is a momentous change in the infant's mind at about 9 months that brings a capacity for co-operation in the performance of joint tasks and a new level of symbolic understanding. Objects handled by the baby in the presence of other people are identified within common interest and given evaluations between them by 'emotional referencing' (Klinnert *et al.* 1983; Rogoff 1984). The feelings that others have about objects or situations are taken up by the infant and projected on to the things to which they refer. Objects become 'good' or 'bad', 'clean' or 'dirty', 'ours' or 'not ours', 'safe' or 'dangerous', and so on. Thus the child moves outside his or her private feelings about objects, to gain from trusted elders a conventional wisdom about the state of the world. Interest in the gestures and utterances of others leads to compliance with instructions and willing performance of a part in a joint task (Hubley and Trevarthen 1979; Rogoff 1984; Rogoff *et al.* 1988). This we have called 'secondary intersubjectivity' or person-person-object awareness (Trevarthen and Hubley 1978). It shows the child imagining that others can have intentions and feelings that may be of interest and use. The new mental state has been called a 'theory of mind' (Bretherton *et al.* 1981) but we would consider the process neither so abstract nor so debatable as a 'theory'. The motives involved are intermental and co-operative, with immediate functional significance and a controlling role in mental growth (Rogoff 1988).

8. Simultaneously with this new compliant interest in the purposes of others, the 1-year-old infant becomes capable of performing 'acts of meaning' in protolanguage (Halliday 1975) conveying wishes, denials, refusals, curiosity, or satisfaction in the accepted way. These messages are made by combining vocalizations with orientations, posturing, and gestures of the hands. A few sounds resembling words of the mother tongue and some conventional hand gestures are now assimilated into the infant's expressive repertoire. This is a clear step across the threshold to language. It is accompanied by an opening of awareness to grasp conventional acts and standard tools and artifacts (Trevarthen 1988b, c). Indeed, the baby is making a first entry into culture itself, beginning to be a person with pride in knowing how to behave and what to do (Kagan 1982), and is so treated by those who know him or her well. Both the conventional uses of things and roles to be played become of consuming interest for the child (Donaldson 1978).

9. When 1-year-olds are separated from the person whom they most love and trust, they lose playful curiosity about the world and no longer learn to understand it in terms that others can understand. These cognitive functions need to be affectionately supported. Fear of being alone, or reception of insensitive response from other persons, make a 1-year-old unable to explore, uncomprehending (Parkes and Stevenson-Hinde 1982), and broken trust can cause depression or anger at this age.

The second year

The great achievement of the second year is speech, bringing all the advantages of the language others understand (Brown 1958). This is not just a learning of word units, or activation of syntactic structures, but a memory and imagination for shareable ideas that can exist in absence of their referents. The child begins to enter the 'real' and symbolic world of a community. Language opens the way for new relationships and new knowledge (Halliday 1975).

As speech begins, and gestures and skilful manipulation mature, a happy child rapidly learns the meanings of many domestic objects and tasks and basic social conventions (Kagan 1982; Rogoff 1988; Trevarthen 1988a, b). The pretence of 2-year-olds is strong enough to bring out what Vygotsky calls the 'emancipation of meaning' from the simple label of a word for an isolated object or action (Vygotsky 1967/1976). The child does not just learn words merely to name foci of interest in immediate surroundings that are shared with others 'here and now', but, even at the start of speaking, he or she carries out performances and creates messages beyond the limitations of present time and space.

Fragments of daily rituals of eating, drinking, using tools, greeting and so on, and friendly exchanges of objects, particularly with peers, make their appearance in a 2-year-old's pretend play, to the enjoyment of everyone in the family (Dunn and Dale 1984; Miller and Garvey 1984; Stambak et al. 1986). This self-confident mastery of social and cultural skills depends on consistent affectionate support from particular familiar people (Rogoff 1988). Absence of this support, or confused response to the need for it, can push a 2-year-old into speechless, unimaginative withdrawal that may persist for years (e.g. Hunt 1982).

Genetic or pathological factors that distort the child's motivation for human contact can produce arrest of growth towards culture. The autistic child, scarcely identifiable before 2-years-old, becomes conspicuous by withdrawn or angry emotions, an obsession with repetitive experience in isolation, and failure to engage in playful acts with others; for these children, communication seems to be avoided because it threatens the protective sameness of the world, or because emotions of human sharing are intolerable (Richer 1978). On the other side of the relationship, a frightened or depressed mother may fail to carry her perfectly normal child through to a speaking mastery of both serious and playful experiences with simple cultural activities that normally are shared in house and family. In severe social deprivation and neglect, or in war, the effect of maternal destitution, illness, and despair on a toddler can lead to chronic fear and mutism.

Young children and roles in peer society

After 3-years-old, a child can increasingly draw on companionship and affection from peers, independent of, and in parallel with, a close involvement with adults or older siblings in family affections and interests. Language gives a bridge to the imaginations of people of the same or different ages who have different homes and families but share a common culture. Fantasy provides possibilities for recreation of all the dramatic and socially meaningful activities and roles of people in the child's world. Peer friendships built in play give a new base for learning and co-operative action, alternative to parents or other trusted adults (Damon 1983). The play world of nursery-school children proves to be an original, self-contained interpretation of how people act in family and society. Still dependent on affectionate relationships from adults, a child of this age can further extend the sharing of understanding by meeting a peer on new ground, established this time around a position of equality unknown to him from his relationship to adults.

In these new engagements among young peers, one encounters much of the emotional and negotiatory dynamics of the adult world. Here, allowances are made for both good and bad behaviour, as the children enter into conflict, persuasion, empathy, obligation, and endless comparisons (Gottman and Parkhurst 1980). Close friendships are often established, in the positive climate of which children feel free to explore and express their individuality, normally without the danger of irreparable conflict. On the other hand, these same

172

children may be capable of acting in cruelly exclusive or exploitative ways in other circumstances, where there appears a confrontation of will or personalities.

In every culture, the period of 3 to 5 years is one in which children begin to discover wider opportunities for co-operation as well as the harsher aspects of human conflict and aggression. They begin by imitating and comparing, and then gain imagination for real co-operation in a narrative drama where pretended roles complement each other. Emotions of liking and disliking are strongly expressed in play. When play breaks down, fights can become mean and bitter. Friendships and antipathies last, but are open to negotiation and change. Confident and joyful sharing of experiences, and of the motives that give them significance, depends on acceptance of rules and the exercise of communicative skills that facilitate agreement. These skills develop considerably in this preschool phase.

It is important that research on the social characters of children at nursery and primary school age leads to the conclusion that children gain increasing proficiency and understanding of their culture, both by following the didactic authority of adults, and by free and spontaneous expression of companionship and imaginative role playing with other children, or with a few most trusted adults who love the children and like to be with them (Trevarthen 1988b). They have active imagination for learning by sharing beliefs, ideas, and evaluations.

Cultures differ in the ways they support the communicative and co-operative needs of young children (Liederman et al. 1977; Field et al. 1981). Some emphasize talk, factual knowledge, and verbal explanation; others assist the child more in observation and adjustment to the activities and communications of other people, including other children. Some keep infants and toddlers more isolated from daily work and responsibilities people have in society, others have them present when their parents or minders are at work and ready for any responsible help a young child can give. They also differ in their expression of feelings, and in the kinds of emotion they will tolerate or encourage in a child. However, all of them give scope for babies and children to practise increasing communication about actions, experiences, and the performing of roles (Rogoff 1988).

THE NEEDS OF CHILDREN IN SOCIETY: WHAT CAN WE LEARN FROM THEM?

We need trace development no further to make the point that human co-operation has powerful inborn motivations. It is obvious from the first protoconversations at 2 months, through the games of mother with child, to the role-taking fantasies of 3- to 5-year-olds who rapidly absorb both the language and conventions of their culture, that children actively seek co-operation. They 'worm' culture out of their companions within a succession of special relationships that are regulated by emotion. They reason in a common cause with others and trust that social moves will assist their minds to grow freely. These principles have been observed to apply in cultures that value different expressions of individuality and that cultivate different uses of emotions (Trevarthen 1988b). The strategy is universal, even if the particular pattern it takes on is special for each tradition of society.

What does the new description of development have to offer about an adult world where peace and violence have quite a different magnitude from the affiliations and fights of children? First, it puts interpersonal relations in direct contact with the individual's comprehension and use of reality. The child learns how to act and what to believe by sharing. Even though an infant shows signs of a rational individuality, of a cognitive mind that in isolation can rehearse a stock of experiences, solve problems, examine arguments for inconsistency or promise, the ultimate reference for meaning is what makes sense to a community of individuals used to working together with common cause. Second, the motives of the child reveal why unfamiliar ideas are received with mistrust and dislike. As soon as they can speak, children argue about what is so and what is not so; they lay down moral as well as cognitive principles, beginning to negotiate a community of ideas — trying to reach a consensus (Stambak *et al.* 1986). This communication is carried forward in joy and affection, defended with aggression, and lost with fear. Third, conflict with unbelievers or rivals in understanding can become a way of co-operating in a group formed to oppose these 'enemies'; dangerous and wasteful, perhaps, but still a means of retaining the essential community of purpose against the opposition. Because children act out roles that seem to attract admiration and loyalty of others, even the act of killing other people who have been designated as enemies is not beyond them. As they develop responsibility within

174

the system of meanings of their society, their actions become virtuous or evil, and innocence leaves them. At adolescence they gain power and autonomy, and a capacity to have motivations directed by scientific, moral, or religious doctrine spelled out in their culture's myths and texts.

Finally, important lessons about emotions and their regulatory function can be learned from abandoned and mistreated children; with this solemn topic we hope to illuminate the dangers of a remorseless state of rational cunning and to engender faith that positive virtues of compassion, altruism, and hope and humour are as deeply innate and durable as any impulse to fear, attack, and destroy, provided they receive support from the co-operative society for which they are adapted.

Infants deprived of adult care and instruction can show remarkable solidarity, can even create peer communities in which they co-operate and help one another survive. Six orphans, infants from a Moravian concentration camp, aged between 6 months and 1 year, whose parents had been shot or gassed, had been fed like farm animals, but deprived of all affectionate interaction and play with adults. They had only each other for company, until they were liberated after nearly three years of incarceration. Anna Freud and Sophie Dann (1951) cared for and observed them in England, keeping them together, because they clearly had formed close bonds of affection that were entirely confined to their group. They showed no care or trust for any other human beings, children or adults. Indeed, they reacted to adults with hostility, screaming, cursing, and flying into violent displays of anger, only accepting food and clothing from them. In the group itself, however, everything was shared. Unlike the fiction in *Lord of the Flies* and unlike some parent–child relations, too, this is a story of a democratic group in which all took turns to decide what to do and how to organize games. The children were kind and solicitous to each other, behaving as equals. In time, they befriended adults and became essentially normal children, overcoming much of the fear and dislike for older people.

Hunt (1982) describes how retarded infants in an orphanage in Teheran transformed when they were given increased affectionate play by their caretakers. Toys or stimulation of other kinds had little effect; the isolated and depressed children, who were not learning to speak, needed to be assisted with communication.

In many tropical cities children from 3 or 4 years are considered to

175

have a capacity to fend for themselves. Poor mothers, short of food, send them to join street groups of their older brothers and sisters who live by theft and prostitution. In these gangs a style of cunning comradeship, rich in expressions of affiliation, enters into a kind of guerrilla war with the adult commercial world, and this has destructive effects on the children's psychological growth. Feuerstein and Hoffman (1982) and Hundeide (1986) document a catastrophic arrest in cognitive growth, street children in their teens being unable to keep a record of their memories of a supporting past and unable to conceive of a realistic social future. Thinking about practical problems was also markedly retarded. A comparable arrest of socioemotional and cognitive growth has been documented among children in war zones. The effects relate, not so much to the danger, as to confrontation with cruel adults absorbed in patterns of violent co-operation that shut out, or even attack, the children.

Reports from Afghanistan, Iran, Lebanon, Uganda, and many other countries where war is traditional or endemic show how children can join in war. A television crew reporting on the effects of a massacre of parents in a camp in Beirut found toddlers arrested in development by horrors they had seen, struck dumb. At the same time they found young teenagers acting as seasoned fighters, gaining an optimism for the future together, declaring their determination to build a new world in which the rival factions of their elders would come to peaceful understanding. They perceive themselves as able to throw away the bad.

THE EMOTIONS FOR COGNITIVE GROWTH IN INFANCY

It is important to underline that even in infancy, powerful emotions arise in defence of a threatened self (Stern 1985). This self has an inherent duality: an inner coherence and vitality (the 'I') and a reflexive evaluation of relations with certain others (the 'me'). It identifies supportive and destructive potentialities in other human beings, showing affection and joyful companionship in response to trusted familiars and fearful withdrawal from strangers. It resists domination by interfering and unsympathetic advances of others, and, though weak, is capable of defending itself with anger. The balance of emotional communication with the human environment is immediately affected from early years by the quality of support that

176

this self-conscious and emotional individual receives from other human beings.

There can be no doubt that an adult world preoccupied with violence or power, unable to give consistent solicitous affection, impulsive and selfish in action, may deeply damage a young child. Indeed, in early infancy, a negative, depressed, or angry human situation, the baby being in immediate proximity to a person or persons who cannot give affection, can lead the child to refuse life. With older infants, fear and mistrust engendered by unkindness or by wooden indifference from the adult world may lead to arrest of language and thought. Even in infancy, children can begin a defensive adaptation that cripples their curiosity and imagination. They become unsociable, uncultured, specialized in survival and remorseless in exploitation of others.

For the early years, when the child is naturally dependent on affectionate support from a family that has stability in itself, in protected separation from the society at large (Winnicott 1964), physical violence, immoral action in others, and psychopathic motivation are beyond the child's mental grasp. In this sense, babies are innocent and 'wholly' good. Furthermore, the evidence from social psychiatric studies is that remarkable powers of recuperation remain in the human psyche until adolescence, and beyond. Nevertheless, consistent affectionless or violent family life, or destruction of the family, may bring out a latent fighting spirit and evil competitiveness in the very young. Case studies and epidemiological and socio-graphic surveys prove that young children may be emotionally damaged if their human world is full of violence and fear. The innocence of a baby is not a state of indifference and insensitivity (Parkes and Stevenson-Hinde 1982).

PSYCHO-BIOLOGICAL CONSIDERATIONS — WHAT A CHILD'S BRAIN IS AFTER

Research on the brain brings evidence that human evolution has provided, not just greater capacity for storing experiences, but new mechanisms for control of mental relationships. Humans have evolved a greater capacity for sharing experiences and purposes, and the instinctive systems for social communication have expanded along with the neocortex that learns. While this evolution has conferred freedom from tight genetic regulation of sensori-motor adaptations (Chisholm 1985), it has entailed more elaborate genetic control of brain development to provide a mechanism that will regulate uptake of experience from the collective knowledge of the social group (Jolly 1986; Menzel 1974; Humphrey 1976). Comparisons of monkey, ape, and human social groups and especially studies of how the young develop in various primate species, confirm this perspective.

Victor Turner argued (Turner 1983) that anthropology should take note of recent advances in neurobiology and neuropsychology. Inherent differences between the cerebral hemispheres that respond to cultural experience and that acquire skills of culture help explain antithetical systems of belief — rational or realistic on the one hand, and intuitive or mythic on the other. Motivating mechanisms of the core of a human being's brain exercise powerful influence over both how other persons are responded to and communicated with, but also over how consciousness of the world is organized and retained in complementary hemispheric memory stores as a guide to future action. These same systems regulate growth of the brain, including growth of the late maturing tissues of the cortex that retain social and cultural knowledge (Trevarthen 1986a, 1988c).

Psychopathological states, and mental illnesses, demonstrate how genetic factors, disease, or injury may also lead to distortion of human emotion, from inside the fabric of the mind, sometimes producing patently maladaptive anger, fear, or depression, or equally abnormal dependence on affection or affiliative attentions (Heilman and Satz 1985). They show that cognitions for culture, or symbolic imagining, can become aborted or out of tune with the collective understanding as a result of brain pathology.

Evidence from children with autism, Rett's Syndrome, etc. shows that motivations for interpersonal and social life can be deformed by genetic fault (Richer 1978; Trevarthen 1988c). The emotional effects in later life resemble closely those produced postnatally by a human environment so grossly abnormal that it fails to respond to natural needs and acts destructively on children's innate impulses for companionship and learning (Curtiss 1977; Fraiberg 1982).

Psychiatric illnesses that distort or cripple participation in community as well as cognitive mastery of culture's tasks and concepts can be explained in terms of changes in the balance of neurochemical systems with different motivating roles. A major distinction is that made by Hess (1954) between ergic, energy-expending action on the

178

environment, with alert attention to the sensory guidance of forceful movement, and trophic, energy-conserving or nurturant states that respond to needs of the body at rest. Ergotropic motivations give energy to social interactions as well as to mastery of physical challenges. Trophotropic motivations give sensitivity and compassion, satisfying needs for affection, care, and protection, or just for companionship. The two kinds of motive act together in regulation of the life of a community, keeping it intact and making it grow. There is an obvious sexual dimension to this difference.

Turner (1983) contrasts ergic 'animus' with trophic 'anima'. While the sexual distinction cannot be accepted as absolute, it is reasonable and in accordance with neuropsychological and medical science to see a tendency for male and female human minds to be different in a way that conforms to the facts of social groups. Care of young children and regulation of intimate personal relations in the community mostly fall to women, while energetic and rule-governed use of force to master the environment is usually organized by men. Gender roles also interact with the hierarchical organization of society and division of work, which can certainly emphasize or conceal 'biological' differences.

Children are endowed with the same pattern of basic system of emotions as adults and a controlled programme of age regulated change in motivation. Much work remains to be done to clarify how the motives of boys and girls develop as they enter, by stages, into co-operative social life. In the process, natural strengths and weaknesses, and individual differences in motivation for learning, can be either greatly reinforced or suppressed. Families and societies differ in the way they condone or discourage the inherent emotions, some permitting greater expression of ergic or violent feelings, that may lead to open conflict, others insisting on much more restraint, or encouraging quiet and nurturant concern. However, the evidence is that the cerebral material is already patterned to respond in all the possible ways, although with inherently different balances being set in different individuals. We see the creation of the ethical and moral individual, a person who has achieved high correspondence with social ideals, as one form of expression of principles carried into society at his or her birth. We would qualify Kohlberg's cognitive approach to morality (Kohlberg 1981) and support the thesis of Hume (Hume 1739–40) that morals begin in the natural feelings in the family.

HUMAN GENESIS IN CHILDREN'S PLAY

Anthropology, it would appear, took it for granted that it was not worth focusing on the intrinsic sources of life and culture in infants and young children, neglecting especially the latter. Infants have indeed been observed, but only with an interest in the duties and rituals of motherhood. In most anthropological accounts, brief reference to what children feel and do is thought to be adequate, since it has been assumed that children, as soon as they acquire a separate self, simply imitate adults. In this literature metaphors such as 'copycat', 'primitive human', 'personality trainee', 'monkey' are used to characterize the growing child who is thus portrayed as an imperfect human person. Yet Schwartzman (1978) introduces a new metaphor, one reflecting the radical changes of ideas about the nature of consciousness and selfhood — that of the child as 'critic'. Communities of children at play are now seen as performing a critical 'interpretation' of the adult world, as well as of their own performance. By transforming the 'here and now' of their existence, drawing themes and roles mainly, if not exclusively, from their social experiences, children are able to produce their own version of the two worlds. Erikson, in his analysis of the developmental stages in the transformation of personal identity, describes the 2- to 5-year-old child's 'conviction' as: 'I am what I can will freely' at first, and later: 'I am what I can imagine I will be', which respectively correspond to the questions of Autonomy vs. Shame and Initiative vs. Guilt, crucial for the development of an integrated self (Erikson 1963).

Now children's play is seen to have a similar function to adult rituals. Both are analysed in terms of their meta-communicative functions, their power to transform and comment upon everyday experience (Geertz 1972; Handelman 1977). A pioneering contribution to the study of children's play through this perspective has been made by the anthropologist Elizabeth Schwartzman (1978). Applying the notions of Gregory Bateson's theory of communicative play (Bateson 1955), she comes to the conclusion that the play of children is both generative and expressive of personality and culture. She thus raises the play of children from a status of triviality to that of source and essence of everything human. Similar ideas on the nature of play can also be found in other literatures — psychoanalytic (Winnicott 1971) and philosophic (Schiller 1967; Fink 1968; Gadamer, 1975).

CONCLUSIONS

To understand peacefulness in the individual and in society, and to measure it against states of violence and aggression, we need to know how intrinsic motives for mental activity attain peace within the individual, and how these same motives operate in the development of a child and in the propagation of systems of meaning and belief from generation to generation in the historic culture. The checks and balances of the framework of emotion hold the secret of the formation of each individual self-consciousness and of the meaningful society with its codes and artefacts of culture.

The psychology of self-awareness in childhood, the becoming of a self, reveals a driving primary need for the human person to attain a feeling of valid and effective motivation in relation to others. From before the child learns language, there are clear and explicit emotional evaluations of relationships and social roles. The child has internally specified needs to gain a place of importance in the consciousness of significant others. Before speaking, the child begins to act as a practitioner of culturally significant acts and as a knower of meanings that have been created in co-operation between conscious members of a culture.

Early infant communication helps explain the process of cultural inheritance, the transmission process that conveys meanings and technical skills from generation to generation. The human mind does not build itself, at least not in childhood, by power of reason and by mastery of emotions, as Descartes thought, but by emotional regulation of a sharing of ideas with others. Private reason, the thinking 'I' postulated by Descartes, stands in contrast with the idea of a self with feelings that flourish in community. The former depends upon the latter.

Discovery of the co-operative mental powers in infants hitherto unadmitted by any established scientific view of the human mind must change the way we categorize the 'innate' and the 'acquired' in human motivation. Bipolar labels like 'biological' and 'social'; 'instinctive' and 'cultural'; 'emotional' and 'rational' change in meaning and explanatory power; they cease to be mutually exclusive categories. Our meaningful world is not constructed by conquest of animal feelings by divine reason. By co-operating, we reason with feelings; we gain emotional satisfaction from sharing clear reasons that appeal to an agreed sense of what is true or right.

181

The positive value of peacefulness and co-operative creativity in society derives from its constructive opening out of both the individual life and the life of the society. In so far as war is co-operative, it acts to open human beings' lives and feelings within the common purpose of defence or conquest. Violence and destructiveness arise from the pent-up isolation of mutual mistrust whether between individuals who feel enmity, or between societies who perceive one another's meanings and customs to be immiscible and mutually corrosive. Violent feelings and actions require interpretation in terms of co-operation and its defence. Peaceful feelings need no interpretation to be perceived as co-operative. However, they incur the risk of generating an unquestioning trust or idealized understanding that papers over fundamental differences in awareness and fundamental incompatibilities of purpose. Violent feelings and violent agonistic actions exist to separate incompatible perceptions, purposes, customs, and beliefs — for the sake of their continued maintenance.

Desires and motives for reciprocity are not based upon optimization of individual benefits — they are of a structure that seeks joint engagement and co-operative achievement of experience and action. From the start of childhood to old age, and in the growth of a society or a culture throughout its history, motives for mutual benefit are powerfully ascendent. Antagonistic motives gain the upper hand when the co-operative motives are deceived or frustrated, or when their mechanisms in the motivational core of the brain are disorganized by disease or injury.

Violence can be controlled only to the extent that the human environment does not make unreasonable advances and demands. This is true between rival cultures who use their technology to prepare for killing each other, as it is between any two persons, or social groups, who refuse to tolerate differences of understanding.

Individual choice exists, and the feeling of individual freedom is necessary, of course; but it is a borrowed or temporary individuality. The motives and morality of individual action (self-reliance) are a reflection of affiliative involvements in a relationship, many relationships, a group, a society, a culture. Our intentions, desires, imagination and purposes are *inherently* social — biologically social and biologically meaningful. Fundamental moral axes are preestablished in the fabric of a child's mind. They are extended by shared evaluation of the circumstances for acting. Autistic morality is

deviant, motivation for life rendered painful by a breakdown of interpersonal awareness and by loss of the engagement of trust.

© 1989 Colwyn Trevarthen and Katerina Logotheti

REFERENCES

Bateson, G. (1955) 'A theory of play and fantasy', *Psychiatric Research Reports*,
2: 39–51.

Bowlby, J. (1969) *Attachment and Loss, Vol. 1: attachment*, London: Hogarth
Press. New York: Basic Books. Harmondsworth: Penguin Books (1971).

Bowlby, J. (1973) *Attachment and Loss, Vol. 2: separation, anxiety and anger*,
London: Hogarth Press. New York: Basic Books. Harmondsworth:
Penguin Books (1975).

Brazelton, T. B. (1985) 'Development of newborn behavior', in F. Falkner
and J. M. Tanner (eds) *Human Growth* (2nd edn), vol. 2, *Postnatal Growth:
neurobiology*, New York: Plenum, 519–40.

Bretherton, I., McNew, S. and Beeghly-Smith, M. (1981) 'Early person
knowledge as expressed in gestural and verbal communication: when do
infants acquire a theory of mind"?', in M. E. Lamb and L. R. Sherrod
(eds) *Infant Social Cognition*, Hillsdale, NJ: Erlbaum.

Brown, R. (1958) *Words and Things*, New York: Free Press.

Bruner, J. S. (1981) 'Intention in the structure of action and interaction',
in L. P. Lipsitt (ed.) *Advances in Infancy Research*, 1: 41–56, Norwood, NJ:
Ablex.

Chisholm, J. S. (1985) 'Developmental plasticity: an approach from evolutionary biology', in J. Mehler and R. Fox (eds) *Neonate Cognition: beyond the
blooming buzzing confusion*, Hillsdale, NJ: Erlbaum.

Curtiss, S. (1977) *Genie: a psycholinguistic study of modern-day 'wild child'*,
New York: Academic Press.

Damon, W. (1983) *Social and Personality Development*, New York: Norton.

Darwin, C. (1872) *Expression of the Emotions in Man and Animals*, London:
Methuen.

Darwin, C. (1877) 'A biographical sketch of an infant', *Mind*, 2: 285–94.

Donaldson, M. (1978) *Children's Minds*, London: Fontana.

Dunn, J. and Dale, N. (1984) 'I am a Daddy: 2-year-olds' collaboration in
joint pretend with sibling and with mother', in I. Bretherton (ed.) *Symbolic
Play: the development of social understanding*, Orlando, Fla.: Academic Press.

Erikson, E. (1963) *Childhood and Society*, New York: Norton.

Feuerstein, R. and Hoffman, M. B. (1982) 'Intergenerational conflict of
rights: cultural imposition and self-realization', *Journal of School Education*,
58: 1.

Field, T. M., Sostek, A. M., Vietze, P. and Leiderman, P. H. (eds) (1981)
Culture and Early Interactions, Hillsdale, NJ: Erlbaum.

Field, T. M., Woodson, R., Greenberg, R., and Cohen, D. (1982) 'Discrimination and imitation of facial expression by neonates', *Science*, 218:
179–81.

Fink, E. (1968) 'The oasis of happiness: toward an ontology of play', *Yale French Studies*, 41: 19–30.

Fraiberg, S. (ed.) (1982) *Clinical Studies of Infant Mental Health: the first year*, London: Tavistock.

Freud, A. and Dann, S. (1951) 'An experiment in group upbringing', *Psychoanalytic Study of the Child* 6: 127–68.

Gadamer, H. G. (1975) *Truth and Method*, London: Sheed and Ward.

Geertz, C. (1972) 'Deep play: a description of the Balinese cockfight', *Daedalus* 101: 1–38.

Gottman, J. M. and Parkhurst, J. T. (1980) 'A developmental theory of friendship and acquaintanceship processes', in W. A. Collins (ed.) *Development of Cognition, Affect and Social Relations* (The Minnesota Symposia on Child Psychology, Vol. 13) Hillsdale, NJ: Erlbaum.

Halliday, M. A. K. (1975) *Learning How to Mean: explorations in development of language*, London: Arnold.

Handelman, D. (1977) 'Play and ritual: complementary frames of metacommunication', in A. J. Chapman and H. C. Foot (eds) *It's a Funny Thing, Humour*, Oxford: Pergamon.

Heilman, K. M. and Satz, P. (eds) (1985) *Neuropsychology of Human Emotion*, London: Guildford Press.

Hess, W. R. (1954) *Diencephalon: autonomic and extrapyramidal functions*, New York: Grune and Stratton.

Hubley, P. and Trevarthen, C. (1979) 'Sharing a task in infancy', in I. Uzgiris (ed.) *Social Interaction During Infancy* (New Directions in Child Development, Vol. 4), pp. 57–80. San Francisco: Jossey-Bass.

Hume, D. (1739–40) *A Treatise of Human Nature*. L. S. Selby-Bigge (ed.); 2nd edn, rev. P. H. Nidditch. Oxford: Oxford University Press (1978).

Humphrey, N. (1976) 'The social function of intellect', in P. Bateson and R. Hinde (eds) *Growing Points in Ethology*, Cambridge: Cambridge University Press.

Hundeide, K. (1986) 'The indigenous approach to early deprivation and development: a rationale for intervention' (International Child Development Program Report. Psychological Institute, University of Oslo and UNICEF). In preparation.

Hunt, McVicar (1982) 'Towards solutions of early childhood education', in Nir-Jamir, Spodek and Steg (eds) *Early Childhood Education*, New York: Plenum.

Jolly, A. (1986) 'Lemur social behavior and primate intelligence', *Science*, 153: 501–6.

Kagan, J. (1982) 'The emergence of self', *Journal of Child Psychology and Psychiatry*, 23: 363–81.

Klinnert, M. D., Campos, J. J., Sorce, J. F., Emde, R. N. and Svejda, M. (1983) 'Emotions as behavior regulators: social referencing in infancy', in R. Plutchik and H. Kellerman (eds) *Emotion: Theory, Research and Experience*, Vol. 2, New York: Academic Press.

Kohlberg, L. (1981) *Essays on Moral Development* (Vol. 1), New York: Harper and Row.

Liederman, P. H., Tulkin, S. R. and Rosenfeld, R. (eds) (1977) *Culture and Infancy*, New York: Academic Press.

Meltzoff, A. (1985) 'The roots of social and cognitive development: models of man's original nature', in T. Field and N. Fox (eds) *Social Perception in Infants*, Norwood, NJ: Ablex.

Menzel, E. (1974) 'A group of young chimpanzees in a one-acre field', in A. M. Schrier and F. Stollnitz (eds) *Behavior of Non-Human Primates*, Vol. 5, New York: Academic Press.

Midgley, M. (1984) *Wickedness*, London: Routledge and Kegan Paul.

Miller, P. and Garvey, C. (1984) 'Mother-baby role play: its origins and social support', in I. Bretherton (ed.) *Symbolic Play: the development of social understanding*, Orlando, Fla.: Academic Press.

Murray, L. and Trevarthen, C. (1985) 'Emotional regulation of interactions between two-month-olds and their mothers', in T. Field and N. Fox (eds) *Social Perception in Infants*, Norwood, NJ: Ablex.

Papousek, M. and Papousek, H. (1984) 'Learning cognition in the everyday life of human infants', *Advances in the Study of Behavior*, 14: 127–63, New York: Academic Press.

Parkes, C. M. and Stevenson-Hinde, J. (1982) *The Place of Attachment in Human Behavior*, London: Tavistock.

Richer, J. M. (1978) 'The partial non-communication of culture to autistic children', in M. Rutter and E. Schopler (eds) *Autism: a reappraisal of concepts and treatment*, New York: Plenum.

Rogoff, B. (1984) 'Interaction with babies as guidance in development', in B. Rogoff and J. V. Wertsch (eds) *Children's Learning in the Zone of Proximal Development* (New Directions for Child Development, No. 23), San Francisco: Jossey-Bass.

Rogoff, B. (1988) 'The joint socialization of development by young children and adults', in M. Lewis and S. Feinman (eds) *Social Influences and Behavior*, New York: Plenum.

Rogoff, B., Mistry, J., Radziszewska, B. and Germond, J. (1988) 'Infants' instrumental social interaction with adults', in S. Feinman (ed.) *Social Referencing, Infancy and Social Psychological Theory*, New York: Plenum.

Sander, L. (1983) 'Polarity, paradox, and the organizing process in development', in J. D. Call, E. Galenson and R. L. Tyson (eds) *Frontiers of Infant Psychiatry*, Vol. 1, New York: Basic Books.

Schiller, F. (1967) *On the Aesthetic Education of Man*, Oxford: Oxford University Press.

Schwartzman, E. (1978) *Transformations: the anthropology of children's play*, New York: Plenum.

Stambak, M., Ballion, M., Breaute, M. and Rayna, S. (1986) 'Pretend play and interaction in young children', in R. A. Hinde, A. N. Perret-Clermont and J. Stevenson-Hinde (eds) *Social Relationships and Cognitive Development*, Oxford: Clarendon Press.

Stern, D. (1985) *The Interpersonal World of the Infant*, New York: Basic Books.

Trevarthen, C. (1979) 'Communication and cooperation in early infancy. A description of primary intersubjectivity', in M. Bullowa (ed.) *Before Speech: the beginnings of human communication*, London: Cambridge University Press.

Trevarthen, C. (1980) 'The foundations of intersubjectivity: development of interpersonal and cooperative understanding in infants', in D. Olson (ed.) *The Social Foundations of Language and Thought: essays in honor of J. S. Bruner*, New York: Norton, 316–42.

Trevarthen, C. (1983) 'Interpersonal abilities of infants as generators for transmission of language and culture', in A. Oliverio and M. Zapella (eds) *The Behaviour of Human Infants*, London and New York: Plenum, 145–76.

Trevarthen, C. (1984) 'Emotions in infancy: regulators of contacts and relationships with persons', in K. Scherer and P. Ekman (eds) *Approaches to Emotion*, Hillsdale, NJ: Erlbaum, 129–57.

Trevarthen, C. (1985) 'Facial expressions of emotion in mother-infant interaction', *Human Neurobiology*, 4: 21–32.

Trevarthen, C. (1986a) 'Brain science and the human spirit', *Zygon*, 21: 161–200.

Trevarthen, C. (1986b) 'Form, significance and psychological potential of hand gestures of infants', in J-L. Nespoulous, P. Perron and A. Lecours (eds) *The Biological Foundation of Gestures: Motor and Semiotic Aspects*, Hillsdale, NJ: Erlbaum, 149–202.

Trevarthen, C. (1988a) 'Sharing makes sense: intersubjectivity and the making of an infant's meaning', in R. Steele and T. Threadgold (eds) *Language Topics: essays in honour of Michael Halliday*, Amsterdam and Philadelphia: John Benjamins, 177–99.

Trevarthen, C. (1988b) 'Universal cooperative motives: how infants begin to know language and skills of culture', in G. Jahoda and I. Lewis (eds) *Acquiring Culture: cross-cultural studies in child development*, Beckenham, Kent: Croom Helm, 37–90.

Trevarthen, C. (1988c) 'Growth and education of the hemispheres', in C. Trevarthen (ed.) *Brain Circuits and Functions of the Mind: essays in honor of Roger W. Sperry*, New York: Cambridge University Press (in press).

Trevarthen, C. and Hubley, P. (1978) 'Secondary intersubjectivity: confidence, confiding and acts of meaning in the first year', in A. Lock (ed.) *Action, Gesture and Symbol*, London: Academic Press, 183–229.

Trevarthen, C. and Marwick, H. (1986) 'Signs of motivation for speech in infants, and the nature of a mother's support for development of language', in B. Lindblom and R. Zetterström (eds) *Precursors of Early Speech*, Basingstoke, Hampshire: Macmillan, 279–308.

Turner, V. W. (1983) 'Body, brain, and culture', *Zygon*, 18 (3): 221–45.

Vygotsky, L. S. (1967) 'The mental development of the child', *Soviet Psychology*, 12: 62–76. Republished in J. Bruner, A. Jolly and K. Sylva (eds) *Play: its role in development and evolution*, Harmondsworth: Penguin, 1976.

Winnicott, D. W. (1964) *The Child, the Family and the Outside World*, Harmondsworth: Penguin Books.

Winnicott, D. W. (1971) *Playing and Reality*, London: Tavistock.

Chapter Ten

SOCIALITY, NOT AGGRESSION, IS THE KEY HUMAN TRAIT

MICHAEL CARRITHERS

The ethnographic papers in this volume illustrate that some societies value peacefulness to a marked degree in their notions of human persons and in their actual social practices. For many socio-cultural anthropologists such evidence has three implications. First, any explanation of human nature which assumes that humans are innately unpeaceful must be incorrect, for there are many counter-examples. Second, since some societies do not so emphasize peacefulness, then peacefulness is a significant dimension in which human societies vary. Hence, third, a successful general explanation of human nature would have to allow for variability in that dimension, as in the many other dimensions in which human societies differ. Such a general explanation is found in the theory of culture, which asserts that humans possess a capacity for culture, for a learned repertoire. The cultural capacity is labile, enabling humans to learn quite different cultural repertoires, and therefore to differ profoundly in their practices and their notions of persons.

Such arguments have shown their usefulness, but they do suffer from important weaknesses. To depend on the counter-examples alone is weak, for someone espousing aggression as the key to human nature could adduce their own counter-counter-examples. The Semai of Malaysia, for example, are a peaceful society who were supposedly turned into deadly soldiers (Konner 1984: 205). Though the Balinese have been thought peaceful, their history is drenched in blood, as Leo Howe observes in his paper. Or a careful investigation of the supposed peaceful societies might in fact reveal innate aggression, as Konner (1984: 204) alleges for the !Kung.

To depend on the theory of culture is also weak, for the aggression-ist has two possible retorts. First, the theory of aggression follows from evolutionary theory and is founded in biological evidence. It shows how other continuities between humans and animals are matched by a continuity in innate aggression. And on this basis it can easily accommodate as well a difference between humans and animals, namely the capacity for culture, so long as culture is not assumed to override the older evolutionary tendency to aggression. Culture, on the other hand, is only a theory of the differences between humans and animals, it ignores the continuities, and to that extent explains less and brings less evidence into play.

Second, the aggressionist could argue that the theory of culture is really just circular. Humans are culturally labile. How do we know that? Because they form very different societies, some peaceful and some not. Why do they do that? Because they are culturally labile. The theory of culture is no better than its examples, while the theory of aggression is a higher level theory, showing hidden causal explanations.

The culture theorist could reply by rejecting the application of grand evolutionary theory to the fine grain of human life . . . and the argument could continue without end, largely because of differences in training and outlook between biologists and anthropologists. I want to make what I hope is a more constructive proposal, a research programme which is consistent with the insights of both culture theory and evolutionary biology — though aggressionism as such will have to be discarded.

The key to such a programme is *sociality*. Sociality points to a continuity between humans and other animals, especially other primates; but human sociality is also significantly different. Evolutionary theory can explain the formation of distinctly human sociality, and sociality in its turn can then account for the fact of diversity among human cultures. My intention is not at all to replace the notion of culture, but to argue that sociality is a necessary precondition for the existence of culture. Sociality allows for peacefulness to vary among societies, though it does imply that some measure of peacefulness is a feature of all societies.

But first it will be necessary to clear the way for sociality by dealing with aggressionism, which has dominated so much of our evolutionary thinking on human nature. Only by dealing firmly with its distractions can we go on to the more fruitful programme of sociality.

THE DEFINITION OF POP, A TERM OF ART

I will interrogate a recent exposition of innate aggression, but let me begin from Philip Kitcher's splendid and rigorous book, *Vaulting Ambition: sociobiology and the quest for human nature* (1985). He writes of 'pop socio-biology' as a distinct historical movement, a collection of writings which appeal 'to recent ideas about the evolution of animal behaviour in order to advance grand claims about human nature and human social institutions' (1985: 14–15). The term 'socio-biology' need not detain us, for it can be used most simply of any attempt to explain social behaviour in evolutionary terms.

'Pop' is more interesting, and I wish to use it as a term of art. I think its sense is twofold. First, Kitcher uses the term to mean 'popular': that which is designed to be, and is, read widely. Pop socio-biology is certainly pop in this sense, especially in the United States. Second — here I go beyond Kitcher — such works can be pop because they speak to some established cultural representation, some generally held view which prepares a readership to accept a work. Carlos Castaneda's hugely successful books, for example, reaffirm an old collective representation in our civilization, that of the hollowness of bureaucratic reason and the wisdom of the apparently uncivilized. But such works can be novel as well, as Castaneda's are novel in using the figure of a Mexican healer. The diagnostic feature of being pop lies in the effect of *re*confirmation, however novel the means of reconfirmation.

We can go further. Such reconfirmations are perceived to be weighty, and therefore achieve popularity, just insofar as they have moral consequences. The reconfirmation is of a moral vision, a view of what human beings are in the light of what they should be.

The ethologist Nicholas Thompson shows how a theory of innate aggression has such force:

> I taught an adult education course under the naive presumption that I would have to sell the significance of animal behaviour to the average man-in-the-street. On the contrary, my chief problem was to convince the man-in-the-street not to take every monkey anecdote to heart in the raising of his children. My students were New York citizens who rode the subways and daily saw the spectacle of hundreds of people . . . compressed peaceably into an intimacy rarely shared between husband and wife in our society, much less by strangers. Yet despite this spectacle, my students were eager to

189

interpret the handful of aggressive incidents which occur daily in the subways as evidence that man's simian nature ill suits him to live in an urban environment. (Thompson 1976: 226)

Here Thompson captures the moral authority wielded by innate aggression, and indeed the appropriateness of the term pop as applied to it. The reconfirmed vision perhaps concerns innate depravity, or conservative authoritarianism, as Rose *et al.* (1984) argue. In any case writings that confirmed such a view would 'satisfy some very deep general moral yearnings'.

This quotation is from Ernest Gellner (1979: 168), who argues that scientific or scholarly empiricism demands the rejection 'of a certain class of possible worlds', namely those which neatly fit some established moral opinion. Gellner's is a strong, indeed too strong, injunction. I would prefer to argue that, if the aggressionist case does not reconfirm a moral vision, reconfirmation creates serious doubt about its reliability; but we should go on to ask whether its supporting evidence is drawn together by that moral vision, or by a dispassionate theory.

AN ARGUMENT FOR INNATE AGGRESSION

Melvin Konner's *The Tangled Wing: biological constraints on the human spirit* (1984) is evidently intended as an introductory text on human behavioural biology, but it is a good deal more as well. It brings together a very large number of references concerning the biological bases of human behaviour; it presents these data in a very readable form; and it clothes the data in evocative literary quotations and wide-ranging reflections on the human condition.

The book begins and ends with the issue of human violence, and its general argument is that a finer understanding of the biological basis of human behaviour may one day allow us some control of violence. The argument can be briefly stated. Physiological evidence shows that there are structures in the nervous and endocrine systems of animal species and humans whose function is aggressive. These structures have evolved under natural selection to enable organisms to survive and reproduce. Ethological evidence further shows that aggression is a widespread, even universal, trait of both animal and human behaviour. And ethnographic and historical evidence only

190

reinforces the conclusion that aggression is therefore inherent in human nature.

Konner is especially concerned with human emotions, such as rage, lust, and fear, which he regards as springing directly from evolved physiological structures. If we are eventually to learn to control emotions and therefore human behaviour, the research underpinning such control will carry us 'from the physiological laboratory through the field setting of the natural historian to the annals of human history' (1984: 188).

Whether we regard the book as pop or not depends on our understanding of the book's form. Someone persuaded by Konner might take the following view. The book is founded upon the frequent passages in which Konner presents evidence. Interleaved with such passages are others which follow logically from the biological evidence and proffer a social and moral interpretation. The third sort of writing, which frames the whole book, blends the biological and the moral together. These passages are the literary dressing which make the book palatable to the non-specialist, but the reasoned substance is found in the biological evidence and its social interpretation.

A sceptic would take a different view. The framing passages set out the moral vision. The moral and social interpretation follows from the moral vision. And the evidence itself is selected and presented to support the moral vision.

The chapter on 'Rage' sets out Konner's argument on innate aggression in a nutshell. That chapter (Konner 1984: 175–207; I will not give page references hereafter) begins as follows:

On July 8, 1977, Richard James Herrin, a twenty-three-year-old Yale senior, went to the bedroom of Bonnie Jean Garland, a classmate and sometime girl friend in whose home he was then a guest, and bludgeoned her to death in her sleep with a claw hammer. He then fled from the scene . . . to Coxsackie, New York, where he surrendered himself to a priest and confessed his crime. He told the arresting officer that he had planned to kill the young woman and commit suicide. The precipitating cause was romantic rejection; Garland had evidently broken off with Herrin.

At the trial, he pleaded not guilty by reason of temporary mental defect or disease.

Konner goes on to recount, in the same style, the trial and sentencing of Herrin ('eight and one-third to twenty-five years'). Then

Konner moves on directly to the case of Wang Yungtai, who did something very similar in Peking with a hammer to a woman of his acquaintance, 'on November 18, 1978, while Richard James Herrin awaited trial'. Wang, too, confessed and gave himself up. Konner recounts Wang's trial and sentencing.

The cases are alike, Konner then explains, in the fundamental structure of emotions. 'The young man experiences lust [though] we would not be able to distinguish [the lust] from what we . . . call love'. 'A deep sense of joy' must then occur, at the prospect of 'shared life'. But then such hopes are frustrated, and at the prospect of loss fear supervenes. 'There arises from this fear a feeling of rage . . . in these cases, the rage is sufficiently strong to produce homicidal violence.' And finally grief appears, 'a mourning for the losses'.

So far Konner argues the similarity between the two events. He then explains their significance, which lies in the 'gamut of emotions' which 'compel our interest more than does many another homicide'. Lust, love, joy, hope, fear, rage, grief, mourning: all human life is there. 'We are able to sympathize with the conflict' because it 'touches every corner of the human unconscious'. Such cases 'exemplif[y] the widest range of human — or, indeed, nonhuman — emotions'.

These passages seem to belong to the literary framework, and Konner admits as much by referring to them as a 'digression'. However, there are two reasons for regarding them as more than mere packaging. First, as the chapter progresses he increasingly takes the homicides to be evidence in themselves. They are used as if they handily summarize all evidence on emotion in human behaviour. Second, the very journalistic or police court prose in which Konner presents the homicides conveys a sense, not of suggestive imagery, but of hard factuality. Moreover the interpretation of the homicides' emotions is presented in an authoritative style, as though it were an actual account of the two murderers' states of mind.

So in fact Konner means the homicides to be evidence, not part of the literary frame. But this in turn creates difficulties. For whereas elsewhere he cites scholarly and scientific sources, here he refers only to a pair of newspaper articles. Moreover, the reconstruction of the homicides' states of mind is wholly unsupported. It is in fact pure speculation, based on no more than the newspaper cuttings alone. The significance of the homicides, and the emotional scenario attributed to them, is Konner's creation, aided perhaps by the sensationalism of his sources.

There is, however, one strong, if far from adequate, reason why someone might accept such an uncritical, unreliable, and deceptive account: Konner's reconstruction touches on some of our deepest collectively held notions about behaviour and the judgement of behaviour. Here is raw emotion as we represent it to ourselves in fiction and myth; here is crime; here is suffering; and here is stern retribution. Konner's story enjoys the same plausibility that a television script might enjoy, the same plausibility which journalists daily recreate through their selective accounts of events. Konner need not support his reconstruction, for it seems intuitively right, another entertaining and morally pregnant narrative of the human depravity with which the newspapers daily regale us.

This is pop moralizing with a vengeance, and in fact Konner does move directly from the speciously interpreted homicides to moral judgement:

> I feel a great impatience with behavioral and social scientists . . . who try to explain away acts of selfishness or brutality by reference to psychological facts and principles. . . . [Such] principles have little place in a court of law. The law is not an instrument of explanation, it is an instrument of justice, of protection, of redress of grievances, and of punishment of wrongdoing.

He then observes that 'to explain is not to explain away, and to understand, in my opinion, is not necessarily to forgive'.

This passage reflects the moral stance taken by Konner throughout the book. In his view humans are to be described ultimately not in biological or psychological, but in moral terms: selfishness, brutality, justice, punishment, wrongdoing. The message is that biology confirms the censurable depravity which we already knew to be deeply graven in human nature. Konner writes as though the discovery of such depravity were an exciting adventure in biological research, but in reality there is no discovery at all, only the reconfirmation of a deeply held view.

Moreover, this pop moralizing deeply affects the evidence which he presents in the rest of the chapter. Let me begin with Konner's reading of ethnographic data. While discussing the two homicides he offers the following remarks; his intention is to connect the murder cases with broader patterns of human behaviour:

> In *many* societies, including so-called primitive ones, young women

193

occasionally meet death at the hands of men who supposedly love them, and in a *wide range of these societies* such crimes make up a *substantial percentage* of homicides. *Frequently* there is a motive of rejection and/or jealousy, there has been no other criminal behaviour, there is suicide or attempted suicide, and there is contrition.

I have emphasized the phrases which evidently refer directly to ethnographic facts, and which seem to constitute a quantitative argument. That argument is difficult to make out, for no figures are offered to give flesh to the terms 'many', 'occasionally', 'wide range', etc. Moreover the piling up of such terms compounds the obscurity. What Konner seems to suggest is that the sort of homicide which he has reconstructed from the newspapers happens so frequently everywhere that we should take notice. But he nowhere offers clear or substantial evidence to support such a notion, and that in a book otherwise richly larded with citations. As regards violent human behaviour itself, the subject of the whole book, Konner is confident that his opinions stand without evidence: he takes his biological/moralizing account as read, and depends on the pervasiveness among his readers of his own pop attitude to bestow plausibility on his remarks.

The ethological evidence is particularly important to Konner's case, for from ethology he draws not only a large number of examples, but also the definition of aggression itself. He writes that ethologists 'classify . . . very distinct sequences of behaviour under the general rubric of "aggressive" because they . . . have the effect, in some sense intended, of inflicting damage upon another creature'. Under aggression he then catalogues phenomena such as predation and fighting behaviour in cats, rough-and-tumble play, intraspecific fighting, defence, forced copulation, the establishment of dominance hierarchies, and the two murder cases.

Konner does mention many of the difficulties involved in drawing such varied behaviour into a single category; but he never deals with these difficulties, and never deviates from the line that aggression is a real entity common to all these behaviours.

Konner draws a great deal of his evidence from the behaviour of cats, so let us turn to the authoritative source, Paul Leyhausen's monograph *Cat Behaviour* (1979), which concerns domestic cats and related species. At the end of his exhaustive description Leyhausen considers the extent to which cat behaviour includes systems —

aggressive, or sexual, or nurturing, for example — which are clearly differentiated from each other. In other words, is aggression (among others) a single behavioural system, which would be underpinned by a distinct physiological system?

Leyhausen assembles some of the individual elements of cat behaviour that seem to relate to aggression (1979: 294-5). He then argues, first, that many of the movements which appear under fighting also appear under attachment behaviour, that is, in mother-infant, sexual, and peer group relations. Hence there are no individual gestures or movements which unambiguously indicate aggression. Second, he notes that sequences or combinations of movements are no better indicators of aggression, for the complexity of actual behaviour transcends such an idealization (1979: 295). Leyhausen concludes that the category of aggression is irrelevant to the actual character of cat behaviour:

> [This evidence presented in a table] shows more convincingly than any amount of words how absurd it is to think it possible to extract . . . 'Aggression' from all this and yet leave the remainder of the system intact. At the outside, only a few of the many possible and actually occurring combinations of a number of behaviour patterns recorded here constitute 'Aggression'! (1979: 296)

So far Leyhausen is only questioning the applicability of the notion of aggression to the actual description of cats. But elsewhere he draws a more general conclusion: 'With a hammer I can knock in a nail, smash a window, or kill a man; there is about as much sense in lumping all these together as "use of hammer" is in calling all the various forms of attack "aggression".' (1979: 133)

In other words, the fault in the category 'aggression' is that it aggregates types of behaviour whose origins, pattern, physiological structure, and consequences or functions are quite different. For example, as Leyhausen demonstrates at length (and as Immelmann [1980: 116, 138] agrees) predation is quite distinct in its behavioural pattern and physiological structure from intraspecific fighting. So we might reasonably regard predation as a function, and treat it as a character which evolves, but we cannot do the same with 'aggression', since aggression is just an arbitrary concatenation of functions and behaviours. Indeed Konner himself is forced to list nine quite different adaptive functions which might be catalogued under 'aggression'. It is a category so broad that, far from explaining an

195

underlying pattern, it obscures the actual patterns in behaviour and the multitude of causes that explain behaviour. As more sober writers on the biological basis of 'aggression' stress (Siann 1985; Rose *et al.* 1984; Klama 1988), 'aggression' is a chimera, one which is now dissolving and being superseded by more complex and interesting biological notions.

But if 'aggression' is not a reliable biological term of art, it nevertheless possesses a strange compulsion, and we cannot dismiss it out of hand. How should we regard the notion?

The Oxford English Dictionary defines aggression as 'an unprovoked attack'. The aggressionist case concentrates on the notion 'attack', but the emphasis should rather be on 'unprovoked', which points to the judgement made concerning the attack, a judgement evoking grievance and a sense of injury. It is true that 'aggression' is a peculiarly English language term. I can think of no exact equivalent in, for example, the South Asian languages known to me. But the notions of grievance and injury can be translated sensibly into those languages, as I suppose into others, and I think such notions point to something general about human nature.

But they do not point to what Konner assumes they do, some grand inherited pattern of violence in humans and animals. Rather, they point to a common human experience, the sense of grievance, and beyond that to a common problem of human life, the fact that our acts affect one another, but our interests, rationalizations, and circumstances differ from one to another. Interests differ, and such differences lead to action, sometimes deleterious to others. Rationalizations differ: one person's crime of passion is another's mere homicide, one group's theft is another's rightful appropriation, one society's notion of manly deportment is another's notion of inhuman behaviour. And circumstances differ, so that one person or group may find it compelling to harm others. What occasions the harm and the sense of grievance cannot be summarized in a single cause, but is complex and diverse, explicable only through a variety of historical, social, economic, political, psychological, or cultural factors.

But all societies do have to deal with differences of interest, deleterious actions, and the sense of grievance. These are experienced as a problem because we are, as I shall argue shortly, social animals who rely greatly on relations with others. And so all societies erect a morality, an aesthetic standard for action which demands some basic level of peacefulness. In this respect the English word 'aggression' is part of English speakers' armoury of peacefulness, part of our way of representing and censuring deleterious actions toward one another. It is perhaps peculiar among us that some, such as Konner, wish to read that moral judgement on to nature and back from nature on to human society. But it is inevitable that words such as 'aggression' possess a coercive and emotive power.

THE KEY HUMAN TRAIT: SOCIALITY

If aggressionism is not a successful research programme, what is? First, such a programme would have to provide a plausible evolutionary story which allowed both for continuity between humans and other species, and for differences. Second, to set the notion of culture on a firmer footing, it would have to show not just that there are different cultures, but some way in which such differences in culture could arise among humans. That is, it would have to allow for cultural change in human history, cultural change that could create the variability in peacefulness which other papers here demonstrate so decisively.

I believe that the notion of *sociality* meets all these criteria. For the moment let sociality simply refer to the capacity for complex social behaviour. Humans share some traits of sociality with social mammals in general, including for example wolves and deer; they share rather more with their close relatives, such as baboons, gorillas, and chimpanzees; but human sociality is evidently more complex and powerful altogether. A research programme on sociality would involve far less physiological or endocrinal research, but far more attention to the actual details of human history and social forms, to social and cognitive psychology, and to the ethology of social primates.

A successful evolutionary explanation of human sociality would have to fulfil two criteria. First, such an explanation would have to be what Kitcher calls an 'ambitious Darwinian history' which would specify 'not only the changes that take place along an evolving lineage but also the causes of such changes' (1985: 57). In the case of human sociality the evolving lineage is that of hominids, humans and their nearest, but extinct, ancestors. We cannot directly compare present-day human social behaviour with that of our nearest ancestors, of whom we have only fossil evidence; so we are left to infer traits of ancestral human sociality from living species of apes and monkeys, humans' next nearest relatives. There might be many evolutionary causes, but I will concentrate on natural selection. My assertion is that specifically human sociality evolved through the selective advantage conferred upon individuals who possessed increasingly powerful sociality.

The second criterion is that the causal account must refer in the first instance to properties of individuals. Evolutionary theorists have come on good grounds to prefer the notion of individual to that of group selection (see, for example, Sober 1984, especially chapters 7 – 9). So, in the first instance, the sociality which evolves must be a property of individual organisms, namely just the capacity to enter into complex social behaviour. This is a departure from the way in which the term sociality has generally been used among biologists, who have stressed it as a quality, not of individuals, but of groups. Wilson, for example, attributes ten qualities to sociality, including group size, cohesiveness, and differentiation of roles (Wilson 1975: 16 – 18). Only one of his criteria, 'fraction of time devoted to social behaviour', refers unambiguously to individual cognitive or emotive properties, and that only indirectly. On this showing sociality is only an attribute of groups or populations, not of individuals, whose attributes are left unspecified.

Groups must necessarily play a leading role in a causal, evolutionary account of sociality, but it is the capacity of individuals to be in groups which evolves, not groups themselves. Groups, we might say, are a consequence of sociality, while sociality itself is a property of the individuals forming the group but not of the group as a whole. Groups have a history, but only individuals have an evolutionary history. In the human lineage the direction of evolution would be for individual capacities to increase, and group complexity would follow.

The argument is drawn chiefly from that of Humphrey (1976, reprinted 1983). He takes as a baseline the already established complexity of social behaviour among primates, and tries to answer the question: how could human social capacities and social complexity have evolved from that of the other primates? The question assumes, in other words, the complexly varied forms of human social life at the end of the story, and the relatively less complex social life of known primates at the beginning.

The core of his argument is this:

Social primates are required by the very nature of the system they create and maintain to be calculating beings; they must be able to calculate the consequences of their own behaviour, to calculate the likely behaviour of others, to calculate the balance of advantage and loss — and all this in a context where the evidence on which their calculations are based is ephemeral, ambiguous and liable to change, not least as a consequence of their own actions. In such a situation, 'social skill' goes hand in hand with intellect, and here at last the intellectual faculties required are those of the highest order. (1976: 309)

He argues that the adaptive advantage of the intellect associated with sociality does not lie in technical invention. 'Even in those species which have the most advanced technologies [such as the Gombe chimpanzees] the exams are largely tests of knowledge rather than imaginative reasoning.' The techniques are either trial-and-error, which are not very effective, or are learned from others. Humphrey emphasizes learning from others. He suggests that the possession of technology at first presupposed little technological intelligence. For the emphasis would have to lie upon achieving and maintaining successful relations with elders from whom techniques are acquired, not on inventing the techniques. On Humphrey's account, there is directed selection *for* social intelligence, since that is the trait related to survival and reproductive success, but only coincidental selection *of* instrumental, technical intelligence, as a sort of unintended consequence of social intelligence.

So society functions in the first instance as a sort of 'polytechnic school' to teach simple subsistence skills. Society allows a long period of dependence in which the young experiment and learn, in continuous contact with the teachers. And since this is an adaptively advantageous pattern, selective pressure will make for longer periods of dependency in childhood and greater age for the elders.

But, as a consequence of the growing diversity of ages and relative positions, there will be a growing complexity of differing interests.

Thus the stage is set within the 'collegiate community' for considerable political strife. To do well for oneself whilst remaining within the terms of the social contract on which the fitness of the whole community ultimately depends calls for remarkable reasonableness (in both literal and colloquial senses of the word). It is no accident therefore that [humans], who of all primates show the longest period of dependence . . ., the most complex kinship structures, and the widest overlap of generations within society, should be more intelligent than chimpanzees, and chimpanzees for the same reasons more intelligent than cercopithecids. (Humphrey 1976: 310)

So far I have sketched the relevant features of Humphrey's essay, which is suggestive rather than exhaustively argued. How might it be refined? First, what more exact account could be given of the proposed Darwinian history?

1.   At the beginning of the story some relatively low level of sociality — social intelligence, in Humphrey's terms — was characteristic of the social primates even before humans evolved. The adaptive advantage was just to preserve certain survival techniques through learning. The form of sociality here is roughly that found in present-day chimpanzee populations.

2.   Then increased sociality arose among one group of social primates, namely humankind's direct ancestors. Humphrey does not imagine that among this group the advantage of increased sociality need have been very great at first, but the difference was enough to separate ancestral humans from the rest. This increased dependence on sociality was associated with increased social complexity within the group, a complexity at first based on increased age differences, but also probably on a more complex division of labour in subsistence activities. The selective advantage bestowed on this now diverging population would probably lie in the increased reliability and productiveness of resource exploitation consequent upon a more complex division of labour and food sharing (Isaac 1983).

3.   The third step also presupposes the selective advantage of a more complex division of labour . . . or rather, to concentrate on individual selection, of successfully reproducing as a member of a group with a more complex division of labour. As social complexity became a yet more important part of the environment in which sociality was expressed, an evolutionary ratchet was set up, so that sociality could only increase. That is, individuals now had to deal, not only with other individuals, but with others in an increasingly wide variety of different relations to themselves. These increasingly complex social relations worked as selective pressures favouring those whose social capacities were superior. Sociality conferred the ability to outsmart

others, but also to understand and co-operate better with others, both of which were advantageous in the new order.

On the other hand, heightened sociality of the members of the population would in turn have allowed groups to vary and grow more complex at a yet faster rate. Indeed the rate of social change and increased complexity must have been more rapid than the change in sociality at every point, or there would have been no selective pressure for increased sociality.

4. But once this evolutionary ratchet had done its work, it had produced a peculiar consequence unforeseen by that 'blind watch-maker', the evolutionary process. For it conferred on our species a powerful capacity to develop and alter social forms far too quickly for evolutionary, genetic changes to track closely. This sophisticated sociality could now allow for very great variation between groups. New forms of interdependence were possible, along with new forms of relations not only within, but between varying groups. Social organizations far larger and more intricate than the gathering and hunting bands of stages 2 and 3 could be created. And the intricacies of relations within, but also between, such groups allowed for new forms of causation, causation we recognize as social, political, economic, or cultural. Such forms of causation are not reducible to those of selective pressure or evolutionary adaptation, but are in fact a feature peculiar to human social life.

In other words: once full human sociality was established, it allowed for human history, a history of change, of development, above all of the proliferation of different forms of social life.

SOCIALITY ANATOMIZED

What then were the features of this ability of individual humans to create ever more intricate and varied forms of life?

One feature of sociality must be what David Premack has called 'pedagogy' (Premack 1984, 1986). Pedagogy involves a complex of abilities through which an individual 'observes another, judges him or her according to some standard, and intervenes to bring the novice's behaviour into conformity with [a] standard' (Premack 1984: 18). Premack argues that the sort of baseline cognitive abilities which we can impute to the chimpanzee in transmitting techniques are not pedagogy proper, but only imitative learning, albeit of a high standard. Chimpanzees may be able to transmit some social skills through training, but such training does not involve an aesthetic standard.

By contrast, full-blown human pedagogy involves, first, a sophisticated aesthetic judgement of what constitutes a good performance, whether in social or technical skills. Second, it involves representing the difference between the pedagogue's own ability and that of the novice, and therefore a high degree of both self-consciousness and consciousness of others. And third, pedagogy presupposes the disposition to invest time in training without any immediate return on the investment of time and energy. In terms of the Darwinian, evolutionary history, the payoff for pedagogy is a deferred one. In this sense pedagogy achieves the functional equivalent of what John Maynard Smith calls 'the social contract game', whose form is this: 'I will [co-operate]; if any other individual [defects], I will join in punishing him; if any other individual fails to join in punishing, I will treat this as equivalent to [defecting]' (Maynard Smith 1983: 452). Maynard Smith assumes that such a stable strategy could only be found in humans, who — to put it in Premack's terms — possess an aesthetic standard on which to judge behaviour. Moreover, Maynard Smith's social contract game is only a functional equivalent, not an exact one, because it does not recognize that 'punishment' and 'joining in punishment' can be achieved in the developmental process, not merely as transactions between adults. But in any case, pedagogy ensured that the aesthetic standard taught through pedagogy had some longevity, some capacity to endure, if only eventually to change.

Let us pursue this reasoning further. In the evolving human lineage, pedagogy was concerned with an aesthetic standard which applied increasingly to action toward others. For it was action between humans, not upon objects, which was the focus of change. There was therefore a specifically *social* aesthetic standard, and that standard had to grow more abstract, more powerful, and indeed more complex just because of the increasing complexity of the group. So the social aesthetic standard came, perhaps very gradually, to resemble what we might think of as morality or social rules. But I will adhere to the term 'aesthetic standard', for it at least allows for an essential fuzziness, an unavoidable indeterminacy, in the application of the standard.

This indeterminacy in fact raised a problem for both the pedagogue and the novice. For the aesthetic standard had to be applied to circumstances which were themselves shifting, ambiguous, and intricate, the ephemeral result of the actions of many individuals, including oneself. From the pedagogue's point of view, the problem was to understand the intentions and propensities of many others and the consequences of well- or ill-formed actions in that more complicated environment. For the novice, the problem was to understand what standard was appropriate in which context.

The powerful cognitive capacity underlying such competence is perhaps best summarized as *narrativity*, which involves two capacities. The first is the capacity to cognize, not merely immediate relations between oneself and another, but many-sided human interactions carried out over a considerable period. We might say: in the evolving lineage humans came to understand *characters*, which embody the understanding of propensities and intentions in oneself and many different others; and *plots*, which show the consequences and aesthetic evaluations of a multifarious series of actions. Narrativity, in other words, is not a matter of telling stories, but of representing long complex series of actions. And as such, narrativity must underlie the developed human propensity for exchange, that is, for prestations and deferred counter-prestations.

Second, narrativity allows for the identification of characters and plots with present circumstances. It allows, in other words, for the application of social aesthetic standards in real situations. In present-day humans narrativity is intimately involved with the use of language to propose interpretations of situations (see Carrithers 1983: Chapter 5; Bruner 1986). And once language enters the picture, narrativity allows the pedagogue to convey moral standards vividly through fictional or historical narration. But narrativity is a social, not a linguistic skill, and we can conceive of narrativity apart from the production and reception of stories in language.

I think we must conceive under sociality another feature as well, that of *creativity*, inventiveness, or imagination. Humphrey writes of calculation, which suggests that sociality is a narrow computative skill which arrives at one correct answer in unvarying circumstances. But from time to time he in fact writes also of creativity and imagination, and that especially when he considers the sheer difficulty of the task of social understanding and social action. Similarly, for practical, every-day thinking, Sylvia Scribner writes that 'beneath the surface of [practical thinking] lie continuing acts of creativity — the invention of new ways of handling old and new problems' (Scribner 1986: 28). She considers relatively simple technical problems, but the social world is more intricate and variegated, so the capacities of sociality must be correspondingly more creative.

Indeed narrativity is inherently creative both in constructing narratives and in connecting them with the real world: as Michelle Rosaldo writes, it is not just a matter of applying 'schematic programs', but of using 'associative chains and images that tell what can be reasonably linked up with what' (1984: 140). The force of 'reasonably' here is that more than one narrative line, and more than one identification of narrative with actual circumstances, are possible, so in any particular case the associative, creative linking may take more than one form.

By the same token, creativity must also be part of both learning and pedagogy. As the evolved human capacity now stands, children (Shotter 1984: 92) bring imagination to the task of learning social aesthetic standards, as indeed do anthropologists, travellers, captives, outmarrying women and inmarrying men when they begin again from scratch in a new society. Pedagogues, on the other hand, must frame the moral rules imaginatively to conform with fluid, changing circumstances; and in so framing the rules, teachers change them. Though we think of creativity as being extraordinary, it is in fact a routine part of the human constitution.

Finally, sociality includes another feature which is not narrowly cognitive, what Trevarthen and Logotheti in their paper here call 'intersubjectivity'. We automatically think of human abilities as being directed toward a world of objects, but sociality is directed wholly toward other individuals. In an evolutionary perspective this must point to an emotive and conative change, an increasing dependency and openness toward conspecifics. Humans are available to each other, and their abilities are only developed and transformed by others and in respect of a social environment. The capacities of sociality may be *in* individuals, but are completed only *between* them.

The full implications of this feature of sociality are radical: for it means that the basic image cannot be of a collection of individuals being subject directly to collective representations, as Mauss proposed (1979: 22–3). Still less can we think simply of an abstracted individual confronting culture, as Geertz sometimes assumes (1975: 67–8). The absolutely minimal image must be of an interacting pair; that pair must be inherently different from each other, their difference involving mutual imaginative construction of each other; and they must in turn be conceived as part of a larger social world possessing its own momentum of change. Only with that image firmly in mind can we write as well of aesthetic standards or collective representations or culture.

Finally, sociality need not imply a purely sunny view of human nature. This case has been put best by Schick (1984), who writes that humans act not only in naked self-interest, but also attend to each other's interests. As he puts it, humans act 'socially' (1984: 89), which might mean some of the following, as expressed in Schick's style of examples: Adam chooses to oblige Eve, or to spite her, to obey her or to disobey her, to foster or to hinder her. So on this account sociality does involve a responsiveness to each other as persons with distinct interests and attributes (1984: 80–7); but such responsiveness is by no means necessarily amicable or harmonious. Enemies in a vendetta, for example, are meticulously responsive to each other. Insofar as social aesthetic standards enshrine particular, local forms of mutual responsiveness, those standards may emphasize peacefulness, or they may not. From the point of view of sociality, human societies are free to be peaceful or bellicose, according to their local histories. The paper by Roy Willis in this volume demonstrates such a history.

SOCIALITY, CULTURE, AND HISTORY

From Franz Boas (Stocking 1982: 161–233) to Marshall Sahlins (1976) the primacy of cultural variability in human life has served to refute simplistic biological stories about humans. The sheer variety of human cultures, great cultural differences between groups genetically very close, close cultural similarities between people with very different genetic heritages, and the failure of human kin arrangements to conform to biological expectations are all evidence to the point. But, as I began by pointing out, the notion of culture (or collective representations) assumed such cultural variability without proffering an explanation for it.

And in fact the case is considerably worse. Once the concept of culture gained ascendancy, then this culture or that, or culture in general, was treated as though it were unchanging, carved in granite. Culture took on a false and unalterable concreteness. It could be thought of as weighing on people as a great mass of tradition, passed on without alteration from one generation to the next. People had the capacity for culture inborn and then were topped up for life with whatever culture their elders possessed. Human life, in this representation, came to seem a frozen tableau of different cultures. Culture could only resist change, could never be part of change, and indeed change itself became very difficult to explain, as Richard Fox (1985) has argued so well. Nor was it any easier to write of anyone who was interstitial, bilingual, or bicultural, because by definition all humans were *in* one culture or another. So, ironically, the very concept, culture, which established the representation that humans vary tremendously, beyond the strict dictates of natural selection, made it impossible to give any account of how that variation came about.

But sociality can give that account. The creative intersubjective capacity, human sociality, evolved among humans under selective pressure. Once full sociality was fixed in the human species, it became possible for enduring change to occur that was not a response to selective pressure. For humans could now respond immediately to an environment in which other humans were the most important feature, and they could respond creatively, coining new forms and reactions. Hence the sorts of variation and change which we associate with history proper became possible: economic and political, social and linguistic events could now alter the shape of human societies and differentiate between them. People could respond to changes, and such historical responses could themselves endure because of the capacity for pedagogy and learning.

Sociality does not wholly explain the *actual* varieties of human experience: only the complexity of local circumstances, local histories, and local causes could provide such a detailed account. But sociality does explain how such a history of variation is possible at all. Indeed, under sociality change and variation would seem natural. First, sociality presupposes a difference of outlook and interests between persons, a difference which gives rise, through imaginative construction, to the give and take of common life. There is no guarantee that what arises in this give and take is the same as before: indeed it would seem more plausible that, apart from other forces, ever new and subtly different patterns of life would inevitably arise, and that these differences would be magnified as the generations pass. Second, learning and teaching could be regarded as sources of variation. What is taught is *not* passed on unchanged. It changes subtly, for

206

at stake is not the teaching of something invariant like arithmetic, but rather teaching how to act in this or that, often unprecedented, circumstance as an accountable person in society.

Third, increasingly complex arrangements in material life, in the distribution of power, in the categorization of persons, and in the understanding of human experience come to have their own effects, which can be explained through economic, political, social, and intellectual history. The accommodation of Pygmies to Bantu agriculturalists, the rise of a working class in Britain, and the translation of Buddhism to China all require explaining through such forces. Such larger changes seem, in their sheer momentum, to be natural and impersonal. But they too are only rendered possible through people with different viewpoints responding to each other, construing each other imaginatively and acting toward each other in the light of that construal. Individuals' sociality is the condition which makes possible collective change.

Of course there is in much human life another momentum, of orthodoxy and orthopraxy. People frequently resist change. The idea of culture as monolithic tradition passed from generation to generation at least made that easy to understand. But following the notion of sociality, we would regard that orthodoxy as something imaginatively created and recreated. We would then ask: under what conditions, what methods of social reproduction, is this seeming orthodoxy achieved? How is the putative stability of these norms, values, rules, this social organization, social structure . . . how is this stability preserved? We would be sceptical that any such stability were as firm, or that any orthodoxy were as monolithic, as it seemed. We would come to expect individual variation and collective change — which are after all the nature of our experienced human world.

'Men make their own history', wrote Marx '. . . but under circumstances directly encountered, given, and transmitted from the past.' This passage embraces the complexity of the human predicament. Anthropologists have accepted the last of these insights, transmission from the past; may we now accept the others as well?

© 1989 Michael Carrithers

REFERENCES

Bruner, J. (1986) *Actual Minds, Possible Worlds*, London: Harvard University Press.

Carrithers, M. (1983) *The Forest Monks of Sri Lanka: an anthropological and historical study*, New Delhi: Oxford University Press.

Firth, R. (1985) 'Degrees of intelligibility', in J. Overing (ed.) *Reason and Morality*, London: Tavistock Publications, 29-46.

Fox, R. (1985) *Lions of the Punjab: culture in the making*, London: University of California Press.

Geertz, C. (1975) *The Interpretation of Cultures*, London: Hutchinson and Company.

Gellner, E. (1979) *Spectacles and Predicaments: essays in social theory*, Cambridge: Cambridge University Press.

Humphrey, N. K. (1976) 'The social function of intellect', in P. P. G. Bateson and R. A. Hinde (eds) *Growing Points in Ethology*, pp. 303-17, Cambridge: Cambridge University Press.

Humphrey, N. K. (1983) *Consciousness Regained: chapters in the development of mind*, Oxford: Oxford University Press.

Immelmann, K. (1980) *Introduction to Ethology*, New York: Plenum Press.

Isaac, G. (1983) 'Aspects of human evolution', in D. S. Bendall (ed.) *Evolution from Molecules to Men*, Cambridge: Cambridge University Press.

Kitcher, P. (1985) *Vaulting Ambition: sociobiology and the quest for human nature*, London: MIT Press.

Klama, J. (1988) *Aggression: conflict in animals and humans reconsidered*, London: Longman Scientific and Technical.

Konner, M. (1984) *The Tangled Wing: biological constraints on the human spirit*, Harmondsworth: Penguin Books.

Leyhausen, P. (1979) *Cat Behaviour: the predatory and social behavior of domestic and wild cats*, New York: Garland.

Mauss, M. (1979) *Sociology and Psychology* (trans. Ben Brewster), London: Routledge & Kegan Paul.

Maynard Smith, J. (1983) 'Game theory and the evolution of cooperation', in D. S. Bendall (ed.) *Evolution from Molecules to Men*, Cambridge: Cambridge University Press.

Premack, D. (1984) 'Pedagogy and aesthetics as sources of culture', in M. S. Gazzaniga (ed.) *Handbook of Cognitive Neuroscience*, London: Plenum Press.

Premack, D. (1986) *Gavagai! or the Future History of the Animal Language Controversy*, London: MIT Press.

Rosaldo, M. (1984) 'Toward an anthropology of self and feeling', in R. S. Shweder and R. LeVine (eds) *Culture Theory: essays on mind, self, and emotion*, Cambridge: Cambridge University Press.

Rose, S., Lewontin, R. C. and Kamin, L. J. (1984) *Not in Our Genes: biology, ideology and human nature*, Harmondsworth: Penguin Books.

Sahlins, M. (1976) *The Use and Abuse of Biology*, Ann Arbor: University of Michigan Press.

Schick, F. (1984) *Having Reasons: an essay on rationality and sociality*, Princeton: Princeton University Press.

Scribner, S. (1986) 'Thinking in action: some characteristics of practical thought', in R. Sternberg and R. Wagner (eds) *Practical Intelligence: nature and origins of competence in the everyday world*, Cambridge: Cambridge University Press.

Shotter, J. (1984) *Social Accountability and Selfhood*, Oxford: Basil Blackwell.

Siann, G. (1985) *Accounting for Aggression: perspectives on aggression and violence*, Boston: Allen and Unwin.

Sober, E. (1984) *The Nature of Selection: evolutionary theory in philosophical focus*, Cambridge, Mass.: MIT Press.

Stocking, G. (1982) *Race, Culture, and Evolution: essays in the history of anthropology*, Chicago: University of Chicago Press.

Thompson, N. S. (1976) 'My descent from the monkey', in P. P. G. Bateson and P. H. Klopfer (eds) *Perspectives in Ethology*, 2: 221–30, New York: Plenum Press.

Trevarthen, C. (1980) 'The foundations of intersubjectivity: development of interpersonal and co-operative understanding in infants', in D. Olson (ed.) *The Social Foundations of Language: essays in honor of J. S. Bruner*, New York: Norton.

Wilson, E. O. (1975) *Sociobiology: the new synthesis*, London: Harvard University Press.

Part Three

THINKING ABOUT 'PEACE' AND 'AGGRESSION': SOME THEORETICAL ISSUES

Chapter Eleven

'PEACE'

ALAN CAMPBELL

'FIERCE PEOPLE'

This is a general paper starting with two specific problems: (a) misgivings about the choice of vocabulary used when describing societies as aggressive and non-aggressive, and (b) misgivings about diagnostic statements of the type 'society X is peaceful' since these mask both the protean nature of interpretations (made by different people in different situations) as well as the vivid complexity of what is being described.

A brief example: suppose we were considering 'goodness' and 'badness'. We might start off saying: 'Let's define goodness and badness', or we could ask: 'Are goodness and badness innate human capacities?' We might also feel we should produce diagnostic statements such as 'the Nuer are a good people and the Dinka are a bad people'. In forced examples like those, I think we can see pretty quickly that there's not much there to take us very far. Similarly, as regards aggression and non-aggression, I'm starting with the view that the effort is neither to define the essence of the words nor to identify the notions as capacities. Furthermore, it does not seem particularly useful to use the words as diagnostic labels.

Rather than chasing around after 'aggression' (or 'non-aggression') catching it here and there — 'Here it is amongst the so-and-so's'; 'It's absent among the such-and-such'; rather than 'finding out what aggression (or non-aggression) *is*'; rather than 'contributing to a theory of aggression and co-operation', instead of any of that, the effort is rather to think about better standards of description, where we can consider all these words (goodness, badness, aggression, non-aggression, fierce, peaceful) as available to us when we think they are

213

appropriate for the story we are trying to tell. One particular advantage of leaving aside these preoccupations of definition and diagnosis is that the way is left less cluttered for the kind of effort reflected in some of the ethnographic papers in this collection: those that deal with the translation of indigenous terms and with the attempt to understand how people are thinking and acting in the various ethnographic settings described.

A simple example: (1) There is a Yanomamo word *waiteri*: *teri* is a 'people' suffix; *wai* is given as 'fierce': so *waiteri* means 'fierce people'. (2) Associated with that are all sorts of ways of carrying on — chest-pounding duels, wife-beating, raiding — that require descriptions of various moral patterns. (3) The end of the line is the diagnostic statement that 'the Yanomamo *are* a fierce people'. Now, without saying that the progression is necessarily faulty, it is worth pointing out that from the *first translation* to the *terminal diagnosis* you've travelled a colossal distance. And it seems to me that writers can slide around within that area unawares. Whereas I can be comfortable with *waiteri* being translated 'fierce people' I am thoroughly suspicious of the Yanomamo being described as 'the fierce people', the point being that the word 'fierce' is doing very different work in each case. Whereas it is capable of its job in the first instance it is not so clear that it is so in the second.

DIAGNOSIS

I want to offer a couple of simple examples that suggest how to get away from the diagnostic habits and idioms of ethnography. We can begin by recognizing that a major difficulty of diagnostic statements ('the so-and-so's are aggressive'; 'the such-and-such' are not aggressive') is that they invite either/or, binary thinking. In indicating that this quality or that state of affairs is present in one case implies that it is absent everywhere else. If *they* are described as violent it indicates that the description is unsuitable for *us*, or for other cases under consideration. That's obviously not adequate. And if we don't mean that, we shouldn't put it like that. (In an everyday context, if you say 'he's a liar, she's a cheat', you imply that you and your interlocutor are not, whereas it would be more helpful to realize that cheating and lying are possibilities open to us all. It's a simple point.) Making the binary contrast more sophisticated by setting up some sort of 'grid and group' graph with plus and minus extremes which one can move between, varying the intensity of the qualities like a moral rheostat, looks like an attractive alternative, but it still leaves us stuck in binary thinking and still leaves us in a thoroughly diagnostic frame of mind.

If we're not going to use these descriptions as diagnostic statements, what are we going to do with them? The notion of 'aggression/non-aggression' is useless in isolation but becomes worthwhile when discussed within various contexts of other related terms. We can usefully talk about aggression/non-aggression when we can see those other related qualities that might interest us in any specific context. How many other related qualities we can think of in any one context depends on how clever and creative we are in establishing a repertoire of terms. I'll give examples of two simple closed repertoires and go on to suggest that we should throw ourselves creatively into open-ended repertoires.

Suppose we wanted to reduce our account of things to the starkness of certain behavioural or ethological views where all human and animal behaviour can be seen in terms of a few basic matters: desire (to consume and gratify), inhibition, flight, and aggression. In a simple little picture like this it would be silly to ask: 'Is society X aggressive?' That would be obsolete. The problem would now be: 'Describe as fully as possible the behavioural patterns of society X within this clutch of categories.' It would be pointless to say: 'In case X nothing takes place that would come into category P (fear, defence, aggression, or whatever)' since we have already decided that our collection of categories are the essential landmarks of what counts as human behaviour. Indeed if we did make a statement like that (that category P was absent) we would be saying that what we were looking at was something obviously incomplete, something damaged, faulty, or limited, like a person suffering from a disability or an amputation. Assuming we're not going to be saying that, assuming that our description is of a bona fide case, we then escape from the cramp of having to make one of these irritating either/or decisions: either aggressive or not aggressive, and we can then get on with describing what's going on as accurately and as vividly as we can. We should then be able to make more pliable, and much more sensitive, comparisons: not 'the Yanomamo are aggressive and the Chewong are not', nor even 'the Yanomamo get a huge plus for aggression while the Chewong get a whopping minus', but something along the lines of 'how do these people or those people deal with certain basic human predicaments?'

215

Obviously we'll have to find something a bit better than that limited set of four or five words in the example. But what it's supposed to show is that once we are released into a worthwhile descriptive vocabulary, the question of whether or not they have this *thing* (aggression) is as redundant a question as those asking whether or not they 'have religion' or 'have totemism'. When left isolated and dangling, these are all bogus categories and the associated questions are bogus too.

Suppose we had a fairly extensive vocabulary of terms used as descriptive labels to indicate the range of what we took to be the basic aspects of human life. 'Passivity', 'aggression', 'restraint', 'violence' would all then be part of that vocabulary. How extensive a vocabulary would we think necessary? It would be like a list of literary *topoi*, a *topos* or 'commonplace' being a basic topic or theme: age versus youth, the quest, contemplative versus active life, paradise, and so on:

> There is basically only a limited number of plots; they can be seen, in different guises, recurring down the ages. The reason is in life itself. Human relationships, whilst infinitely varied in detail, reveal — stripped down to fundamentals — a number of repetitive patterns. . . . Goethe quoted Gozzi's opinion that there were only 36 tragic situations — and he added that Schiller, who believed that there were more, had not even succeeded in finding as many as that. (Brandt 1953: 422)

If we could plunder this view of literature and put it to work in ethnography, and if we had a word for each situation, we would have a vocabulary of thirty-six terms to work with; a considerable improvement on the ethologist's four. But it is still a move towards simplifying and classifying in a radical way, like finding archetypes everywhere, noticing, for example, that the story of 'The Rape of the Lock', of *Pamela*, of Hero in *Much Ado*, and of Hermione in *The Winter's Tale* are all examples of the Proserpina or Persephone story: the rebirth of the female figure; or where Tom Sawyer, in the caves, is seen as an example of the minotaur myth. I think we should accept that there's nothing necessarily *wrong* with this activity. We may find a particular example ridiculously far-fetched, but we should accept that the activity may well produce interesting and productive results. We *can* reduce all these women's predicaments to Persephone. We *can* say that a cod piece, a Gê penis sheath, and a sporran are all *the same thing.* We *can* reduce all descriptions of our motives and our emotions to the limited repertoire of animal behaviour. But the important clue is to notice that these reductions are *idiosyncratic.* There's nothing objective, scientific, apodeictic about them. Reducing everything to fours or thirty-sixes, to Persephone or the minotaur, may be cookey and weird in one case or original and perceptive in another. It depends how it's done. Each reduction is a unique creative endeavour and must be judged interesting or not, adequate or not, as the case may be.

That's the first direction, then: to stop worrying about aggression and non-aggression in terms of diagnostic statements, and to place these words within a vocabulary that includes everything else that's going to count as the human predicament. There are other worthwhile directions too:

> There are many thoughts and feelings, but only a few gestures . . . human beings have only a limited number of noises and grimaces with which to express the multiplicity of their emotions, [e.g.,] she laughed as though she had been amused by something, when in fact she was only surprised. (Huxley 1955: 156, 268)

Talking in terms of fours or thirty-sixes is like describing ourselves and others by talking in grimaces. And we don't have to limit ourselves to that. A check through some of the cross-references in Roget's *Thesaurus* shows vividly how limited were our previous attempts at describing what was going on. Look at the fine discriminations we *could* be making, but can't because we're not good enough with words.

So, as well as these reductions, we could try another direction: creative processes of description and redescription, not necessarily in the sense of 'ever finer discriminations' (it's not a matter of quantity where *more* words will always guarantee ever *finer* nuances), but in the sense of appreciating the freedom to move amongst so many different possibilities of describing and redescribing, the freedom to make new connections, to choose this word today and that one tomorrow.

Once we are released into the creative resources of our language anything can happen. What we will now be looking for will not be a thumpingly simple answer to a thumpingly simple question, but will be that kind of vivid description that can appreciate the growing complexity of what it is trying to grasp. When Signe Howell was being interviewed recently by a radio commentator on the subject of non-aggression, I found myself initially irritated when the interviewer began to ask the usual 'how did you meet them and what did you eat' sort of question: those innocent questions that require anecdotal answer. This line seemed to be getting away from the point, until it quickly became obvious that it was through the vivid anecdotes that the 'non-aggression' business found its context. The 'lack of aggression' feature went along with *this* feature and *that* feature and *the next* feature (including, for example, a certain kind of independence, a reluctance to interfere with others, where one does not make the most extraordinary efforts to rush and help someone in trouble). What was happening was not that the notion of non-aggression was becoming clearer; what was happening was that an increasingly livelier and recognizable picture was emerging, making it less and less necessary to come to a terminal decision on the nature of this society. Suppose, for instance, in response to the description of their being, let us say, a bit relaxed about helping others in trouble, I were to say: 'This is not a "peaceful" society; this is a society that is morally lobotomized', then Signe Howell would quite properly resent the description as inadequate.

Emphasizing the open-ended nature of descriptions is not a plea to 'get back to Mauss' and his notion of 'totality'. Marcel Mauss's notion of 'total social phenomenon' is too formal. Moreover, nowadays the phrase is little more than an incantation. Neither is it saying 'back to "holism" ', General Smuts's word, since that too has become a slogan. Expectations like that are best seen in efforts such as 'the four drives' descriptions, which attempt a complete account of the basics of human behaviour, or 'the thirty-six plots' descriptions, which attempt a complete account of the basic predicaments of human life. There, we would expect aggression and non-aggression to fit comfortably into any suggested repertoire. But in this case there is no closed repertoire. Each new attempt at description is another guerrilla raid or another hunting sortie with unsure outcome. Rather than 'holism' or 'total social fact', I'd suggest 'only connect' from *Howard's End* as the most appropriate catch phrase to describe this kind of effort (especially if it refers to the prose and the passion).

While 'four drives' and 'thirty-six plots' offer simple images of alternatives to diagnostic statements, arguing for open-ended descriptions should see them off entirely. There will be no room in this idiom either for diagnostic types, such as Apollonian and Dionysian, nor diagnostic stereotypes, such as The Fierce People and The Gentle

People, nor rheostats to slide between the two extremities. Yes, it may be argued against this that it's frightfully precious to say: 'it's wrong to describe the Yanomamo as fierce.' Common sense seems to suggest that such a description is comfortable enough. Well, as a description I think it is thoroughly inadequate, and the best that can be said for it is that it's a minimal starting point, indicating, like a sign-post in the wilderness, an unknown direction towards a heap of unanswered questions.

Being aware of the inadequacies of diagnoses also resolves the question of negative descriptions. We should be properly careful of those accounts that describe other people as lacking this or that, where, for instance, the Brazilian Indians were described from the beginning of the European invasions as being *sans foi, sans roi, et sans loi*, that being backed up by bogus evidence about certain 'deficiencies' in their speech: they were said to be unable to produce the sounds 'f', 'r', and 'l'. Marshall Sahlins astutely turns the tables on such descriptions in the opening section of *Stone Age Economics* where those 'hunters and gatherers' previously said to lack material goods and agricultural techniques are redescribed as possessing leisure, affluence, and so on. But the problem of negative descriptions is not resolved simply by turning all of them into positive ones. It really doesn't matter whether the description is a positive one or a negative one. First, it is easy to find negative descriptions that are 'positive': no capacity for cruelty, for evil, or perhaps, no capacity for aggression. Not having nasty qualities can obviously be a plus. But second, possessing nasty qualities can be very interesting indeed. If certain primates are said to be *capable* of playing tricks on each other, of deceiving each other, of 'lying' (a capacity that George Steiner once suggested is peculiarly human), then we really are on to something interesting, not because the quality is mysterious or unfamiliar, which this one obviously is not, but because of the implication that if *this* quality is present, what on earth *else* might be present. A nasty quality might suggest a whole range of other capacities. Once again the problem is not the quality we have isolated, but how far we can get with an adequate description of what we have found. In other words, the diagnosis is simply an invitation, a 'prompt', to get on with doing something. Whether it's a positive or a negative, a moral positive or a moral negative, is neither here nor there. All diagnoses simply say: 'OK, that's the start. Now what on earth is going on?' Stating that the Yanomamo are aggressive or that the Chewong are non-aggressive are both statements at point zero.

THE FACTS

I mentioned how exciting it was to be led by Signe Howell's anecdotes away from the query about non-aggression into the vividness of a recognizable picture. Once there, we would be giving up a lot to retreat back into generalizations and stereotypical statements. Surely we'd find them too lazy, too bland. Yet after these copious and lively descriptions have been created, can we really say once and for all that any kind of statement of general features is misleading? Are there really no essences? Watching the casual conversations amongst Neopolitan traders, the gestures, the touches, the embraces, it is so striking how wholly inappropriate such behaviour would be, say, amongst a group of Scottish farmers gathered at the mart. I don't feel at all on sure ground when looking at questions like this. Certainly to *assume* that there *are* essences, different essences, is one of the most widespread of human dispositions. And that includes anthropologists — they get up to it all the time. Against this, I'm inclined to hold that there are none. In the example I've just given of Neopolitans and Scottish farmers, the differences, though immensely interesting in a folksie sort of way, are flimsy accidentals, like traditional fashions in dress. We may find one fashion preferable to another, but we have not come across any profoundly significant essential difference in human possibilities. Our own ability to imitate and move between one fashion and another is enough to show that.

Looking at ethnographies, there are some compelling examples. In *Wayward Servants* Colin Turnbull creates a breathtaking contrast between the Mbuti pygmies and the Bantu cultivators surrounding them particularly as regards their views of the forest and their views of misfortune, illness, and death. The Bantu cultivators appear to live in a fearful world of baleful influences and witchcraft accusations, while the pygmies appear thoroughly relaxed and happy as regards, apparently, pretty well everything. Napoleon Chagnon's description of the Yanomamo is a desperately violent picture, backed up by their own accounts of their origin myths (being descended from the blood of the moon and so on), and their own notions of *waiteri* (fierce people). Once these extensive and vivid images are in, isn't it asking too much of us to hold back from our stereotypical diagnoses? Surely the Yanomamo *really are* pretty horrible and the Mbuti pygmies *really are* very attractive people indeed? Surely the essences *are* there?

I don't think so. And I justify that scepticism on the basis of two queries, both of which are questions of relativity. First of all, who is doing the telling? I'm not querying the veracity or competence of any of these ethnographic descriptions. I think it's silly to go around saying 'So and so got it all wrong' as was done recently to Margaret Mead's work. If all you have to assess is whether something is right or wrong, you're at a pretty trivial level of judgement, as a look at some of the actual blunders will show. (The ones that come to mind are faulty translations at the pedestrian level of relationship terms.) If we accept wholeheartedly that each ethnographic venture is an inter-pretation, and accept the whole baggage of expectations that goes along with that, our judgements will be a little more complicated than just assessing correctness. They will include some consideration of the perspective and preoccupations of the author. 'You don't find Indians in the forest — you find yourself' is an old and useful cliché. Certainly Turnbull saw a lot of a most placid way of getting on with life and certainly Chagnon saw a lot of violent behaviour. Others, though, saw other things. Judy Shapiro described a widespread relaxed and co-operative atmosphere amongst Yanomamo *women*, who gave the impression that all this violence business was a matter of these stupid men and their factions. Women suffered beatings from their husbands, but were not involved in the factional fights and did not let factions get in the way of their relations with other women. Ken Taylor and Alcida Ramos have frequently said that it's too easy to make too much out of the violence in Yanomamo life and overlook all the more ordinary aspects: of love for their children, of humour, and of happiness. Again, these are examples that show the inade-quacies of simple diagnostic labels. These labels always impoverish our view. And that we get stuck on them shows how anxious we are to deny that our descriptions are the result of our own preoccupations and perplexities. It's as if we deny responsibility for what we see, nervous of being accused of 'impressionism' or 'subjectivity', and anxious to purvey the facts, pure and simple. We *want* the Yanomamo to be thoroughly violent and we *want* the Pygmies to be thoroughly nice. It's so much easier that way.

My first query, then, is 'Who is telling the story?' What's that relation? The second is 'What is the historical predicament of the people who are described?' What is the nature of their relations with others? Ever since Malinowski, in the name of scientific objectivity, deliberately wrote out of his description of the Trobrianders that Europeans, missionaries and officials, were present in Kiriwina, ethnographic descriptions and characterizations have tried to maintain neat edges. Economic problems and community difficulties are fine under the heading of social change. But making a description a function of relations with others doesn't get a lot of emphasis.

In frontier Brazil there is a well-established popular distinction between *indios bravos* and *indios mansos*, 'wild' and 'tame' Indians, adjectives that, along with other animal similes, make up a way of talking of Indians and treating Indians that is all too familiar. *Indios bravos* is not principally meant to refer to a people such as the Yanomamo who raid amongst themselves. Both *bravo* and *manso* refer to the state of the relations between the frontier and the Indians. When Indians resist contact by fighting back they are called *bravos*. Under relentless pressure, all of these will eventually give up and become *pacificados*. Those who do not resist, or whose resistance is too far in the past to be remembered, are called *mansos*.

The first contact between Brazilian Indians and Europeans took place in 1500. Those particular groups of Indians then living along the Atlantic littoral were, from then on through the next couple of centuries until they were wiped out, always described as a pretty bloodthirsty lot, and the Tupinamba especially got the lurid reputation of being cannibals. It is important to remember that those involved in the wiping out were those involved in doing the describing. That all these reports were being sent back to Europe by Portuguese, French, Dutch, Spanish, British, and German travellers; colonizers, soldiers, and missionaries, whose own peoples were engaged in a brutal scramble amongst themselves for territory and resources, and whose treatment of Indians was as savage as anything recorded in our history — none of that is allowed to have any obvious effect on the story. Indeed it seems to be forgotten that the first contact in 1500, described in a letter to the Portuguese king by one of the men on Cabral's expedition, is of as idyllic a picture as you could wish for of an innocent close encounter of the third kind. And many of the early accounts sent back by the first missionaries emphasize the child-like innocence of the natives, giving rise to a nice theological puzzle that if they were innocent (naked, without shame, sinless, unfallen), what was the point of trying to convert them? — not, alas, a direction of thought that got very far. By the time Hans Staden's account comes in (published at Marburg in 1557, an account of cannibalism taken to be one of the most famous on record) the Indians who captured him were already said to be allies of the French and to regard the Portuguese as as their hated enemies; in other words, they had already become drawn into the violent squabbles of the Europeans.

Nowadays, hearing those frontiersmen from their predicament of poverty, ill-health, insecurity, on the margins of our society, describing Indians as animals, is a convincing example of the relativity of descriptions. It is so obvious that the *bravo/manso* distinction refers to a relation and not to essential characteristics of the people to whom the descriptions are applied. In *Os Indios e a civilizacao* Darcy Ribeiro refers to cases where, following 'pacification', the Indians concerned explained that while all the previous trouble had been going on, it was they who had regarded themselves as the ones who had been trying to pacify the Brazilian invaders. There are so many examples of previously hostile Indians who, pretty well overnight, become docile and amenable to contact — not those of the next generation, but the same people, a little older, who find themselves suddenly at the mercy of a vastly different world.

I have no idea how to explain in each case why this group will resist contact violently, while that will enter into contact submissively. But it's quite clear that a great deal of the violent hostility of *indios bravos* has to do with fear of the encroaching strangers; an utterly justified fear of being wiped out. It is equally clear that the docility of *indios mansos* has to do with fear of being finished off by disease, together with a perceived opportunity to escape from previous violence. They hope that this particular contact with outsiders will protect them and give them a chance. It's hard to be a warrior people when there's only thirty of you left and when there's nowhere left to go.

The point is, then, that when we talk of violent behaviour or submissive behaviour in these contexts we are not diagnosing the collective temperament of these people. We are describing a particular moment in their history and their response to the changing circumstances in which they find themselves in relation to other people. Symptoms, qualities, characteristic features — these are not what is at issue. Once again, the job becomes the appreciation of processes, not the identification of things.

LOOKING AT RELATIONS

Some brief comments in conclusion:

1. The problem is not one of trying to find out what 'aggression/

non-aggression' is by looking for evidence from all over the place, collating examples, and filling out a terminal definition.

2. The problem is not one of finding an initial definition of 'aggression/non-aggression' as quality or attribute and then setting off to see if it fits in this case or that case as a descriptive label.

3. 'Aggression/non-aggression' can take its place in a descriptive vocabulary alongside whatever else we want to accept as a repertoire of human attributes, whether in closed vocabularies that reduce everything to basic aspects and basic patterns, or in an open-ended and creative use of the resources of our language.

4. Our perplexities and our preoccupations make up the productive grounds of our openness to the world, 'the conditions by which what we encounter says something to us'. Our account of others is based on these conditions. These conditions are changeable.

5. People are not 'violent' or 'non-violent' in any essential sense. People act aggressively or non-aggressively towards others — in other words, we are looking at relations between people. In certain circumstances these relationships will be characterized by certain forms of behaviour. These circumstances are changeable.

Panta rhei. They always called Heraclitus by lugubrious epithets like 'the weeping philosopher' or 'the obscure one' (*o skoteinos*). I can't imagine why an appreciation of process should always be held to be gloomy.

© 1989 Alan Campbell

REFERENCES

Brandt, G. W. (1953) 'Plot', *Cassell's Encyclopaedia of Literature* 1: 421–3.
Huxley, A. (1955/1928) *Point Counter Point*, Penguin Books.

Chapter Twelve

IDENTIFYING PEACEFUL SOCIETIES[1]

PAUL HEELAS

Is it possible to assert that one society is more peaceful than another, or indeed that some societies are simply peaceful? Although most anthropologists have become highly suspicious of reducing socio-cultural complexity to 'types' (few today compare societies in terms of the shame – guilt contrast, for example), the tradition of designating cultures 'peaceful' or 'aggressive' remains in force. This is what I question. What follows is as savage an attack as I can muster on the idea that it is possible to grade societies along the 'peaceful' – 'aggressive' scale. Questioning the widespread assumption that some societies are obviously more peaceful than others has rather important implications. Not least, doubt is thrown on the strategy of attempting to find correlations between 'peaceful' societies and other factors (certain kinds of childrearing, for example) to explain the management of aggression.

I should immediately make clear that I concentrate on what is involved in establishing the presence or absence of aggressive acts. It is, of course, possible to explore what is involved in characterizing acts by using the contrast between 'peaceful' and 'non-peaceful' ways of life. I prefer to work with the non-aggressive – aggressive distinction. My justification is that those who call societies 'peaceful' have attached considerable weight to what they take to be the unimportance or relative absence of aggressive acts in daily life. It should be borne in mind, however, that societies which appear to be peaceful by virtue of their non-aggression might not be peaceful in other regards. This non-aggression can go together with states of mind, such as fear or anxiety, which are far from peaceful.[2]

Is an act non-aggressive? A widely adopted strategy is to assume that a cross-culturally applicable definition, capturing the 'essence' of

225

aggression, can be devised, and then employed to 'read off' the nature of acts. An act is non-aggressive if it runs counter to the definition being used. My specific target is this 'essentialist' comparative strategy. It does not work. But I also want to attend to another form of comparison. Whether or not acts are aggressive depends on socio-cultural context. Contextual considerations, the fact that acts are embedded within semantic complexes which show little cross-cultural constancy, result in a version of relativism which might work in favour of ethnographic accuracy, but which raises problems for those (perhaps including contributors to this volume) aiming to locate societies along the aggression – non-aggression scale.

CONTROVERSIES

Most of us readily assume that some societies are less aggressive than others. Having presented two illustrations of the kind of material which prompts easy judgement, I introduce controversies, controversies which make us wonder whether assessment is so self-evident.

At first sight it looks as though there is nothing to make a fuss about. Signs of non-aggression or aggression appear to be obvious. For example, who would want to conclude that the !Kung (a hunter-gatherer people of the Kalahari Desert) are not more peaceful than Australian Aborigines living on Mornington Island, northern Queensland? Thus Draper writes of the former,

the !Kung are a people who devalue aggression; they have explicit values against assaulting, losing control, and seeking to intimidate another person by sheer force of personality. Furthermore, on a daily basis and over months of fieldwork one finds that overt physical acts by one person against another are extremely rare. In two years I personally observed three instances in which people lost control and exchanged blows (1978: 33),

whereas McKnight observes,

During my three years of fieldwork on Mornington Island hundreds of fights occurred. Indeed, fighting appeared to be the main social activity. At one period I calculated that there were several arguments every day with antagonists angrily trading harsh words; every day there was usually one fight — about once a month there was a mêlée involving at least a hundred people; and every once in a while there was a tremendous upheaval which involved most of the community. . . . In fact, eventually I became so used to violence that I often failed to record that a fight had occurred (1986: 138).

But are matters so straightforward? The claim that the !Kung are 'the harmless people', as Thomas (1958) describes them, has been criticized by a number of people, including Fox and Eibl-Eibesfeldt. Thus Fox observes, 'Pueblo Indians, Eskimos, Bushmen have all been cited as examples of non-violent people, and all turn out to have high rates of personal violence. The Bushmen have a higher homicide rate than Chicago!' (1975: 131; see Draper 1978: 31). And Eibl-Eibesfeldt has the !Kung in mind when he writes, 'The often-repeated claim that hunters and food gatherers in general are more peaceful than people at a higher cultural level is certainly false, and so obviously false that one wonders how it can survive so stubbornly in the face of the overwhelming abundance of long-known facts' (1979: 161). One of the more arresting pieces of evidence he draws on in connection with the !Kung is provided by Heinz:

A man was playing a musical instrument that another man wanted. 'You've been playing long enough. Now let me play', he said. The first man ignored the request and went on playing. When he refused a second time, the other man tried to grab the instrument and, when he failed, lost his temper and struck the first man on the head with his digging stick so hard that the stick end broke; he then took the instrument and made off. Thereupon the first man took a poisoned arrow from another man's quiver, ran after the assailant, and stuck the arrow into his arm. The other members of the group pursued the assailant with bow and arrow. He escaped in the dark, but died the next day' (cited by Eibl-Eibesfeldt 1979: 158).

Another illustration of disagreement is provided by the (male) Yanomamo Indians of the Venezuelan jungle, portrayed by Chagnon (1983) as violent, vengeful aggressors who kill their unwanted baby girls, beat their women savagely, war constantly among themselves, and drink the crushed bones of their recently dead; portrayed by Lizot (1985) as a people who, though sporadically violent and occasionally cruel, are in no obvious sense 'the fierce people'. Or consider the divergent descriptions of Samoan behaviour given by

227

Freeman (1983) and Mead (1943), the former dwelling on manifestations of violent emotional reactions, the latter on the extent to which Samoans are motivated by emotions witnessed as mutuality, agreeableness, and submissiveness. Finally, mention can be made of the Semai Senoi, portrayed (to varying degrees) as 'bloodthirsty killers' by Konner, Eibl-Eibesfeldt, Paul, and Wilson; as 'inhumanly blissful and serene' by others; as 'notably free of interpersonal violence' by Robarchek and Dentan (Robarchek and Dentan 1987: 356–8; see Robarchek in this volume).

ESSENTIALISM AND COMPARISON

Why do these (and many other) disagreements occur? Of reasons which can be adduced, I draw attention to what is almost certainly an important factor, namely that researchers often employ different definitions of what counts as the 'essence' of aggression, and so arrive at differing judgements of the nature of social activities. I illustrate how disagreements can arise by applying various definitions to Yanomamo, Samoan, Ilongot, and Semai activities.

Yanomamo husbands appear to be classic wife-beaters, or worse: 'some of them chop their wives with the sharp edge of a machete or axe, or shoot them with a barbed arrow in some nonvital area, such as the buttocks or leg' (Chagnon 1983: 112). Yet,

> Women expect this kind of treatment. Those who are not too severely treated might even measure their husband's concern in terms of the frequency of minor beatings they sustain. I overheard two young women discussing each other's scalp scars. One of them commented that the other's husband must really care for her since he had beaten her on the head so frequently! (Chagnon 1983: 113)[3]

In terms of Eibl-Eibesfeldt's definition, behaviour is aggressive 'if it leads to another party's being hurt; this includes not only physical hurt (injury or destruction) but any kind of hurt including annoyance, taunts, or insults' (1979: 29); husbands are aggressive indeed. However, in terms of another definition (Baron and Byrne's 'aggression is any form of behavior directed toward the goal of harming or injuring another living being who is motivated to avoid such treatment' (1977: 405)), it would seem that something else is occurring. That 'women expect this kind of treatment' presumably diminishes or qualifies their 'motivation to avoid' it, a consideration also supported by the suggestion that beatings can signify being 'cared for' rather than (simply) being 'harmed or injured'.

Remaining with the two definitions just introduced, Gerber's material from Samoa provides a perhaps more powerful illustration. She writes,

> When I asked Samoan informants about the feeling of *alofa* 'love' which exists between parents and children, I was surprised to learn that many of them believed a father's beating was an appropriate sign of his love. . . . Several informants told me that if their fathers failed to beat them, they would be sad, since it would be a proof of paternal indifference (1985: 131).

In terms of Eibl-Eibesfeldt's definition, 'love' is seen as signifying aggression. For Baron and Byrne the strong implication that there is no (apparent) 'motivation to avoid' results in a different picture.

Next, consider Ilongot (northern Luzon) and the head-hunting activities of youths. Employing a definition of aggression as 'the intentional injury of another', Berkowitz (1980: 337) would treat head-hunting as aggressive. Another psychologist, Marsh, would not. More exactly, he would not see youths as acting aggressively to those whose heads they lop off. For Marsh, aggression is 'the intentional process of subduing or achieving dominance over a rival' (1978: 33); and Rosaldo (1980) provides no evidence that victims are seen as rivals.

Finally, Robarchek (in this volume) writes that Semai show 'a resistance to co-operative activities growing out of a reluctance to surrender one's freedom of action or to subordinate one's own wishes to the will of others'. None of the definitions introduced would treat this 'resistance' as indicating aggression. It is possible, however, that Hogan's definition would find aggression. For he defines 'passive-aggression' as 'behaviour characterized by indirect resistance to demands for adequate performance in either social or work settings' (1983: 446).

A RELIABLE DEFINITION?

These examples serve to illustrate the extent to which definitions can inform comparison. A major problem facing those who adopt the essentialist comparative strategy is that different definitions, capturing different essences, result in different, if not contradictory, assessments. The obvious solution to this problem is for researchers to employ a generally acceptable, because 'true', definition.

Few who have pondered the 'semantic jungle' (Bandura 1973: 2) which immerses one on addressing the term 'aggression' would want to dispute Johnson's claim that '. . . it is difficult if not impossible to isolate the necessary and sufficient conditions to produce a satisfactory definition' (1972: 4). With this in mind, I now criticize the two approaches which have been used to provide definitions to capture the essence of aggression. None of these definitions serves as a reliable diagnostic tool, a fact with obvious implications for the search for a single 'true' option.

One approach, clearly positivistic, relies on the assumption that aggression essentially belongs to the natural world. It is thus possible to compare in terms of the presence (or absence) of some set of natural signs. The second approach assumes that aggression is primarily to do with human intentions and meanings. It is thus possible to compare in terms of the presence (or absence) of what might be called the 'natural meaning' of aggression, that is in terms of the most basic definition that can be derived from cultural understanding. The difference is between relying on nature to provide the marks of aggression, and asking culture to do the job.

Natural signs

Signs are taken to include physical hurt, 'threatening and fighting behavior' and the like (Eibl-Eibesfeldt 1979: 34). If this were true, we could measure the incidence of aggression much as we can measure the incidence of physical illness, or, somewhat more controversially, 'prototype' emotions (the latter by way of natural facial expressions and so forth (see Rosch 1975: 186; see Leventhal 1980). There is no need to worry about all those problems, discussed later, which arise when meanings are taken into account. Hitting someone is hitting someone, an aggressive act simply by virtue of the fact that 'physical hurt' is inflicted.

But does human biology provide any basis for holding that certain kinds of behaviour are aggressive? Whatever 'aggression' might owe to biology (an issue I have discussed elsewhere (Heelas 1982, 1983)), the fact remains that researchers have not made much progress in specifying what behaviour is aggressive (see Hinde 1982: 234). Siann paints a bleak picture, concluding her discussion of biological approaches with the observations, 'the term aggression is taken for granted' and 'substantive attention is not paid to defining the term' (1985: 50). She also points out that those who adopt ethological and socio-biological approaches use the term 'very broadly' (1985: 90). Such vague 'definitions' leave us unclear as to what counts as aggressive behaviour.

The criteria on offer — for example, 'hurting' (Siann 1985: 50) and 'a generalized determination to succeed or overcome obstacles' (1985: 90) — are not exact enough to avoid serving to encompass more than what can plausibly be considered to be aggressive in nature. Eibl-Eibesfeldt, who it will be recalled advocates a 'hurting' definition, would surely not want to claim that activities such as going to the dentist, accidentally hurting somebody, or disciplining children by slapping them are aggressive in nature. Given the experiential and moral characteristics of these activities, the attribution of 'aggression' would result in the inclusion of activities which go well beyond any sensible biological specification of this 'kind' of behaviour. Physical hurt and so forth, in other words, does not function as reliable natural signs of aggression.

Johnson writes, 'there is no single kind of behaviour which can be called "aggressive" ' (1972: 5). To function as a natural sign, a particular kind of behaviour must be intimately and reliably bound up with aggression. It is no use relying on 'any kind of hurt' (Eibl-Eibesfeldt) as a sign if this could be indicating other things. And there is also the problem that virtually any kind of behaviour (say wearing a 'tribal' scarf at a football match) can signal aggression. 'Natural' signs could be everywhere.

There is perhaps a more fundamental problem with the idea that biological events can be used to define aggression or identify forms of aggressive behaviour. Science relies on establishing causally significant correlations, when cause and consequence must be identified in such a fashion as to avoid conceptual entailment. Thus it is not possible to say, for example, that fighting is aggressive because it is associated with particular states of brain chemistry or frustration. Thinking of one of the best-documented biological theories, one which advances a close connection between frustration and aggression (Berkowitz 1980: 344), aggression has to be defined in terms other than frustration (see e.g. Dollard et al 1969: 9). That this can be done is shown by evidence that frustration need not result in

231

aggression (Robarchek 1977, 1979). But by doing this, frustration no longer serves as a natural sign.

The criticism I want to emphasize rests on the assumption that aggression is a variety of human action; that aggression is meaning-dependent. Argued forcefully by philosophers, there can be no natural signs. Thus Winch writes, 'it is impossible to go far in specifying the attitudes, expectations and relations of individuals without referring to concepts which enter into those attitudes . . .', a point illustrated by 'war' — 'The concept of war belongs essentially to my behaviour' (1971: 128).

Anthropologists are interested in the human significance of aggression. We are interested in how people experience, understand, evaluate, and manage what we might decide to call aggression. For this reason alone, there is little point in ignoring how participants understand their actions. As has already been indicated, supposed natural signs can diagnose aggression even though participants would not (recall 'accidently hurting somebody'). This does not result in good ethnography of human experience. Eibl-Eibesfeldt's definition enables him to characterize Semai 'blood drunkenness' (manifested by a few during the participation in an Aborigine counter-insurgency unit during the 1950s) as evidence of raw aggression (1979: 238), but Robarchek and Dentan, attending to contextual meanings, discredit the natural sign: ' "blood drunkenness", rather than designating the eruption of innate homicidal frenzy, describes an acute state of nausea, fear, disorientation, and disgust which the sight of human blood evokes among the Semai' (1987: 361).

Natural meanings

The second (essentialist) comparative approach has the great virtue of being meaning-dependent. Rather than activities being treated as aggressive (or non-aggressive) by nature, as mere behavioural episodes, their 'nature' is taken to be socially constructed — and thus should be assessed by reference to what they are taken to mean. If members of a particular society conceptualize an activity (say 'hitting someone') in terms other than what we want to translate as 'being aggressive', the activity should not qualify as being aggressive in nature. It should no longer be possible to argue that Samoans, for example, 'mistakenly' understand aggressive beatings in terms of 'love'.

Not surprisingly, theorists seeking meaning-dependent definitions generally introduce the notion of 'intentionality'. The theorists about to be discussed would all agree with Marsh's advice, 'the concept of intention must be an essential component of any satisfactory definition' (1983: 13). (See MacIntyre: 'An action is identifiable as the action that it is only in terms of the agent's intention' (1971: 253).) But in exactly what ways does an act have to be meaningful for it to be assessed as aggressive or non-aggressive? Explaining why meaning-dependent definitions are unsatisfactory, I begin with our own society. If they fail to provide reliable assessments in this context, the omens for cross-cultural comparison are clearly not promising.

According to Berkowitz, it will be recalled, 'aggression is the intentional injury of another' (or, as he elsewhere writes, 'What is most important about aggression is that the aggressor wants to hurt or perhaps even destroy the victim, either physically or psychologically, and is reinforced when this particular goal is achieved' (1983: 15)). Such definitions might owe much to what we mean by aggression, but they do not capture what we mean. At one and the same time, they are too general and also too limited. They include activities which are not considered to be aggressive, and they exclude activities which should be counted as cases of aggression. To illustrate: concerning the first objection, do we really want to say that parents who 'hurt' their disobedient children by taking away their pocket money are acting aggressively? What about the possibility that parents are attempting to fulfil a non-aggressive goal, for instance teaching responsibility? As well as including activities which few would consider to be aggressive, there is also the problem that the definitions include activities which many do not regard as aggressive; for example, fox-hunting. As for the second objection, the role accorded intentionality serves to exclude many of those activities characteristically regarded as aggressive — for example, those associated with 'blind' unthinking anger, as when we simply 'lash out', or with drunkenness.

Can anything be done to arrive at a more satisfactory definition, one which circumvents the problems of including what should not be included and excluding what should not be ignored? Baron and Byrne attempt to avoid the first trap. To remind the reader, their definition runs, 'Aggression is any form of behaviour directed towards the goal of harming or injuring another living being who is motivated to avoid such treatments.' The last clause is designed to avoid including activities which appear to be aggressive but which are held to satisfy non-aggressive ends: '. . . some individuals seem to enjoy being hurt in various ways by their lovers and make no effort to shun such treatment. Similarly, but in more dramatic fashion, persons who commit suicide actively seek the fatal injuries they suffer' (Baron and Byrne 1977: 408).

Unfortunately, this attempt not to include too much renders the definition too narrow to take account of activities which surely should be included in the register of aggression. Baron and Byrne are not able to consider the possibility that someone kicking a wall, an innocent dog, and the like is aggressive (or, for that matter, that an aggressive person hitting someone who enjoys it is actually being aggressive). Council housing estates, where vandalism is not uncommon, could well be presented as less aggressive communities than they are when viewed in terms of everyday usage of 'aggression'.

It is apparent that the more the researcher tries to solve the problem of including too much, the harder it becomes to avoid excluding cases of aggression. Conversely, of course, the more the researcher tries to avoid the problem of not including enough, the harder it becomes to avoid including too much. As we have seen, Baron and Byrne define aggression as they do in order to avoid including non-aggressive acts. But if the 'too limited' problem raised by their definition is met by developing a broader definition, we are back with the problem with which they began — finding a definition which is not too broad. Thus if their last clause ('. . . another living being who is motivated to avoid such treatment') is dropped, their definition becomes more or less identical to Berkowitz's ('. . . the intentional injury of another'), which has already been criticized for being too inclusive.

The problems facing those who aim to define aggression in line with what the term means derive from the richness of our indigenous understanding. 'Aggression' is what Weber called 'an historical concept', a concept which 'covers a whole world of different things' (1985: 78). The richness of the term is shown by the variety of 'essences' which have been identified: to do with 'intentional injury'; to do with 'dominance' (Marsh: 'the intentional process of subduing or achieving dominance over a rival' (1978: 33)); and, to give one example taken from Fromm's analysis of varieties of aggression, to do with 'the aim of obtaining that which is necessary or desirable' (1977: 264). That so many essences have been identified shows that usage is too complicated and divergent to be captured by any one definition.

On the grounds that comparison must be in terms of something, researchers aim to provide definitions which enable them to identify what counts as aggression and thus compare like with like. Unfortunately, the only way of establishing a clear-cut, operational definition is to ignore much participant usage. Thus as Berkowitz himself implies, his 'wanting to hurt or perhaps even destroy' definition is inadequate in that 'Aggression in this sense has very little in common with the forcefulness shown by an "aggressive" salesman or the boastfulness demonstrated by a youthful male who is trying to impress someone by acting tough' (1983: 15). As a result, a particular definition might be able to capture aspects of what we mean by aggression, but much will be left out. Bearing in mind that such a definition will also include too much, it is clearly the case that the assessment diverges from participant understanding and thereby becomes unreliable.

A polythetic term such as 'aggression' (see Marvin 1986: 121; Parkin 1986) cannot be handled in a nomothetic fashion.

Another consequence of essentialism is that comparison is bound to remain controversial. Different definitions result in different activities entering the aggressive register. For Marsh, classroom rivalries count as aggressive in nature (recall his 'subduing or achieving dominance over a rival'); for Berkowitz they probably would not (children do not so much 'intend to injure' as intend to do well). And it is not as though progress can be made by arguing that one definition is better than others. Each has its advantages and disadvantages. The fact that there is so little agreement among researchers strongly suggests that no single definition has fewer disadvantages than its rivals. Finally, problems cannot be solved by compiling a 'multiple definition': the sum would be no better than its parts.

FROM ESSENTIALISM TO CONTEXTUALISM

Ignoring aggression when it is understood to exist, counting it when it does not, arriving at differing assessments — the definitional approach to comparison does not inspire enthusiasm. Used cross-culturally, the idea that some core meaning of aggression permits the reliable identification of cases is even less plausible.

This is because there are great cross-cultural differences in how apparently 'aggressive' acts are understood. The essentialist is not able to take these properly into account. It follows that there is great scope for misidentification. To make matters worse, the essentialist has most probably derived his or her definition from Western understanding. Assessments provided by such definitions are thus likely to be reinforced by ethnocentricism. 'Intentional injury of another' might suggest aggression for us in the West; the definition has been derived from this understanding; so when 'intentional injury of another' is seen in another culture, it 'obviously' has to do with aggression. It might be objected: but surely the essentialist can attend to participant meanings and so avoid erroneous characterization? Bearing in mind what has already been said on this matter, I should emphasize that to pay attention to the richness of participant understanding can only too readily undermine the assumption, for example, that the 'intentional injury of another' naturally means aggression. To show that such 'injury' is relative to, indeed necessarily bound up with, 'non-aggressive' meanings is to undermine the claim that comparison can be effected by using a universally applicable core meaning of aggression.

Faced with Yanomamo husbands beating their wives, use of the 'intentional injury' definition, combined with our natural inclination to regard this as aggressive, leave us convinced that this is an aggressive activity. Attention to full context might well make us pause (recall how wives talk about their beatings). But the essentialist has to rely on information provided by the fact that a definition suits the case (wives are 'injured').

It is not difficult to find examples which illustrate the dangers of using a definition to pick out 'etically' discerned features of 'aggression', ignoring context to the extent of claiming that activities as a whole are aggressive in nature. To be content with one graphic illustration, consider Girard's (general) claim that 'sacrifice is primarily an act of violence without risk of vengeance' (1972: 13).[4] Even supposing that sacrifice involves an intention to injure or destroy, the fact remains that a great many (if not virtually all) instances of sacrifice have more to them than can be successfully characterized as 'violent' or 'aggressive'. It is more than likely that meanings apparently to do with these characterizations are subsumed, better transformed, by semantic context. (See Fromm (1977: 243) and Storr (1970: 43).) A good example is provided by Old Testament accounts, where the central feature of the temple sacrifice is a peace-offering.

In short, that which only appears to be aggressive (or violent) in nature when divorced from full context cannot provide the basis for claiming that activities as a whole are aggressive. The 'etic' cannot override the 'emic'. Reliance on those core meanings which are meant to aid comparison only too readily result in impoverishment and distortion. Full justice must be done to participant understanding.

CONTEXTUALISM AND COMPARISON

Everything points to taking context seriously. The investigator, as Winch puts it,

> has to take seriously the criteria which are applied for distinguishing 'different' kinds of action and identifying the 'same' kinds of actions within the way of life he is studying. It is not open to him arbitrarily to impose his own standards from without (1971: 109).

Now to the central issue. Comparison has to be in terms of something. The great virtue (and sin!) of the essentialist strategy is that the researcher aims to provide a standard measure. That such measures do not work — fighting, to put it graphically, neither provides a natural sign of aggression nor naturally means aggression — raises the question: what is to be put in their place?

Discussing two types of comparison — one where what is compared are ' "concretely" fixed objects', the other where comparison is of 'social facts' which only 'exist in any meaningful way insofar as they are constructed and sustained by acts of interpretation' — Holy goes on to make the point that 'generalizations can be arrived at through the first type . . . but . . . the second can lead only to the highlighting of cultural specificity' (1987: 10–11). Dwelling on the second strategy, he explains why 'cross-culturally valid generalizations seem to be conspicuous by their absence:

> In a way this is understandable, for the formulation of such generalizations through comparative research in interpretative anthropology is hampered by one basic problem which did not face the positivists, namely how to guarantee that the culturally specific meanings of phenomena are not altered or violated in the process of comparison by applying our culturally specific models to other peoples (1987: 13).

The way is paved for the extreme relativist to argue: introduction of our culturally and historically sited terms ('aggression', 'non-aggression', 'peaceful') to characterize activities in other societies only results in 'altering' or 'violating' their meanings; all we can do is 'highlight cultural specificity'. According to this argument, the very title of the volume to which I am contributing — *Societies at Peace* — is questionable.

But, of course, cultural specificity can only be highlighted by reference to our indigenous understanding. The path between essentialism and extreme relativism is to use that 'diagnostic tool' provided by the interplay of our own discourse and that provided by other cultures. The endeavour is to see what happens to our understanding when it encounters the understanding of the other. This is what generates interesting interpretations. So what conclusions can be drawn from the comparative enterprise when it is informed by how participants — so to speak all of us — make sense of activities?[5]

First, relativist or 'cultural specificity' claims should not make us lose sight of the possibility that 'alien' cultures 'share' much of our discourse. To the extent that their characterizations of acts map relatively well on to Western usage, it is possible to apply words such as aggressive or non-aggressive.

However, it is also possible that examination of context, examination of all the clues provided by 'thick description', will suggest that our terms are only 'half-appropriate'. Given the complexity and fuzzy-edged nature of our polythetic notions, and given the difficulties which result when we try to establish the extent to which they map on to alien conceptual configurations, we might have to conclude that determinate characterization is impossible.

Of particular significance in this regard is that many activities do not lend themselves to being characterized as either aggressive or non-aggressive. They are both. When 'aggression and violence are aspects of social interaction in general, rather than unique categories of social behaviour', as Siann (1985: 175) puts it, activities are not simply 'aggressive'. A good illustration is provided by the Dani of New Guinea, who battle and on occasion kill. Whatever the role played by 'aggression', battles transcend characterization as mere aggressive activities. Thus Heider reports 'a tremendous amount of joking', and one of the reasons why he feels entitled to describe Dani menfolk as 'peaceful warriors' is because they fight to prevent ghosts from causing misfortune (1979: 96, 101). Clear-cut assessments of the kind promised by the essentialist founder when 'aggression' is a (perhaps qualified) aspect of action — an aspect which cannot be isolated and then 'weighed' to help locate the Dani on a comparative scale. Thus whether it be 'fighting', 'punishment', 'sacrifice', 'revenge', 'injury', 'competition', or 'forceful presentation of self', the contextualist has to face the possibility (often a strong one) that such activities do not fall into neat categories.

Another reason for this is that assessments of activities are frequently relative to viewpoint. A shared activity can be differently assessed. Thus Yanomamo wives understand their 'beatings' in one way, their husbands (quite possibly) in another. Countless illustrations can be provided from our own society to make the general point that aggression frequently lies in the eye of the beholder, people making different judgements of the same thing. Thus those to the left of the political spectrum see the new Trident shed at Barrow as aggression incarnate, those to the right see it as contributing to peace; what is rampant aggression for middle class people (say what Marsh (1978) calls football 'aggro') might well have a different complexion for participants. Where is the neutral vantage point to decide on assessment? And if decisions are left to those doing the judging, there is no one comparative picture.

Finally, the fact remains that it is often possible to show that apparently aggressive acts are less 'aggressive' than they might appear. It might be concluded that it is best not to call them aggressive at all. Context shows that 'aggressive' acts are not informed by the kind of discourse which the Westerner is prepared to apply.[6] To show that 'beatings', 'fighting', 'sacrifice', 'blood drunkenness', and so forth are deeply imbued with non-aggressive meanings is to show (the essentialist notwithstanding) that these activities are not aggressive in nature. If both Samoan fathers and children understand beatings in terms of love, aggression has little (if anything) to do with the matter. The same point applies to Ilongot head-hunting, an activity understood to effect the transformation of youths from a life dominated by passion (*liget*) to a life of knowledge (*beya*). Conversely, it can be mentioned, context can show that apparently non-aggressive activities are little of the sort. Whilst engaged in field work in Thailand, I was often shaken to find that my attempts at gentle and constructive verbal criticism were construed as being far from non-aggressive in intent.

CONCLUSION

An important concern has been to criticize the two essentialist approaches. Despite the fact that essentialism in general has received a bad press (by Winch and Foucault, for example), and despite the fact that anthropologists have tended to abandon the approach (see Holy 1987), many of those who study aggression and non-aggression continue to rely on core definitions. After all, many are scientists.

Attention to context has the great virtue of dispelling 'myths' generated by essentialism. Although it runs counter to our ethno-centric commitments, evidence suggests that we must resist asserting that Ilongot youths are aggressive simply because they lop off heads; that Samoan fathers are aggressive simply because they beat their children; or, for that matter, that the British were aggressive when they lined up to exterminate the indigenous people of Tasmania. (As Passmore points out, the aboriginal inhabitants were thought of as 'lying beyond the bounds of morality' (1975: 210).) Apparently aggressive (and non-aggressive) acts are relative to more perspectives than our own.

Replacing nomothetic with polythetic definitions and attending to context certainly advances the cause of those wanting to do justice to different ways of making sense of activities. I have argued that con-textualism does not leave us floundering in a welter of cultural specificities. Activities can be shown to be less (or more) aggressive than they might appear, and can sometimes be characterized in deter-minate fashion. Contributors to this volume adopt the contextualist approach. That they appear to successfully identify societies which are 'at peace' shows what can be done. And progress can be made in settling the controversies with which we began: as when Robarchek and Dentan contextualize Semai 'blood drunkenness'.

However, attention to context does not advance the cause of those who want to draw arresting and simplistic contrasts between the aggressive and the peaceful. The more we attempt to remedy the defects of the definitional or yardstick approach by doing full justice to participant understanding, the more difficult it is to decide whether many acts are aggressive or non-aggressive. Such activities do not lend themselves to clear-cut typification. Recall the 'peaceful warriors'.

There is no magic key. Semantic anthropology provides con-testable interpretations, not hard facts or measurements. Contextual analysis might well persuade us that the activities of a particular society add up to a 'peaceful' picture. In general, though, the expectation is that the great majority of societies cannot be labelled 'peaceful' or 'aggressive'. The often 'alien' and rich configurations of those meanings which constitute activities ensure they transcend our diagnostic distinctions. Overall, perhaps all that can be hoped for is a scale running from 'clearly' peaceful to 'clearly' aggressive societies, with the majority falling in a land where the scale collapses — primarily because 'aggression' comes into play with the 'non-aggressive'.

NOTES

1 I owe my thanks to Russell Keat for his philosophically informed comments, comments which have been encouraging and which have led to increased realization that underlying issues deserve further exploration.
2 Concerning the point that importance is attached to the (relative) absence of aggressive acts, book titles are significant: Dentan's *The Semai: A Nonviolent People of Malaya* (1968) and Montagu's (ed.) *Learning Non-aggression* (1978), for example. As for the point that non-aggression can go together with states of mind which are not peaceful, see Robarchek's (1979) argument that 'fear' is a major factor behind Semai Senoi non-aggression.
3 Another somewhat similar illustration is provided by Lewis (1987: 594).
4 Girard's use of the term 'violence' rather than 'aggression' does not diminish the relevance of the illustration.
5 Of particular relevance to the topic under consideration are papers by Marvin (1986, e.g. pp. 118–22; 133–4), Parkin (1986) and Riches (1986, e.g. pp. 1–3). In a general discussion of the comparative method, Parkin draws attention to the crucial point that comparison of meanings is necessarily comparison in terms of 'overlapping resemblances' (1987: 52): with profound implications for those who want to resist 'dissolving' comparative tools. For other general discussions, see contributions to Holy (ed.) (1987); MacIntyre (1971: 260–79) and Winch (1971).
6 One of the most outstanding demonstrations of this way of proceeding is provided by Foucault in his analysis of classical Greek society, which ' "tolerated" what we call "homosexuality" ' (1987: 187). As he continues, 'But perhaps it would be just as well if we avoided those two terms here. As a matter of fact, the notion of homosexuality is plainly inadequate as a means of referring to an experience, forms of valuation, and a system of categorization so different from ours.'

REFERENCES

Bandura, A. (1973) *Aggression. A Social Learning Analysis*, Englewood Cliffs: Prentice-Hall.

Baron, R. and Byrne, D. (1977) *Social Psychology*, London: Allyn & Bacon.

Berkowitz, L. (1980) *A Survey of Social Psychology*, London: Holt, Rinehart & Winston.

Berkowitz, L. (1983) 'Aggression and emotions', in R. Harré and R. Lamb (eds) *The Encyclopedic Dictionary of Psychology*, Oxford: Basil Blackwell, 15–17.

Chagnon, N. (1983) *Yanomamö. The Fierce People*, London: Holt, Rinehart & Winston.

Dentan, R. (1968) *The Semai: A Nonviolent People*, New York: Holt, Rinehart & Winston.

Dollard, J. *et al.* (1969) *Frustration and Aggression*, London: Yale University Press.

Draper, P. (1978) 'The learning environment for aggression and anti-social behavior among the !Kung', in A. Montagu (ed.) *Learning Non-Aggression*, New York: Oxford University Press, 31–53.

Eibl-Eibesfeldt, I. (1979) *The Biology of Peace and War*, London: Thames & Hudson.

Foucault, M. (1987) *The Use of Pleasure*, Harmondsworth: Penguin.

Fox, R. (1975) *Encounter with Anthropology*, Harmondsworth: Penguin.

Freeman, D. (1983) *Margaret Mead and Samoa: the making and unmaking of an anthropological myth*, Cambridge, Mass.: Harvard University Press.

Fromm, E. (1977) *The Anatomy of Human Destructiveness*, Harmondsworth: Penguin.

Gerber, E. (1985) 'Rage and obligation: Samoan emotion in conflict', in G. White and J. Kirkpatrick (eds) *Person, Self, and Experience*, London: University of California Press, 121–67.

Girard, R. (1972) *Violence and the Sacred*, London: John Hopkins.

Heelas, P. (1982) 'Anthropology, violence and catharsis', in P. Marsh and A. Campbell (eds) *Aggression and Violence*, Oxford: Basil Blackwell, 48–61.

Heelas, P. (1983) 'Anthropological perspectives on violence: universals and particulars', *Zygon*, 18 (4): 375–403.

Heider, K. (1979) *Grand Valley Dani. Peaceful Warriors*, London: Holt, Rinehart & Winston.

Hinde, R. (1982) *Ethology*, Glasgow: Fontana.

Hogan, R. (1983) 'Passive-aggression', in R. Harré and R. Lamb (eds) *The Encyclopedic Dictionary of Psychology*, Oxford: Basil Blackwell, 446–7.

Holy, L. (1987) 'Description, generalization and comparison: two paradigms', in L. Holy (ed.) *Comparative Anthropology*, Oxford: Basil Blackwell, 1–21.

Johnson, R. N. (1972) *Aggression in Man and Animals*, Philadelphia: W. B. Saunders.

Leventhal, H. (1980) 'Toward a comprehensive theory of emotion', in L. Berkowitz (ed.) *Advances in Experimental Social Psychology*, London: Academic Press, 149–207.

Lewis, G. (1987) 'A lesson from Leviticus: leprosy', *Man*, 22 (4): 593–612.

Lizot, J. (1985) *Tales of the Yanomami*, Cambridge: Cambridge University Press.

MacIntyre, A. (1971) *Against the Self-Images of the Age*, London: Duckworth.

McKnight, D. (1986) 'Fighting in an Australian Aboriginal supercamp', in D. Riches (ed.) *The Anthropology of Violence*, Oxford: Basil Blackwell.

Marsh, P. (1978) *Aggro. The Illusion of Violence*, London: J. M. Dent.

Marsh, P. (1983) 'Aggression: conceptual issues', in R. Harré and R. Lamb (eds) *The Encyclopedic Dictionary of Psychology*, Oxford: Basil Blackwell, 13–15.

Marvin, G. (1986) 'Honour, integrity and the problem of violence in the Spanish bullfight', in D. Riches (ed.) *The Anthropology of Violence*, Oxford: Basil Blackwell, 118–35.

Mead, M. (1943) *Coming of Age in Samoa*, Harmondsworth: Penguin.

Montagu, A. (ed.) (1978) *Learning Non-aggression*, New York: Oxford University Press.

Parkin, D. (1986) 'Violence and will', in D. Riches (ed.) *The Anthropology of Violence*, Oxford: Basil Blackwell, 204–23.

Parkin, D. (1987) 'Comparison as the search for continuity', in L. Holy (ed.) *Comparative Anthropology*, Oxford: Basil Blackwell, 52–69.

Passmore, J. (1975) 'The treatment of animals', *Journal of the History of Ideas*, 36: 195–218.

Riches, D. (1986) 'The phenomenon of violence', in D. Riches (ed.) *The Anthropology of Violence*, Oxford: Basil Blackwell, 1–27.

Robarchek, C. (1977) 'Frustration, aggression and the nonviolent Semai', *American Ethnologist*, 4: 762–79.

Robarchek, C. (1979) 'Learning to fear: a case study of emotional conditioning', *American Ethnologist*, 6: 555–67.

Robarchek, C. and Dentan, R. (1987) 'Blood drunkenness and the bloodthirsty Semai: unmasking another anthropological myth', *American Anthropologist*, 89 (2): 356–65.

Rosaldo, M. (1980) *Knowledge and Passion*, Cambridge: Cambridge University Press.

Rosch, E. (1975) 'Universals and cultural specifics in human categorization', in R. Brislin *et al.* (eds) *Cross-Cultural Research Methods*, New York: Wiley.

Siann, G. (1985) *Accounting for Aggression*, London: George Allen & Unwin.

Storr, A. (1970) *Human Aggression*, Harmondsworth: Penguin.

Thomas, E. (1958) *The Harmless People*, New York: Random House.

Weber, M. (1985) *The Protestant Ethic and the Spirit of Capitalism*, London: George Allen & Unwin.

Winch, P. (1971) *The Idea of a Social Science and its Relation to Philosophy*, London: Routledge & Kegan Paul.

NAME INDEX

244

NAME INDEX

Thompson, Nicholas S. 189–90
Thomson, Joseph 135–6, 138
Tiger, L. 9, 11
Trevarthen, Colwyn ix, 3, 20–2, 140, 165–83, 204
Turnbull, Colin 31, 33, 100, 220–1
Turner, Victor W. 17, 150–1, 178–9

Vayda, A. P. 2
Vygotsky, L. S. 171

Walters, R. H. 128–9

Weber, M. 234
Whitehead, A. N. 6
Wikan, U. 107
Willis, Roy 1–26, 133–44, 150, 205
Wilson, E. O. 9, 18, 31–2, 198, 228
Winch, P. 232, 237, 240, 241n
Winnicott, D. W. 177, 180
Wolf, E. 32

Zillmann, D. 9

SUBJECT INDEX